The Conservatives under David Cameron

D1390425

The Conservatives under David Cameron

Built to Last?

Edited by

Simon Lee
Senior Lecturer in Politics
University of Hull, UK

and

Matt Beech
Lecturer in Politics
University of Hull, UK

First published 2009 by
PALGRAVE MACMILLAN

Palgrave Macmillan in the UK is an imprint of Macmillan Publishers Limited,
registered in England, company number 785998, of Houndmills, Basingstoke,
Hampshire RG21 6XS.

Palgrave Macmillan in the US is a division of St Martin's Press LLC,
175 Fifth Avenue, New York, NY 10010.

Palgrave Macmillan is the global academic imprint of the above companies
and has companies and representatives throughout the world.

Palgrave® and Macmillan® are registered trademarks in the United States,
the United Kingdom, Europe and other countries.

ISBN-13: 978-0-230-57564-6   hardback
ISBN-10: 0-230-57564-1   hardback
ISBN-13: 978-0-230-57565-3   paperback
ISBN-10: 0-230-57565-X   paperback

This book is printed on paper suitable for recycling and made from fully
managed and sustained forest sources. Logging, pulping and manufacturing
processes are expected to conform to the environmental regulations of the
country of origin.

A catalogue record for this book is available from the British Library.

A catalog record for this book is available from the Library of Congress.

Printed and bound in Great Britain by
CPI Antony Rowe, Chippenham and Eastbourne

Contents

Foreword

Peter Oborne

From the collapse of the Major government in the mid 1990s till the Brownite putsch which did for Tony Blair in the early summer of 2007 Britain remained in important respects a one party state. The official Tory opposition was reduced to peripheral status, while the Liberal Democrats failed to rise to the historical opportunity with which they were presented. As a result, political rivalry was suppressed.

Conflict did show itself, however, in two primary ways. One was the rise of political movements from outside the Westminster establishment, such as the UK Independence Party, the British National Party and the anti-war coalition. All of these were able to exploit the monolithic structure of public discourse that established itself for a decade after 1997.

The second manifestation of conflict was the emergence of an extraordinary level of feuding inside the governing party itself. From 2001 onwards this became increasingly menacing as the suppression of public argument on issues such as foreign policy, immigration and the economy led to convulsions inside New Labour. Most of these disputes were fought out in secret, and normally publicly denied. Eventually, however, they erupted in the short-lived New Labour civil war of the autumn of 2006. Tony Blair was obliged to surrender to the threat of mass ministerial resignations, which had been orchestrated by allies of his rival Gordon Brown, and duly promised to resign. He reluctantly fulfilled this pledge in June 2007.

New Labour has never fully recovered from this catastrophic toppling of a successful party leader. Tony Blair's successor Gordon Brown was greeted with a sharp rise in the opinion polls, as John Major was after the fall of Margaret Thatcher in 1990. But Brown was now ruling a divided party. There have been attempts to establish unity, above all through the return of Peter Mandelson in the 2008 reshuffle. However the Blairite faction never felt any abiding allegiance to Gordon Brown, any more than supporters of ex-premier Margaret Thatcher did towards John Major. Tony Blair's supporters have never forgiven Gordon Brown for what they believe to be his role in first poisoning, and then destroying, a Labour government.

These deadly divisions inside New Labour threw a lifeline to the apparently defunct Conservative Party. Today, for the first time since 1992, a Conservative leader stands a strong chance of becoming Prime Minister. It has become of first rate importance to understand who David Cameron is, what he stands for, and what he would do in office.

The first thing to note is that David Cameron marks a reversion to a type of Tory leader widely assumed to have become extinct. His socio-economic status is comparable to the leaders who governed Britain in the Conservative ascendancy during the immediate post-war period: Winston Churchill, Anthony Eden, Harold Macmillan and Sir Alex Douglas-Home. Educated at Eton and the son of a stockbroker, he comes from the landed upper-middle class. It was assumed after the defeat of Sir Alex Douglas-Home in the general election of 1964 that such a figure could never again become the prime minister. Indeed, David Cameron is the first Tory leader since Sir Alex even to have been educated at a public school.

In short, the emergence of Cameron as Tory leader and future prime minister represents the re-emergence of the former British governing elite into mainstream public life (a phenomenon observable in other areas, for example the appointment of Radley-educated Andrew Strauss as England cricket captain). This promotion to a front-line political role would have been unthinkable only a generation ago. In 1990 the foreign secretary Douglas Hurd's Old Etonian and landed background was held against him when he battled to succeed Margaret Thatcher. Hurd was reduced to making the thoroughly misleading claim that he was the son of a 'tenant farmer', and eventually retired from the contest comparing the Conservative Party of the late 20th century to 'some demented Marxist sect'. David Cameron cannot be understood until it is grasped that he will be the first prime minister who was born to rule in half a century.

However, it is misleading to attach too much significance to Cameron's Establishment credentials. It is also important to understand that he has built his career as a core member of the so-called 'modernising' movement. These modernisers are a cross party phenomenon. This means they are hostile to core structures of ideology or belief, and therefore tend to join parties mainly for pragmatic reasons of career advancement. They form a metropolitan clique, and are collectively highly skilled users of political technology: focus groups, state of the art psephological methods, voter targeting, consumer advertising etc. These modernisers are especially fluent and confident at using the media. Modernisers will always tend to manipulate voters rather than directly articulate mainstream concerns. They are political insiders who typically find themselves at odds with the mass of the party membership. Their rise as a factor in British mainstream politics was anticipated in Richard Katz and Peter Mair's brilliant essay: 'Changing Models of Party Organisation and Party Democracy: the Emergence of a Cartel Party', written in 1995. Though the idea of British modernisation was invented on the left, they represent a collective attempt to restore elite dominance after the post-war collapse of the British governing class.

The Labour cabinet minister Peter Mandelson is the godfather of British modernisation, which is why he is revered by political insiders from all parties. He put the idea into practice first as a senior aide to Neil Kinnock, then with the New Labour coalition he subsequently assembled under the apparent leadership of Tony Blair. At the core of the modernisation project is the very simple idea that it is possible to create at any rate an illusion of progress by repudiating core party supporters and ideological positions. It took many years for the Conservatives to copy this technique. Michael Portillo endeavoured to put it to work inside the Tory Party after the general election landslide of 2001, but was defeated by an unforeseen backwoods revolt under the eccentric captaincy of Iain Duncan Smith. David Cameron is the first outright moderniser to lead the Conservative Party, just as Tony Blair was the first outright moderniser to lead the Labour Party. This is what Cameron surely meant when, very early on in his leadership, he told a group of newspaper executives that he was the 'heir to Blair'. Many of Cameron's closest political friends, such as Benjamin Wegg-Prosser, the former Downing Street director of strategic communications, and the Downing Street press officer Tim Allan, come from the Blair inner circle. Allan gave private strategic advice to Tory modernisers during the 2005 election. Both men are likely to emerge as informal advisers to Cameron once in government. Cameron has far more in common with either of those two skilled Westminster operatives than with any of his backbenchers.

So Cameron embodies a contradiction. On the one hand the Tory leader is a throwback to political leadership by the traditional landed class. On the other hand he is an assiduous student of Peter Mandelson, the inventor of British political modernisation.

The twin identities will always struggle inside him. Insofar as he is a member of the British Establishment, the idea of duty, a concept that has partly been lost in recent decades, will come naturally to Cameron. He will seek to reclaim what the political philosopher David Marquand has fruitfully labelled the 'public domain'. Modernisers, in sharp contrast, do not really understand or admire this proposition. They have consistently been scornful of the traditional British governing methodology, and in particular deeply contemptuous of the ideals of service and fastidiousness embodied in the traditional British public servant. Modernisation has determined (among other things) the capture of many areas of state activity by the businessmen through outright privatisation, the private finance initiative and the ubiquitous use of management consultants to address problems of public sector management. Bonuses, once a phenomenon confined to the City of London, have become a significant feature of civil service remuneration. Modernisers have uncritically accepted the neo-liberal economic settlement which has formed the base for economic policy-making from Thatcher to Gordon Brown. Cameron appears to accept almost all of these modernising insights, and will try to build on Blairite public service reforms in his first years in government.

Cameron the Establishment figure is an entirely different matter. He will be reverential of traditional institutions like the monarchy, parliament, the Anglican Church, the civil service, the trade unions and the armed forces. As Matt Beech observes in his essay, Cameron 'is rooted in institutions – institutions to which he ascribes value: Eton College; Oxford University; and the Conservative Party'. But Cameron the moderniser will be automatically scornful of all these institutions. The Establishment Cameron would aim to strengthen civil society: Cameron the moderniser would build up the strength of the centre and capture or destroy alternative power bases.

The Establishment Cameron and the modernising Cameron are therefore at war with one another. They represent rival aspects within his political and intellectual formation. Each identity will tend to provide a contradictory solution to any given problem. It is unlikely that this battle between the two sides of Cameron's personality will ever be resolved. How Cameron resolves this conflict will determine the nature of the government he leads. At this early stage of his political career – and from the narrow and frequently misleading vantage point of opposition – the following tentative observations can be made.

In terms of technique Cameron is a moderniser. This means that he is a consumer of the most advanced political technology. He devours the findings of focus groups and accepts the core modernising strategy of triangulation – the opportunistic adoption of political positions for situational advantage. His speeches are littered with short sentences and verbless grammatical formulations. This arid literary style, apparently clear but in reality designed to manipulate, is a hallmark of the modernisation movement and contrasts with the more thoughtful and homely style of discourse used during the period of Establishment rule.

Cameron has also repudiated the modest and unobtrusive leadership style of the British Establishment, which had been based on the ancient ideal of gentlemanly conduct. This mode was challenged first by Margaret Thatcher, then repudiated wholesale by Tony Blair, Britain's first celebrity prime minister. Blair evolved an alternative mode, founded on knowingness, ostentation and the deliberate collapse of long-established dividing lines between public and private. Indeed Tony Blair's fusion of the two spheres represented what was in effect a return to pre-modern modes of political leadership in which the sovereign's entire life took place in full public view. It is likely that Cameron will pursue this methodology even more remorselessly and with yet greater success than Tony Blair. The Tory leader, even more than Tony Blair, has lived out his private life in public. This is why the death of his son Ivan, though a matter of intense private tragedy, was also an event of first rate political importance.

Certain consequences of this new type of politics have already become obvious: others are not yet so clear. David Cameron's wife Samantha, daughter of Sir Reggie Sheffield Bt, is destined to become an iconic national and international figure, eclipsing over time the mesmerising public presence even of Carla Bruni, wife of the French President Nicolas Sarkozy. The Camerons will become one of the most glamorous power couples in world politics.

Cool political utility lies behind this apparently transient and insubstantial modernising political methodology. A celebrity party leader is able to rise far above the constraints of conventional party machines or cabinet government. He can outshine political rivals by appealing over the heads of party and parliament and direct to the voter. This nakedly populist method sits uncomfortably with traditional governing structures. Once in office David Cameron is likely to find it irresistible.

But this not all there is to David Cameron. Born into the ruling class, educated at Eton and taught politics at Oxford University by the con-stitutional historian Vernon Bogdanor, Cameron has a surer grip of the theory of British government than any prime minister since Harold Wilson. Once elected Tory leader, he was quick to attack the centralised, top-down governing technique which Tony Blair introduced in 1997 and which has been sustained by Gordon Brown since the handover of power in 2007.

Cameron has frequently reasserted the primacy of cabinet government and supported certain measures (such as secret votes to elect chairmen of Commons select committees) which will strengthen the legislature against the executive. Right from the start Cameron has stressed the need to weaken the state and strengthen civil society. He has pledged to restore the independence of institutions and voluntary organisations which have been captured by the government over the past two decades. He has also promised to devolve power from the centre to localities.

Meanwhile Cameron has strongly criticised the hyperactive model which has been one of the core features of the modernising system. Cameron has some of the attributes of a Tory in the tradition of Michael Oakeshott. That means that he does not believe in the ability of the state to pursue grand projects of social change and regeneration.

So Cameron is torn between two opposite systems: the modernising dogma and frenzied activity driven from the centre, and his inherited Tory scepticism about the range and functions of the state. So far Cameron's public statements, in particularly his strong defence of civil society and decentralisation, have been at war with his actions. He has led the Tory Party from the centre, refused to tolerate internal dissent, showed a brilliant feel for publicity, and completely overshadowed all but a handful of rival spokesmen at the top of the Conservative Party. Cameron does not merely welcome the modernising technology he has copied from New Labour, but also New Labour's neo-liberal analysis. The achievement of this brilliant volume of essays, the first really well-informed analysis of Tory policy at the end of the New Labour era, is to show that the incoming Tory leader would represent continuity more than change.

David Cameron does not challenge the core principle of British foreign policy under New Labour, i.e. allegiance at all costs to the United States of America. Nor is there any fresh analysis on defence. Indeed Cameron's early 2009 reshuffle left in place Liam Fox, best known for his impeccable connections with the now discredited neo-conservative faction which surrounded George W. Bush, as defence spokesman. It is admittedly the case that Cameron will enter Downing Street as a euro-sceptic. However pragmatism will almost certainly pull him towards the centre ground, just as force of circumstance obliged Tony Blair and Gordon Brown to betray their own pro-European rhetoric. Simon Griffith's essay shows how Cameron fully supports engaging the New Labour vision on public services.

The contributors to this volume reflect Cameron's own contradictions in their analysis of Tory policy towards the welfare state. Simon Lee rightly responds to the poetry and imaginative reach of Cameron's idea of the 'Broken Society'. But Stephen Driver notes the enormous practical difficulties in using the voluntary sector as a solution to intractable social problems, while Philip Lynch demonstrates how British membership of the European Union will act as a constant drag on David Cameron's attempts at change. Only in issues of secondary political importance, above the environment, do the Cameron Tories diverge in a tangible way from the New Labour analysis. It remains to be seen whether the Tory flirtation with green voters can be sustained for long in office.

Yet there have been certain signs this year that David Cameron's political identity is starting to change. At the start of 2009 he began to widen his circle beyond the small group of Tory modernisers who placed him in power four years earlier. One sign of this was the appointment of former Chancellor Ken Clarke to the shadow cabinet in a powerful blow to the authority of David Cameron's friend and guru George Osborne, the shadow chancellor. Another sign was his private dinner with Margaret Thatcher and a group of her loyal supporters at the Goring Hotel. He could never have dared do this during the early years of his leadership when he was trying to change the Tory Party image. This series of rapprochements with the *ancien régime* suggests that Cameron is slowly turning back into a more traditional type of Tory leader.

The sheer scale and severity of the economic crisis is also forcing Cameron to become a different kind of leader. In his early years David Cameron and George Osborne's modernising analysis caused them to adopt a strategy of adopting New Labour's economic policies. As Simon Lee shows in an original and eye-opening essay, the severity of slump has already forced Cameron to abandon his early allegiance to governing spending targets. Changed circumstances will now force Cameron to take an axe to spending – just as Margaret Thatcher did in 1979. Mass unemployment, civil unrest, financial instability and structural deficit of approaching £100 billion may all lie ahead. 42 year old David Cameron will define himself by how he confronts these disparate, unexpected and perhaps insoluble problems.

The Centre for British Politics

The Centre for British Politics is a research centre that promotes the study of British Politics; in particular, it conducts research on British political parties, their ideologies and their public policy. It was designed to unify the research interests of Philip Norton, Simon Lee, Richard Woodward and Matt Beech, thereby creating a research cluster with a British Politics identity and collaborative ethic in the Department of Politics and International Studies at the University of Hull. The establishment of the Centre for British Politics reinforces the tradition of teaching and research in the area of British Government and Politics that the Department has had for over 30 years. The Centre for British Politics strives to produce internationally renowned research in the form of monographs, edited volumes and articles in peer-reviewed journals. It is represented in this volume by Philip Norton, Simon Lee and Matt Beech.

This book was inspired by a symposium of the Centre for British Politics at the University of Hull on 24–25 September 2008. The 'David Cameron and the Conservatives' symposium evaluated developments in the Conservative Party's ideology, policy, and strategy since David Cameron's election as Conservative Party leader in December 2005. The event brought together some of the key thinkers in this area.

Acknowledgements

The Centre for British Politics would like to thank and acknowledge Simon Lee for providing the inspiration for this project, and for organizing both this publication and the symposium upon which it is based. The project would not have been possible without the funding provided by the Department of Politics and International Studies at the University of Hull, for which the editors are extremely grateful. In addition, the Centre would like to thank colleagues in the Department of Politics and International Studies for their help in establishing the Centre in June 2007 and for their continued support.

We have been greatly fortunate to have as contributors a team of first rate scholars who made the 'David Cameron and the Conservatives' symposium, 24–25 September 2008 at the University of Hull a pleasure to participate in. We are also particularly grateful to Peter Oborne for agreeing to write the foreword to this book. We would like to thank the publisher and especially Amy Lankester-Owen for commissioning this project, Alison Howson for overseeing it, and Gemma d'Arcy Hughes and Katherine Bullas for their work in bringing the book through to publication. The authors are also grateful to Oliver Howard and Ray Addicott for their work on the manuscript.

Finally, Matt as ever would like to thank his wife Claire, for her continued support. Simon's contribution would not have been possible without the love and support of Helen McGarry.

Notes on Contributors

Matt Beech is Lecturer in Politics and Director of the Centre for British Politics at the University of Hull. His research interests include New Labour, social democracy and conservatism. He is co-editor of *Ten Years of New Labour* with Simon Lee.

James Connelly is Professor of Politics at the University of Hull. He writes primarily on political theory and environmental politics. He is the author (with Graham Smith) of *Politics and the Environment: From Theory to Practice* (second edition, Routledge, 2003) and several articles and chapters on political theory and the environment. He is currently working on the concepts of environmental citizenship and environmental virtues. His book *Sustainability and the Virtues of Environmental Citizenship* will be published by Routledge.

Stephen Driver is Principal Lecturer in the School of Business & Social Sciences at Roehampton University. He has co-written two studies of New Labour with Luke Martell, *New Labour: Politics after Thatcherism* (1998) and *Blair's Britain* (2002). Stephen completed a second edition of *New Labour* in 2006. He is also Director of the Social Research Centre at Roehampton, which has been working with Amnesty International UK on a project on political activism.

Mark Evans is Professor of Governance and Director of the ANZSOG Institute of Governance at the University of Canberra. He is the author of (amongst others) *Constitution-making and the Labour Party* (2004), *Policy Transfer in Global Perspective* (2005), *Public Administration and Development* (2006) and *Understanding Governance* (2007).

Simon Griffiths is a Lecturer in Politics at Goldsmiths, University of London. He is also Senior Research Fellow at the Social Market Foundation, where he heads the organization's work on public service reform. He is the co-editor with Kevin Hickson of *British Party Politics and Political Thought after New Labour* (2009).

Victoria Honeyman is a lecturer in Politics at the University of Leeds. Her first book *Richard Crossman: A Reforming Radical of the Left* was published in 2007. She is currently working on projects on both the Labour and Conservative Parties and British Foreign Policy.

Simon Lee is a Senior Lecturer in Politics at the University of Hull. His teaching and research interests are principally in the field of political economy, with a particular emphasis upon the politics of globalization and governance, and the politics and national identity of contemporary England. A second edition of his monograph, *Best for Britain? The Politics and Legacy of Gordon Brown* (2007) will be published in June 2009 as *Boom to Bust: The Politics and Legacy of Gordon Brown*. He is co-editor of *Neo-Liberalism, State Power and Global Governance* (2007) with Stephen McBride, and *Ten Years of New Labour* (2008) with Matt Beech.

David Lonsdale is Lecturer in Strategic Studies at the University of Hull. Prior to his current appointment, David worked at King's College, London, based at the Joint Services Command & Staff College, and the University of Reading. His publications include *The Nature of War in the Information Age: Clausewitzian Future* (2004) and *Alexander The Great: Lessons in Strategy* (2007).

Philip Lynch is a Senior Lecturer in Politics at the Department of Politics & International Relations at the University of Leicester. His main research interest is in contemporary British Conservative politics, on which he has published a number of books and articles, including the edited volume, *The Conservatives in Crisis* (2003), which examines the fortunes of the Conservative Party under William Hague.

Philip Norton [Lord Norton of Louth] is Professor of Government and Director of the Centre for Legislative Studies at the University of Hull. He is the author or editor of 27 books covering British politics, the constitution, the Conservative Party, parliament and legislatures in comparative perspective. He was elevated to the peerage in 1998. He chaired the Conservative Party's Commission to strengthen parliament and has served as chairman of the House of Lords Select Committee on the Constitution.

Peter Oborne is a journalist, author and commentator. He is a political columnist for the *Daily Mail* and was Political Editor of the *Spectator* from 2001 to 2006. He is the author of *The Rise of Political Lying; Alastair Campbell: New Labour and the Rise of the Media Class* and, in a different vein, a biography of the cricketer Basil D'Oliveira (for which he won the William Hill Sports Book of the Year in 2004). His most recent book, *The Triumph of the Political Class*, was published in September 2007.

1
Introduction: David Cameron's Political Challenges

Simon Lee

When David Cameron was elected to the leadership of the Conservative Party in December 2005, barely seven months had passed since his party had suffered its third consecutive general election defeat. Cameron found himself confronting six major political and personal challenges. First, in electoral terms, his four immediate predecessors – John Major, William Hague, Iain Duncan Smith and Michael Howard – had delivered three consecutive general election defeats. Despite having been in opposition for more than eight years, there was little evidence that the Conservative Party had convinced a disenchanted and highly sceptical electorate that it could offer them a better alternative to New Labour's programme of political, economic and social renewal. Second, in ideological terms, the party appeared to have lost the battle of ideas decisively to New Labour's modernization project. Third, in policy terms, the Conservative Party had failed to identify a policy agenda that would resonate with the British electorate. It had also failed to resolve the extent to which there would need to be continuity with or departure from the legacy of Thatcherism.

Fourth, in organizational terms, the party possessed a declining and ageing membership, and a parliamentary party with little representation of women or ethnic minorities and over-representation of public school-educated, white middle-class Englishmen-traits shared by the majority of constituency parties. It had also faced electoral oblivion in Scotland and Wales at the three previous general elections, and seen its vote decline in the five northern-most English regions at the 2005 general election.

Theresa May, a recent Conservative Party Chairman, had described her party as 'the nasty party' (May, 2002), a label which it had found difficult to dislodge. Fifth, in personal terms, the Conservative Party had failed to find politicians who could provide a credible challenge to the polished double act of Tony Blair and Gordon Brown, despite their own well-publicized rivalry. Sixth, in financial terms, the Conservative Party remained heavily dependent upon funding from a limited number of rich individuals, laying it open to the charge that it had failed to cast off the sleaze that had so damaged the party during the Major government.

The Conservative Party's prospects of not suffering a fourth consecutive general election defeat would depend critically upon whether David Cameron could succeed, where his four predecessors had failed, by providing the necessary leadership and vision to identify Conservative ideas, policies and an electoral strategy, built to last, which could meet each of these six challenges. This book provides an evaluation of how the Conservative Party has performed under the leadership of David Cameron to meet those challenges. This introductory chapter provides a brief overview of Cameron's approach to his task before summarizing the contributions of our team of authors. Although, at the time of researching and writing the book, there were still a possible 18 months to go before the next general election, already Cameron had been leader of his party for three years. Consequently, it was possible for a detailed scrutiny of his leadership, ideas, policies and strategy to be undertaken.

Cameron's electoral challenge: smelling the coffee

The Conservative Party is not accustomed to spending long periods in opposition, let alone to suffering three consecutive general election defeats. Indeed, the twentieth century had been depicted as 'The Conservative Century', because the party had held office for more than twice as long as its political opponents (Seldon and Ball, 1994). At general elections from 1918 to 2005, the Conservative Party was the largest political party on 14 occasions, with the best post-war result in 1983, when it won 397 seats. However, in 1997, the Conservatives had won 165 seats, the worst performance since 1906, and 9.6 million votes, their lowest total since 1929. Indeed, the party's share of 30.7 per cent of the vote was its lowest since 1832. Not a single seat was won in Wales or Scotland. In 2001, the Conservatives won 8.36 million votes, 31.7 per cent of the vote, and just 166 seats. This was an increase in the share of the vote of only 1.0 per cent, with one additional seat won. Not a single seat was won in Wales, and only one won in Scotland. On 5 May 2005, the Conservative

Party won only 8.8 million votes and 198 seats, or 32.4 per cent of the total, and up only 0.7 per cent on 2001. Of its 198 seats (31 per cent of the total at Westminster), 194 or 98 per cent of the total were won in England, an increase of 29 seats and a 0.5 per cent rise in the votes, and 65,000 more votes than won by the Labour Party in England. However, the Conservatives' share of the vote in the four northern-most regions of England actually fell. Indeed, the total number of votes it won in the United Kingdom was its fewest in post-war general elections, with the exception of 2001 (Tetteh, 2008a).

Michael Howard greeted his party's third consecutive general election defeat, unprecedented in modern British political history, by expressing his pride in the campaign that had been fought. Indeed, he proclaimed confidently that the Conservatives had taken 'a significant step towards our recovery' (Howard, 2005). The implication of his statement was clear. One more heave would be sufficient to dislodge New Labour at the next general election. Others did not share Howard's optimism, believing that, as had been the case following previous Conservative defeats in 1945, 1966 and 1974, a more fundamental review of party ideology, policy and strategy might yet be required. One of the most important contributions to this debate came from the former Conservative Party Treasurer, Lord Michael Ashcroft. He issued a vehement rallying cry for the Conservatives to heed the wake-up call from the electorate and 'smell the coffee' (Ashcroft, 2005). Ashcroft had already attracted personal opprobrium from sections of the media sympathetic to the Blair government because he had provided substantial funds to the Conservatives to target winnable seats in marginal constituencies. He was soon attracting similar sentiments from sections of his own party because his detailed study of public opinion during the 2005 general election campaign did not pull any punches. Among its principal findings, the study found the Conservative Party to be out of touch with the attitudes to contemporary social and cultural issues of ordinary people. The party was also 'thought less likely than their opponents to care about ordinary people's problems, share the values of voters or deliver what they promised. Majorities in key marginal seats thought that the party was out of touch, had failed to learn from its mistakes, cared more about the well-off than have-nots, and did not stand for opportunity for all.' Indeed, voters actually possessed 'a more negative view of the Conservative Party at the end of the campaign than they did at the beginning' (Ashcroft, 2005: 3).

If this was not damning enough in its own right as a verdict upon Michael Howard's leadership and David Cameron's role as policy coordinator, Ashcroft's study also found that 'To the extent that the party had identified concerns that people shared, it had failed to articulate solutions, and on the issues that mattered most to people, Labour's lead remained unassailable – or at least, unassailed.' In short, Ashcroft concluded that 'The Conservative Party's problem is its brand', which was not associated with 'opportunity for all, or economic competence, or the delivery of good public services, or with looking after the less fortunate, or with life in modern Britain' (Ashcroft, 2005: 4). Above all, to Ashcroft it was evident that 'To the extent that the voters who rejected us in 2005 associate the Conservative Party with anything at all it is with the past, with policies for the privileged few and with lack of leadership. We cannot hope to win a general election while this is how we are seen by people who should be our supporters' (Ashcroft, 2005: 4).

As a consequence of these damaging revelations about public opinion of the Conservative Party, Ashcroft identified five clear lessons for the party to learn, irrespective of who was chosen to succeed Michael Howard as leader. First, party resources must be targeted more effectively. Second, campaigns must be fought hardest 'on the things that matter most to people, rather than things we hope can be made to matter'. Third, given the number of parties competing for votes, Labour's unpopularity could not be assumed to translate automatically into support for the Conservatives. Fourth, any appeal to the conservative or reactionary instincts of people would be at the expense of attracting the real core vote and the support of minority communities. Fifth, to avoid the party becoming a rump, it must recreate the real core vote among 'the election-winning coalition of professionals, women, and aspirational voters' (Ashcroft, 2005: 5). However, as a measure of the scale of the challenge confronting the successor to Michael Howard, to persuade the Conservative Party of the need to change to win, Ashcroft's survey had also found that while only 38 per cent of voters thought the Conservative Party was actually making progress and on the right track to return to power before long, no fewer than 79 per cent of Conservatives thought this was case. Despite an unprecedented eight years of opposition for the modern Conservative Party and three consecutive general election defeats, many Conservatives were still refusing to face up to the need for substantive change in their party's ideas, policies and strategy.

Cameron's campaign challenge: change to win

Despite this unpromising political inheritance, both during the campaign for the Conservative Party leadership and in the months immediately following his election, David Cameron appeared to approach the task confronting him with a confident optimism that seemed to defy his party's position on the opposition benches. That confidence appeared to flow from an analysis of modern British politics, shared with George Osborne, the Shadow Chancellor of the Exchequer and Cameron's campaign manager. Historically, the development of Conservative Party ideology, policy and electoral strategy, in the wake of electoral defeat, had presented something of a paradox. On the one hand, British conservatism historically had stood for a limited number of core tenets, notably the maintenance of social order, the defence of private property and the rule of law, an organic society and orderly change, and a limited role for the state (Seldon and Snowdon, 2001). The Conservative Party had not been a pressure group for capitalism (Gilmour, 1978). On the other hand, ever since the establishment by Margaret Thatcher and Sir Keith Joseph of the Centre for Policy Studies in 1974, the Conservative Party had sought to win the battle of ideas by abandoning the social democratic middle ground, and occupying instead the 'common ground' in British politics. This common ground entailed a new agenda, embracing the moral and material benefits of the market, and a politics founded upon a descending hierarchy of 'values, aspiration, understanding, policies'. The common ground was that political territory occupied by politicians aspiring to transform the expectations of government in pursuit of prosperity, low inflation, private profit and investment, 'housing choice, decent education, less dependency, less crime' and 'freedom within the law to run our own lives' (Joseph, 1976a: 27–33).

From May 1979 to April 1992, the Conservative Party's success in occupying the common ground, by building institutions for the market, through policies such as privatization, deregulation and liberalization, had enabled it to secure four consecutive general election victories. The Conservative Party's traditional core electorate had been joined by a new generation of aspirational voters, keen to share in the property-owning, share-owning democracy of Thatcher's popular capitalism. Thereafter, John Major, William Hague, Iain Duncan Smith and Michael Howard had all struggled and ultimately failed to identify a means of reoccupying the common ground. In seeking to consolidate and rally the party's core vote, each leader had alienated the floating voters who had deserted en masse to New Labour in 1997, and not returned to the Conservatives thereafter.

David Cameron and George Osborne's route out of this political and policy conundrum was simple. Their analysis had concluded that, despite its consecutive general election defeats, the Conservative Party had actually won the vital battle of ideas. Indeed, the very election of Tony Blair and the creation of the New Labour project were themselves the ultimate evidence of that Conservative ideological triumph. New Labour's '"Social justice and economic efficiency" are the common ground of British politics' (Cameron, 2006a). Therefore, the task confronting the Conservative Party was straightforward. Modern conservatism simply had to come to terms with that triumph, and its previous problem in eight years of opposition of not knowing how to deal with it (Cameron, 2006a).

In launching his leadership bid on 29 September 2005, Cameron dismissed his relative youth and parliamentary inexperience as obstacles to his candidacy. In being equally dismissive of the 'one more heave' approach to winning the next general election, upon the back of New Labour's unpopularity or faltering economic performance, Cameron identified the key obstacle to electoral success as the absence of popular trust in the Conservative Party. The party had to change, but this would entail something more fundamental than mere changes in organization or presentation. The essential task was ideological, namely 'to explain to people what it means to be a Conservative in 2005' and how Conservative principles would make a difference in future. Cameron identified a series of ideas that illustrated his thesis. First, the party's commitment to personal responsibility should mean freedom to choose, but 'must not mean selfish individualism because there was "a we in politics as well as a me"'. Second, support for the family to redress what he portrayed as 'an increasingly atomized society' would mean 'a shared responsibility among individuals and families, government and business'. Third, a commitment to lower taxes should mean a commitment to sharing the proceeds of economic growth 'between better public services on the one hand and lower taxes on the other hand'. Fourth, in identifying the idea of limited government, Cameron stated that he desperately wanted 'the State to be our servant and not our master' but that rolling back its frontiers must mean 'a whole new compact with the voluntary sector and social enterprises' which would enable social problems to be tackled but without leaving behind the weak and defenceless (Cameron, 2005a).

From the outset, Cameron and Osborne built their conception of modern Conservatism and their political strategy for reviving their party's political fortunes upon the need for change. Throughout his leadership campaign, Cameron was adamant about the direction his party should take. For the Blair era to end, the Conservative Party would have to change. The three choices confronting Conservative MPs and ordinary party members in the leadership contest were: to move to the right (with David Davis), or fight from the centre ground (with Cameron); to 'stick to our core vote comfort zone' (with Davis), or 'reach out' (with Cameron); and to 'repeat the mistakes of the past' (with Davis), or 'change to win the future' (with Cameron) (Cameron, 2005b).

In his keynote speech to the Conservative Party conference, which proved a decisive moment in the campaign given David Davis' own faltering performance, and the lukewarm reception the latter received both from the party faithful and the media, Cameron chose the theme 'Change to Win'. Cameron began by reminding his audience that their party had lost to a government that had made a litany of mistakes and 'won fewer votes than any in history'. No comfort could be taken in 'solid, but slow progress'. The government had failed, but so had the Conservative Party. The answer was not to move to the right, because that would turn the Conservatives 'into a fringe party, never able to challenge for government again'. The party must recognize that it was 'in third place amongst under 35s', had lost support amongst women, while public servants no longer thought the party was 'on their side'. To reverse these trends, there would have to be change and modernization of the party's 'culture and attitudes and identity'. This could not be 'some slick re-branding exercise', but had to be 'fundamental change', not least of the party's culture 'so we look feel, think and behave like a completely new organization'. The task would be 'to build together a new generation of Conservatives'; 'to switch a new generation on to Conservative ideas'; and to dream 'a new generation of Conservative dreams'. In short, the party should commit itself to 'a Modern Compassionate Conservatism', which would lead 'a new generation of social entrepreneurs tackling this country's most profound social problems' and 'a new generation of business men and women who are taking on the world, creating the wealth and opportunity for our future' (Cameron, 2005c).

Cameron's organizational challenge: a positive action plan

In the immediate aftermath of his election as Conservative Party leader, David Cameron identified the task confronting his party as being to 'give to this country a modern and compassionate conservatism'. Having campaigned on the theme of the need to change to win, the Conservative Party would now change. First, it would change the way the party looked. The fact that nine out of ten Conservative MPs were white men had led to 'a scandalous under-representation of women'. That would change. Second, the party would change the way if felt, so that there was 'No more grumbling about modern Britain'. Third, the party would change the way it thought, so that it didn't just talk about tackling problems, but actually developed all of the right ideas. Fourth, the party would change the way it behaved, to end 'the Punch and Judy politics of Westminster' name calling and point scoring, by working with the government when it did the right thing, and calling it to account when it didn't and was wrong (Cameron, 2005d).

All of these changes would be necessary to address the big challenges confronting the United Kingdom, namely economic competitiveness, reform of the public services, the quality of life, national and international security, and, above all, 'social action to ensure social justice, and a stronger society'. This would entail mending 'our broken society' by first recognizing 'There is such a thing as society, it's just not the same thing as the state', and then sweeping away New Labour's 'command and control state, the quangos, the bureaucracy, the regional government' (Cameron, 2005d).

One week later, Cameron reaffirmed his commitment to change by reminding his party that because he had won a convincing victory in the leadership contest, he now possessed 'a clear mandate to make that change'. That mandate included the under-representation of women, ethnic minorities and disabled people within the Conservative parliamentary party. As an example, Cameron cited the fact that the 17 women MPs in the current parliamentary party was only four more in total than in 1932. Women accounted for only 6 per cent of the new 2005 intake of Conservative MPs, and there were only six women candidates in the top fifty winnable seats. Similarly, only 6 per cent of Conservative candidates were from ethnic minorities. To create 'a balanced party', Cameron announced 'a positive action plan', composed of five 'decisive steps' to dramatically increase the number of women, black and minority ethnic Conservative MPs.

First, all candidate selections would be frozen with immediate effect, until a new system of selection had been established which guaranteed 'increased diversity, fairness and meritocracy'. Second, a priority list of 'our best and brightest' would be drawn up by the Party Board's Committee on Candidates from the existing candidate list, but at least half the people on it would be women and a significant proportion would be disabled or ethnic minority candidates. In future, all target and Conservative-held seats would be expected to select from it. Third, after three months of selections, there would be a review of progress, with further action taken if necessary. Fourth, and led by Theresa May and Bernard Jenkin, the Deputy Chairman for Candidates, there would be an intensive programme of headhunting for new women, black and minority ethnic candidates, supported by a mentoring programme, and supplemented in turn by prepared guidance to local constituency associations 'to help them understand the need for change'. Fifth, to engage the local community in the candidate selection process, non-party members would be expected to be involved in candidate selection through either a panel of local community stakeholders, or an open or closed primary system (Cameron, 2005e).

To transform the Conservative Party's policy agenda, Cameron announced the creation of six policy groups to address the six major challenges Cameron believed to be confronting the United Kingdom. The groups would address social justice; the quality of life; globalization and global poverty; national and international security; economic competitiveness; and public service improvement. They would be given 18 months to report and to engender 'the most exciting and creative 18 months of political discussion this country has ever seen' (Cameron, 2005e). However, despite this highly optimistic prediction of the policy groups' likely impact, which in the event proved to be a gross exaggeration, none of their recommendations would be binding upon the shadow cabinet. For all of his past and subsequent critique of Tony Blair and Gordon Brown as centralizing, control freaks, Cameron was keeping tight central control over the formulation of the agenda of modern compassionate conservatism.

Cameron's ideological and policy challenge: built to last?

When Tony Blair had become Labour Party leader in June 1994, he had wasted little time in rewriting his party's archaic 1918 constitution, including its Clause Four definition of socialism. To convince a sceptical British electorate that the Labour Party really had changed its aspirations, Blair's New Labour project began by redefining the Labour Party's aims and values themselves, before undertaking major revisions of the party's economic and social policy agenda. In a similar vein, to convince voters that the Conservative Party was equally committed to change, within three months of becoming leader of his party, Cameron had drawn up *Built to Last: The Aims and Values of the Conservative Party*, and sought the approval of the party's membership for the statement of aims and values. *Built to Last* was intended to provide the foundation upon which the policies and agenda of Cameron's modern compassionate conservatism could be constructed. In his foreword, Cameron made two major claims. First, that when confronted by changing economic, environmental, social and security challenges, at home and abroad, the 'old answers' provided by top-down government and monolithic, unreformed public services were not working well. Second, that he was clear about the 'new direction and new answers' needed by the United Kingdom to meet the challenges of the twenty-first century. The solution would lie in Cameron's 'responsibility revolution', which in turn would require respective revolutions in personal, professional, civic and corporate responsibility. Indeed, the mission of the modern Conservative Party would be 'a responsibility revolution to create an opportunity society – a society in which everybody is a somebody, a doer not a done-for' (Conservative Party, 2006: 2–3).

Cameron's values and aims for the modern Conservative Party immediately aligned themselves firmly with the era of Thatcherism, rather than the pre-Thatcher traditions of One Nation conservatism which had seen successive Conservative governments in the post-war era roll forward the frontiers of the social democratic welfare state in a series of technocratic state-led modernization projects, from the Industrial Charter of 1947 to Edward Heath's 'Quiet Revolution' of 1970. At the same time, *Built to Last* reaffirmed Cameron's insistence that the Conservative Party would need to end its preoccupation with economic policy, and switch its attention to society, and a new approach to tackling social problems. This was because the biggest challenge facing the United Kingdom was 'not economic decline, but social decline' (Cameron, 2005d). However, that new approach would remain true to Thatcherite means and values because the agency of social change chosen to reduce welfare dependency and heal the 'broken society' would be the entrepreneurial initiative of business leaders and civil society organizations.

Margaret Thatcher and Sir Keith Joseph had based their quest for a return to the political common ground of a property-owning democracy by seeking to restore an enterprise culture in which individual entrepreneurial initiative would replace state intervention as the primary agency of economic and social change. To maintain this focus upon entrepreneurship, the very first of the eight aims of the party would be the encouragement of enterprise 'in all its forms – in the economy and in the community' because of the Conservative Party's belief that 'the enterprise of our people is the source of our progress' (Conservative Party, 2006: 4). The second aim of the party would be the construction of 'a strong society' to fight social injustice and assist the most disadvantaged (but by implication, not all the disadvantaged). This responsibility would not fall upon the state alone but be shared by social entrepreneurs and the voluntary sector.

The third aim would be to enhance the environment, and meet 'the great environmental threats of the age', because 'there is more to life than money' and 'the quality of our relationships and the sustainability of our environment are central in building a strong and just society'. This aim would include supporting 'families and marriage, and making high quality childcare more available and more affordable'. The fourth aim would be the provision of 'first-class healthcare, education and housing that respond to the needs of each individual'. However, rather than state administration of public services, trust would be placed in professionals and choice given to parents, patients and families to demonstrate that excellence could be engendered 'through vocation, flexibility and local initiative' (Conservative Party, 2006: 6–7).

The fifth aim would be 'to take a lead in ending global poverty'. Indeed, the party had 'a moral obligation' to fight global poverty as 'a priority, not an afterthought' because it would contribute not only to long-term security, but also be 'a necessary counterpart of controlled immigration' and a means to 'stronger, more cohesive communities at home and abroad'. The sixth aim of protecting 'the country we love' would reflect the Conservative Party's pride in the United Kingdom's past, confidence in its future, and commitment to being hard-nosed defenders of freedom. The seventh aim of giving power to people and communities, and recognizing the limitations of government, would reflect the party's belief that centralized government alone could not change society for the better. The eighth and final aim would be for the Conservative Party to be 'an open, meritocratic and forward-looking Party', representing 'all parts of our country in all its diversity' (Conservative Party, 2006: 8–11).

Cameron was much later depicted as 'a new kind of Tory, the sort of Tory no one had ever seen before', a Conservative who was 'fundamentally non-ideological' (Cameron cited in Jones, 2008: 10, 13). However, what *Built to Last* had revealed was that whatever else he might be, David Cameron most certainly was not 'fundamentally non-ideological'. *Built to Last* demonstrated that, like Margaret Thatcher before him, Cameron was determined to win the battle of ideas in British politics, not by abandoning Thatcher's principles, but, on the contrary, by extending them into the sphere of Britain's broken society. After all, Cameron's formative political years had been the 1980s – the decade of Thatcher and Thatcherism. He had first become a passionate reader of newspapers during the Falklands war. He described Thatcher as 'a big influence, yes', but denied she was a role model. In his words, 'I thought she was doing the right thing' (including fighting the miners' strike and being passionately pro-NATO). Her ultimate vindication was the fact that New Labour, 'the people who thought she was doing the wrong thing came to terms with what she had done and then successfully won three elections in a row' (cited in Jones, 2008: 34). Thatcher had 'mended the broken economy in the 1980s', so now Cameron wanted 'to mend Britain's broken society in the early decades of the twenty-first century' (cited in Jones, 2008: 308–9).

The structure of our book

To evaluate the Conservative Party's performance under the leadership of David Cameron, and to establish the degree to which it and its leader have risen to the many political challenges confronting it, our book evaluates developments in party ideology, policy and strategy since December 2005. First, it begins with three chapters devoted respectively to the development of Cameron's ideas; his leadership style and strategy in opposition; and Cameron's approach to policy development. Second, the book then provides five analyses of the Conservative Party's agenda on domestic policy, ranging from the economy, social policy and public services, to the competition state and the environment. Third, three chapters explore the Conservatives' European Union, foreign policy, and defence and security policy agendas. Finally, the book concludes with an overview of the Conservative Party's prospects for winning the next general election and beyond. As with our team's previous work, *Ten Years of New Labour*, the evaluation of the Conservatives under David Cameron provided here does incorporate a variety of perspectives, reflecting the different insights and political convictions of the editors and those contributing.

The book begins by exploring the ideas, leadership and approach to policy development that have characterized the Conservative Party under David Cameron. In his chapter on the development of Conservative ideology, Matt Beech explores Cameron's political thought in order to arrive at a deeper understanding of the type of Conservative that he is, and also the type of conservatism that will guide his government if Cameron becomes the next Prime Minister. Beech demonstrates how Cameron has presented the electorate with a clear choice between the Labour Party's faith in the state, and the Conservatives' faith in the market. As a serving Conservative peer in the House of Lords, Philip Norton provides a fascinating insider's perspective on the role played by Cameron, as Leader of the Opposition, in securing a significant opinion poll lead during much of 2008. By comparing developments in party strategy since December 2005, with the strategy pursued after May 1997 under William Hague, Iain Duncan Smith and Michael Howard, Norton shows that for the Opposition to win a forthcoming general election, it has not only to face an unpopular Government but also to demonstrate that it is itself electable, or at least not unelectable. In my chapter on

Cameron's policy review and strategy, the development of Conservative policy is explored to highlight how Cameron has centred upon the importance of moving Conservative Party policy away from a narrow focus upon economic policy towards a concentration on fixing the broken society and improving the quality of life.

In the following five chapters, we explore the development of a domestic Conservative Party policy agenda under the leadership of David Cameron. In my chapter on the development of economic policy under David Cameron, three distinct phases are identified in the Conservative Party's economic policy agenda. An initial period of convergence and consolidation, during which Cameron and Osborne assumed that neither the United Kingdom economy nor the Blair government's economic policies were broken, is shown to have been followed by a period during which the Conservatives developed a critique of the Brown government's economic policies, in the wake of the Northern Rock crisis. Finally, a third phase of divergence in economic policy is shown to have emerged at the time of the 2008 pre-budget report. This marked Cameron's abandonment of his party's commitment to match Labour's planned public spending on public services.

In his chapter on social policies and welfare reform, Stephen Driver addresses one of the most important policy areas, at the very heart of Cameron's political agenda. Cameron's identification of the 'broken society' as the most urgent domestic policy challenge confronting the United Kingdom has ensured that it will be vital to the Conservative Party's prospects of winning the next general election, and central to the legislative agenda of a future Cameron-led Conservative government. Driver therefore locates the policy debate about the broken society within the context of the Conservative Party's relationship with the post-war welfare state, before exploring the major challenges that Cameron's welfare reform agenda will face. The capacity of a future Conservative government to fix the broken society will also depend critically upon the development of an effective agenda for the reform of the public services. In his chapter, Simon Griffiths analyses this vital area of Conservative Party policy by identifying the contemporary challenges facing the public services, and the emergence of a new generation of Conservative 'modernizers', and what separates them, if anything, from the ideas and policies of the other major political parties.

In his chapter on the competition state, Mark Evans addresses the Conservative Party's agenda for redefining the role of the state. His thesis is that Gordon Brown's flirtation with Keynesianism will be short-lived and is best understood as crisis management rather than a paradigm shift.

A return to neo-liberalism but practised within a stricter competition regulatory approach seems to be the more likely new orthodoxy of the competition state. David Cameron is therefore likely to follow the trajectory of the competition state fostered under New Labour in an attempt to adapt state action to cope more effectively with what political elites perceive to be global imperatives.

One of David Cameron's most prominent policy slogans has been 'Vote Blue, Go Green'. In his chapter on the Conservative policy towards the environment, James Connelly evaluates the extent to which the Conservative Party under Cameron has gone sloganizing to embrace a real commitment to environmental concerns. Connelly's evaluation both compares and contrasts this Cameron with previous Conservative leaders' attitudes towards the environment and asks whether there has been a significant shift in policy or (despite appearances) an underlying continuity.

We proceed to explore developments in Conservative Party policy towards defence and security, foreign and international policy, and the European Union. In his chapter on defence policy, David Lonsdale evaluates the continuities and changes in Conservative policy since December 2005, by placing them within the context of developments in the security environment since the early 1980s. Lonsdale shows how a future Cameron government will face some important security choices, including the question of the retention and replacement of the United Kingdom's nuclear weapons, against the context of major constraints upon the defence budget. In her chapter on foreign policy, Victoria Honeyman explores the ideas underlying the policy choices and priorities which Cameron and his Shadow Foreign Secretary, William Hague, have identified, including the vital 'special' relationship with the United States, the wars in Iraq and Afghanistan, the reform of international organizations and the role of the Commonwealth. Particular attention is paid to Cameron's 'liberal conservatism' as the ideological underpinning for the foreign policy of a future Conservative government.

The Conservative Party's policy towards the European Union has been a major source of tension and internal debate and conflict for party leaders ever since Margaret Thatcher. It has also proven an obstacle to the party's attempts to present an image of unity to the wider electorate, and a major source of political capital for rival political parties, not least during general election campaigns. In his chapter on Europe, Philip Lynch shows how where it was a highly divisive issue during Cameron's formative years in politics, the Conservative Party under his leadership has maintained a settled policy on which it is largely united. Lynch also identifies how the issue of Europe may yet have the potential to destabilize a future Conservative government.

In the conclusion to our book, Matt Beech evaluates the prospects for the Conservative Party under David Cameron in the run-up to the next general election and beyond. Beech provides a picture of what a Cameronite United Kingdom would look like through the lens of existing constraints, not least the onset of recession and the serious deterioration in the public finances, policy commitments and the political relationships that will likely be encountered. The choice still lies open for the Conservative Party under Cameron to opt for the well trodden path of post-Thatcherite British conservatism or the newer path of a more moderate politics for the twenty-first century.

The challenges ahead for Cameron

David Cameron has summarized his political project as follows: 'I'm going to be as radical a social reformer as Mrs Thatcher was an economic reformer, and radical social reform is what this country needs right now' (cited in Jones, 2008: 315). To achieve this objective, Cameron has conceptualized modernization in terms of three components. First, modernization of the Conservative Party itself. This was necessary because it had 'lost touch with the country, and so we didn't look like the country we were trying to govern'. This was manifested in 'the shortage of women candidates, the underlying representation of ethnic minorities, the fact that we were representing mainly rural seats, mainly in the south of England'. Consequently, the Conservative Party 'literally needed to be more reflective of the country we wanted to govern' (ibid.: 293). Second, modernization of the Conservative Party's ideas and policies because Cameron thought 'For too long the party had got rather intellectually idle' (ibid.: 293). Third, modernization of the Conservative Party's organization, through 'a properly run Central Office and press office and better organization all round' (ibid.: 293). Cameron's analysis was that the Conservative Party had failed not because 'we were insufficiently pro-business or pro-markets, our problem was people didn't think we had a good vision of society, of what constituted good public services, of how you actually improve the quality of life and well-being' (ibid.: 312). Cameron has asserted that 'The focus on those social aspects of modern Conservatism was right and they'll be a very big part of my premiership if I get elected. Social responsibility is the essence of liberal conservatism. This is the Britain we want to build' (ibid.: 312).

Whether Cameron's agenda for modernization has fashioned a party, ideas, policies and organization built to last and capable of winning a general election, let alone governing against the backdrop of a global economic slump and seriously depleted public finances, remains to be seen. The evidence from trends in public opinion polls, by-elections and local government elections remains ambiguous. For example, following the June 2008 local government elections, the Conservative Party now holds 9,657 or 48 per cent of the council seats in Great Britain, more than twice as many as the Labour Party's 4,589 or 23 per cent. In England, the Conservatives control no fewer than 211 councils or 57 per cent of the total. The Labour Party controls only 47 councils or 13 per cent (Tetteh, 2008b: 13). In each of the years of Cameron's leadership, the Conservative Party's estimated national equivalent share of votes cast at local elections has risen. In 2005, the party had managed only 33 per cent, against Labour's 36 per cent; but under Cameron, that share has risen to 39 per cent in 2006, 40 per cent in 2007 and 43 per cent in 2008. Labour's share had collapsed to a record low of 24 per cent in 2008. However, it should be remembered that prior to its landslide general election victory in 1997, New Labour had performed even better under Tony Blair, scoring 47 per cent in 1995, 43 per cent in 1996 and 44 per cent in 1997 (Tetteh, 2008b: 11).

This mixed picture has been confirmed in opinion polls. For example, the Ipsos MORI Political Monitor poll carried out between 12 and 14 September 2008 saw the Conservative Party on 52 per cent, and the Labour Party on 24 per cent – both the largest ever Conservative share of the vote and the largest ever Conservative MORI poll lead. Moreover, the largest ever survey of opinion in 238 marginal seats conducted by PoliticsHome.com predicted a Conservative margin of 146 seats at the next general election, with the Conservatives winning 398 seats, Labour 160 and the Liberal Democrats 44 (PoliticsHome.com, 2008: 6). No fewer than eight current cabinet ministers would lose their seats in such an electoral landslide. With the onset of recession, these polls might have been regarded as clear vindications of Cameron's strategy had they been part of a secular trend. The problem for Cameron had been that until 16 March 2008, and the publication of a 16-point opinion poll lead, his strategy failed to generate the sort of opinion poll leadership achieved by New Labour between June 1994 and May 1997, especially in the face of an unpopular and error-prone incumbent government. Until March 2008, the trend in consecutive opinion polls had suggested a failure to restore decisively the general public's trust in the Conservative Party's capacity to deliver effective policies, especially in relation to the reform of the public services and the management of the United Kingdom economy. A sizeable minority of public opinion remained undecided about the Conservative Party's fitness to govern. This book is therefore devoted to a detailed statement and critical evaluation of the ideas and policies of David Cameron's Conservative Party to enable the reader to decide for him/herself whether Cameron's Conservatives have developed an agenda built to last.

2
Cameron and Conservative Ideology[1]

Matt Beech

> In 1979, James Callaghan had been Home Secretary, Foreign Secretary and Chancellor before he became Prime Minister. He had plenty of experience. But thank God we changed him for Margaret Thatcher.
>
> (Cameron, 2008a)

> The central task I have set myself and this Party is to be as radical in social reform as Margaret Thatcher was in economic reform. That's how we plan to repair our broken society.
>
> (Cameron, 2008a)

One of the most contemplated questions in contemporary British politics is, 'what type of Conservative is David Cameron?' For many voters it is a question that will be pondered in the lead up to the next general election. Those citizens in particular who for over a decade have abandoned Britain's most electorally successful political party in favour of New Labour, are now reconsidering their electoral options. The Conservative Party was once regarded as the ubiquitous party of British government until the emergence of Tony Blair and Gordon Brown. But now, under a new leadership the Conservative Party is experiencing a renaissance, in England, at least. This is largely due to the charisma, character and, more substantively, the perception of political moderation of David Cameron. Of course, it is accurate to state that New Labour is a victim of its own success inasmuch as it has governed for 12 years and won three successive general elections. Electorates eventually choose one of the opposition parties to rule and in the British case, with the first-past-the-post electoral system, that choice is in reality one of one. The British electorate may well be inclined to opt for Her Majesty's Opposition at the next election and that means a Conservative government led by David Cameron.

As New Labour's politics of dominance wanes the Conservative Party has been remodelled and relaunched. But, perhaps the most interesting and the more salient question for a student of British politics to ask is, 'whether and to what extent, has the Conservative Party been meaningfully reformed?' This collection of essays is in part a contribution to that debate. The precise purpose of this chapter is to evaluate Cameron's political thought and, by so doing, arrive at a deeper understanding of the type of Conservative that he is and the type of conservatism that will guide his government if he becomes the next Prime Minister. The process of evaluating Cameron's political thought involves scrutinizing policy announcements, keynote speeches, biographies and interviews with him. My approach to this investigation is to analyse Cameron against three notable classifications of conservative ideology: One Nation conservatism; New Right/Thatcherite conservatism; and his preferred terminology – liberal conservatism.[2]

David Cameron fully emerged in frontline British politics by winning the leadership of the Conservative Party in December 2005. His leadership campaign saw him defeat a stalwart of the Tory right and former Shadow Home Secretary, David Davis. Cameron's rise inside the ranks of the Conservative Party has been well noted (Elliott and Hanning, 2007) but it is worth stating that on becoming party leader aged 39, he had been MP for Witney since May 2001, thus his parliamentary career was approaching four and a half years long. Cameron left Oxford in 1988 and began work in the Conservative Research Department until 1992 when he was offered a position as an adviser to Chancellor Norman Lamont; after Lamont's demise he found employment at the Home Office, and then decided to embark on a career in the private sector for Carlton Communications as Director of Corporate Affairs in 1994 (Elliott and Hanning, 2007). He stayed with Carlton until he won his seat in 2001. The usefulness of summarizing Cameron's career lies in the fact that he is rooted in institutions – institutions to which he ascribes value: Eton College; Oxford University; and the Conservative Party. This is the first clue to the type of Conservative that he is.

The 2008 pre-budget report has arguably changed the Brown government's ideological course. New Labour's political economy has altered, as the pattern of interventions has changed, including the scale of borrowing. New Labour has announced its intentions to raise taxes in the form of a 0.5 per cent increase in National Insurance contributions. Moreover, it has broken with its 'golden rules' about the level and conditions of borrowing by stating that it aims to borrow £118 billion mainly as a fiscal stimulus to see the country through the recession. Most dramatically of all, it has set out plans for increasing the level of direct income taxation to 45 per cent on incomes of over £150,000. These measures are historic, pragmatic in terms of political strategy, and ideological. These measures are historic because New Labour's political economy is predicated on 'Brown's golden rules', which in fairness have been stretched several times but never abandoned. These measures are pragmatic in terms of political strategy because this recession is global and possibly without equal. Darling and Brown have suspended their usual rules of politics and economics and embraced a Keynesian style fiscal stimulus that borrows more than any British government has borrowed to fund welfare bills, public services and programmes of public works. The prospect of mass unemployment and rising poverty has in effect replaced the perceived New Labour virtue of economic moderation. These measures are ideological because they substantially extend the remit of the state to salvage an economy in crisis and require taxpayers, especially the better off, to help contribute towards the cost of the rescue plan. New Labour is not some swift convert to Bevanite democratic socialism but its present means and anticipated ends are more obviously social democratic than before.

This is relevant for a study of the ideological make-up of David Cameron because the pre-budget report has by definition moved New Labour's political economy to the left, and Cameron's Conservative Party who aggressively countered the logic of much of the Brown government's intentions to borrow, bring forth public works and then raise taxes after the next election, are clearly well to the right. These measures have not merely repositioned New Labour, they have repositioned Cameron's Conservative Party as being quite far from the government. Whether or not this will prove to be an advantage for Cameron is still unclear, but it has presented the electorate with a clear choice at the next general election. The centre ground is less centrist than before and the electorate has to choose between faith in the state or faith in the market.

Cameron as One Nation Conservative

The One Nation tradition in the Conservative Party began terminologically in the nineteenth century with Benjamin Disraeli in his novel *Sybil: or*

The Two Nations (Disraeli, 1998). In his novel Disraeli intimates that Britain can only thrive as one nation and this is shown in the marriage of the two main characters from divergent social backgrounds. However, as a school of thought, One Nation conservatism formally emerged in the post-war era and refers to a type of conservative politics on the party's left wing.[3] Politicians who personify One Nation conservatism include Harold Macmillan (Macmillan, 1938), Rab Butler (Butler, 1971), Ian Gilmour (Gilmour, 1977, 1992), Iain Macleod (Macleod and Maude, 1950), and Edward Heath. Broadly speaking, One Nation politics embodied an active state approach to governance and saw the state as the key player in ameliorating social problems. From the 1950s One Nation conservatives accepted the post-war consensus of the welfare state, the mixed economy and a tripartite approach to industrial relations (these were instituted by the Attlee governments, 1945–51). This post-war consensus or post-war policy settlement that existed between Labour and Conservative moderates is regarded by the Conservative right as a democratic socialist consensus.

Today, despite the continued activities of the Tory Reform Group, One Nation conservatism is not a force in the parliamentary Conservative Party. However, it does represent moderate Conservative Party voters who are normally not card carrying members. The attitude towards what is now the European Union became a totem for what it meant to be a Conservative and partly defined One Nation conservatism as being sympathetic to the idea of a supranational body that could cooperate on many issues to solve mutual problems. Moreover, the idea of a common market or single European market was the centrepiece of Edward Heath's desire for Britain to become a member of the club of European nations. Therefore a tension developed from the early 1970s in the Conservative Party and intensified throughout Thatcher's tenure and culminated with such deep divisions that they nearly toppled Major's administration. This same period saw the demise of One Nation conservatism as a strong, even dominant approach to conservative politics in Britain.

As I have stated elsewhere, it does appear that Cameron has intentionally tacked his party's policies and ideas to the left in search of centre-ground conservatism (Beech, 2008). Thatcher would not approve. It is obvious that Cameron has felt the impact of New Labour's politics of dominance in the area of public services by initially endorsing their investment strategy and calling for further reform. However, it ought to be noted that Cameron's speech to the CBI Conference in London in December 2008 was a departure from his acquiescence towards Labour's high public spending. Cameron stated that his Conservative Party would no longer pledge to match Labour's level of public spending from 2010 (Cameron, 2008b). Cameron focused in his first period as leader on issues such as public services, the environment and international development, and one could conclude from engaging with such issues that he hopes to be a new Macmillan charting a middle way between New Labour and Thatcherite conservatism. There is some truth in this statement. For example, Cameron has not advocated swingeing cuts in direct taxation or privatization of frontline public services but in response to the recession and to Labour's economic step change, outlined in the pre-budget report, Cameron's tone and approach has altered. Whereas in his first three years as Tory leader he did not argue for a smaller level of public expenditure, now his rhetoric has hardened towards public expenditure and the services that it pays for:

> The first step is to set realistic targets for public spending ... Borrowing is now going beyond acceptable limits. Taxes are already too high – and Labour's plans for even more taxes will act as a drag anchor on recovery. They'll put people off from investing here and help to destroy jobs not create them. So the choice is clear, and it's a tough one – we need to restrain public spending. (Cameron, 2008b)

The idea of social justice has been given a blue shade partly by the work of Iain Duncan Smith's Centre for Social Justice and partly because Cameron and his allies have argued that conservatism must reconnect with the tradition of social reform in the history of the Conservative Party. Cameron appears at ease with Labour's programmes such as the National Minimum Wage, Tax Credits and the Pensioner Credit. The welfare state and the progressive income tax system which funds it are taken by Cameronite Conservatives as a public policy given. He does wish to reform the welfare state; place more welfare services in the voluntary sector and private sector; advocate greater personal responsibility to counter dependence on state entitlements and advocate the importance of marriage and family (Cameron, 2008b), but he does not desire to aggressively roll back the welfare state and shrink it in size and purpose as Thatcher had wished but ultimately failed in so doing. Nonetheless, Cameron's free-market economic ideals, euroscepticism and his claims to 'give people back power over decision-making' position his politics outside of the traditional One Nation conservative stable. There are certainly shared emphases but too much of his politics are Thatcherite to classify him as in the tradition of Macmillan, Butler, Heath, Gilmour or Macleod. That tradition, despite the best efforts of the Tory

Reform Group, has dwindled intellectually and numerically throughout the membership of the Conservative Party.

Cameron as New Right/Thatcherite Conservative

The terms 'New Right' and 'Thatcherite' are not synonyms yet they do cohere. The New Right pertains to an intellectual movement in Britain and the United States that began in the mid-1970s within the Conservative Party and the Republican Party respectively. Key thinkers of this movement included Friedrich von Hayek (Hayek, 1960, 1976), Milton Friedman (Friedman, 1962), and to a lesser extent Barry Goldwater (Goldwater, 1960), and Sir Keith Joseph (Joseph and Sumption, 1978). The New Right was 'new' in reaction to the established interpretations of conservatism that existed in both the Conservative and Republican parties which were perceived to be moderate at best and acquiescent with the left, at worst. It is also important in a discussion of the New Right to note that the British and American experience of the development of New Right politics was not identical and nor would one expect it to be. The divergent histories, political structures and cultural contexts affect this. Nevertheless, the New Right broadly sought to connect free-market liberalism with social conservatism and to reassert the traditions of social order and public morality to conservative politics in the face of the emergence of the permissive society (Gamble, 1988). Therefore, the New Right imported classical liberal ideas about the economy, taxation, the size and remit of the state, a purely negative conception of liberty, an anti-egalitarianism and an instinctive individualism whilst remapping traditional conservative concerns about ethical behaviour, authority and order to fit the age in which they were living. It was in the personalities of Margaret Thatcher and Ronald Reagan that New Right ideas flourished on both sides of the Atlantic.

At the heart of Thatcher's New Right politics was the view that British social democracy had since the Attlee governments succeeded at being the dominant ideology and the Conservative Party especially the government of Edward Heath 1970–74 had capitulated to its demands. For Thatcher, her politics and therefore the British New Right was defined against British social democracy and its institutions: the Labour Party, the trade unions, the public sector and Keynesian demand management. To be a Thatcherite is to support the policies of Thatcherism and by implication to support and usually to deeply respect Thatcher as the Prime Minister who saved Britain during the 1980s. Thatcherites can be understood today as the heirs of a political movement in British conservatism that established the New Right.

Is therefore David Cameron a Thatcherite? How much does his thought owe to the New Right? Whilst the previous leaders of the Conservative Party since Major (Hague, Duncan Smith and Howard) would all feel strongly proud of Thatcher, all hail from the Conservative right wing and could have been described at one point as Thatcherites, this cannot be said for a significant minority in the parliamentary Conservative Party during and shortly after her premiership. It is worth noting that today Tory MPs are more Thatcherite in outlook than at any time in the past. This has a lot to do with the demise of the One Nation tradition of conservatism in the parliamentary party. Cameron I believe can be understood as a Thatcherite inasmuch as he is a free-marketeer who desires less state intervention in the economy and in the lives of British citizens. His political economy owes a great deal to Thatcherism which itself is predicated on classical liberal economics or what is often termed neo-liberal economics. In discussions with Dylan Jones about taxation, Cameron gave an illuminating insight into his own attitude towards personal income taxation and demonstrates that on matters of economics he is a neo-liberal:

> What I and George Osborne have been saying is, we're low tax Conservatives, we're believers in a low-tax economy. It's good for the economy, it's good for all of us. We believe in it for economic reasons, for moral reasons; we think it's good to leave people with more of their own money to spend as they choose. (Cited in Jones, 2008: 280)

His generation of conservatives have been imbued with Thatcherite political economy, but also with Thatcher's euroscepticism. As Lynch and Whitaker assert, 'David Cameron pledged to pull Conservative MEPs out of the EPP-ED [European People's Party-European Democrats] during the 2005 Conservative leadership contest only to announce in June 2006, after a troubled search for allies, that a new group would not be formed until after the next elections to the European Parliament in 2009' (Lynch and Whitaker, 2008: 31). Cameron's motivation for such a pledge is that he believes that the British Conservative Party should oppose European federalism and economic protectionism which EPP members support. In discussion with Dylan Jones on the topic of Europe the following exchange occurred:

Is the EU good for business? The single market is good for business, but the regulation that surrounds it can be terrible. Some regulation is inevitable in creating a single market, but it's far too prescriptive as it is now ... *Do you feel instinctively that European integration should be put on hold or reversed?* I think it has gone too far, and too far in the wrong direction. We need a European Union that works as a looser and more flexible, open organisation. (Jones, 2008: 255–6)

Cameron is clearly a neo-liberal in economic terms but is he fully a neo-liberal conservative in philosophical terms? Hayek (the godfather of the neo-liberal philosophy) loathed democratic socialism and his toleration of 'moderate' conservatives was – similarly to Thatcher's attitude – only marginally milder (Hayek, 1991). Neo-liberal philosophy is more coherent and ideologically robust than the New Right or Thatcherism because it is philosophically consistent despite being more extreme. For advocates of a pure neo-liberalism the individual resides at the centre of life not family, class or nation. The individual must be set free from the big state's lust for his or her taxes and therefore, his or her liberty. No overarching notion of social justice can be legitimate as injustice is not social but individual in its effects and impacts on the lives of private citizens. A socialist or egalitarian narrative about class or poverty finds no support in the mind of the neo-liberal. At the same time, individuals must be protected from other people – usually groups of moralizers and agents of the state – who wish to prescribe a code of ethics by which all citizens should behave above the concerns of natural law. In the thought of the New Right the liberal and conservative tendencies collide and must broker compromises in terms of power, emphasis and policy. Though few full neo-liberals have flourished in the post-war British political tradition their case, however radical it appears, is consistent. Cameron, a conservative who believes in the social values of institutions such as marriage, family and nation to name but a few, can never subscribe to full neo-liberalism or what is called in American political parlance, libertarianism. As he stated in his 2008 party conference speech:

My values are Conservative values. Many people wrongly believe that the Conservative Party is all about freedom. Of course we care passionately about freedom from oppression and state control ... But freedom can too easily turn into the idea that we all have the right to do whatever we want, regardless of the effect on others. That is libertarian, not Conservative – and it is certainly not me. (Cameron, 2008a)

Cameron as Liberal Conservative

The term 'liberal conservative' is Cameron's preferred political designation but this itself does not mean that it is an accurate summary of his brand of conservatism. He set out what he means by the term in a speech in Bath in 2007 whereby he called upon supporters of the Liberal Democrats to join his Conservative Party:

> I am a liberal Conservative. Liberal, because I believe in the freedom of individuals to pursue their own happiness, with the minimum of interference from government. Sceptical of the state, trusting people to make the most of their lives, confident about the possibilities of the future – this is liberalism. And Conservative, because I believe that we're all in this together – that there is a historical understanding between past, present and future generations, and that we have a social responsibility to play an active part in the community we live in. Conservatives believe in continuity and belonging; we believe in the traditions of our country which are embedded in our institutions. Liberal and Conservative. Individual freedom and social responsibility. (Cameron, 2007a)

By using the term 'liberal' as an adjective to describe his brand of conservatism Cameron is undertaking the tasks of ideological positioning and political marketing. Cameron means to employ the term for the following three reasons. Firstly, I believe he uses the term liberal conservative because it gives identity to certain outlooks he has and to distance himself and his politics from what he perceives as unsavoury elements of his party's past. He wants to use liberal to denote a belief in social liberalism as opposed to social conservatism. For example, social liberals are comfortable with a variety of social relationships and family units, including homosexual families; they believe that immigration and the ethnic diversity that stems from it is inherently virtuous, and often (but not in Cameron's own case) argue that the British state should assert a multicultural approach as opposed to an assimilationist approach to settled immigrants.

Secondly, Cameron wants to use the term liberal conservative to demonstrate that he is not a Tory right-winger but a moderate in terms of the Conservative Party. In short that he is different from Thatcher, Major, Hague, Duncan Smith and Howard and that under him the Conservative Party is revising its creed and its policies. Moreover, the argument suggests that those liberal conservatives such as Cameron, George Osborne, Ed

Vaizey and Michael Gove are Conservatives within the mainstream of British politics; centre-right not right-wing.

Thirdly and finally, Cameron uses the term liberal conservative to suggest liberty or freedom. That he is first a conservative who wants to restore freedoms to the British people that have been lost under New Labour; lost due to a tax-hungry and authoritarian nanny state operated by social democrats. Liberal in this context enables Cameron to stress his party's commitment to liberty for the individual, for a smaller state, for less taxation, for civil liberties, for market provision and choice in public services but in a less full-blooded form than neo-liberalism has previously offered. It is possible that Cameron views his foreign policy position as liberal internationalism as opposed to neo-conservatism which has been the dominant approach from which to view world affairs by the Republican Party during the presidency of George W. Bush.[4] Liberal internationalists prefer a multilateral approach to global problems and assert the importance of nation-state sovereignty and universal human rights. Neo-conservatives believe that unilateralism is often required and that breaches of human rights invalidate nation-state sovereignty, hence the moral imperative for regime change.

Cameron in context: Hague, Duncan Smith and Howard

The idea of defining himself as a liberal conservative is in part to distance his politics and his brand of conservatism from the more right-wing approaches that have embodied the leaderships of Hague, Duncan Smith and Howard. Cameron has learnt lessons from the unsuccessful leaderships of his last three predecessors and is striving to move his party and their policies to the centre ground of British politics. In the following extract Cameron reveals his attitude to a more moderate, centrist conservatism that Hague initially presented before adumbrating a right-wing agenda:

> If you go back to 1997, 1998, Hague was saying then that the party had to modernize, had to shake off the dust of the previous twenty years, and he really did try and set off down that path ... I was very pro-Hague at the time, but then he changed tack, and, as I have discussed many times, he was stuck and nothing was working for him, and I think it was the wrong decision and he regrets it. (Cited in Jones, 2008: 75)

The Hague years from 1998 were characterized by the campaign to 'Keep the Pound' (to prevent Britain entering the European single currency); the debate about immigration and asylum; pro-motorist positions such as cutting the price of fuel; increasing the number of police officers; making prisoners work; and of course an article of faith for the Tory right – tax cuts. Whilst some or perhaps all of these measures may be deemed worthy of frontline political attention and debate they still appear as secondary political concerns. Economic management; investment and quality of state schools; investment, efficiency and cleanliness of NHS hospitals; the level and security of pensions; and British foreign policy were and are all regarded as more important than the aforementioned list of concerns, with the exception of immigration. Hague's 2001 general election manifesto, *Time for Common Sense* (Conservative Party, 2001) is quite different in tone and approach than the emphases and topics found in Cameron's speeches. One theme does continue and has done throughout the post-war period; that of freeing people from Labour's big state and returning power and choice to individuals and their families:

> We present here the most ambitious Conservative programme for a generation. Its aim is to release the wisdom, decency and enterprise of British citizens. We can achieve that by handing back to individuals and families the ability to shape their own lives and communities. We will free entrepreneurs to build businesses and to create prosperity, free those who use public services to choose what is best for them and free those who work in our schools and hospitals and police service from endless political interference. (Hague/Conservative Party, 2001: 3)

This theme was Churchill's, Thatcher's, Hague's and is now Cameron's. It is a ubiquitous argument for British conservatives.

Duncan Smith was leader of the Conservative Party from 2001 to 2003. He did not contest a general election and never authored a manifesto. Nonetheless, his brief tenure was in the same mould as Hague's. His main policy document was *Leadership with a Purpose: A Better Society* (Conservative Party, 2002). The content of this document is indicative of Duncan Smith's priorities for the Conservative Party. Its key aims are to use market forces in health and education provision to extend opportunity for patients and parents and improve the quality of service. It sets out plans for state funded scholarships for the brightest pupils to leave the state sector and attend private schools, and state funded treatment for patients in private hospitals. One does not need to be overly cynical to suggest that these measures seek to use state resources to bolster private sector provision at the disadvantage of the state sector. What Duncan Smith cannot be accused of is inconsistency, as these policy prescriptions are entirely consistent with the economic tenets of

Thatcherism. Duncan Smith's document also argues for an increased use of the third sector in the provision of certain services, especially for the most vulnerable in society. This argument has been strongly made ever since by his Centre for Social Justice which has influenced Cameron's shadow cabinet on issues such as poverty and deprivation.

Michael Howard led the Conservative Party from 2003 until the election of Cameron in December 2005. He fought and lost the general election of 2005 and his manifesto *Are You Thinking What We're Thinking? It's Time For Action* (Conservative Party, 2005) like Hague's appealed mainly to Conservative members and voters on the right. Howard's key theme was immigration and it was a notable issue at that time for much of the electorate, so unlike Hague, Howard chose an issue of significance for much of the voters. However, the nature of the issue meant that it was relatively straightforward for people to interpret Howard's message and for the government to argue that the Conservatives are for limits on immigration because they are not disposed to groups of people different from themselves. The accuracy of this interpretation was less politically important than its perception. Howard's Tories were regarded as right wing and therefore unelectable.

There are, however, similarities as well as differences, continuities of policy and ideology as well as discontinuities between Cameron's leadership and that of the previous leaders since 1997. For example, two important ideological continuities of all four are their support for neo-liberalism and euroscepticism. A wider point is that all four leaders are admirers of Thatcher, and in their political economy and in their attitudes towards the virtues of the European Union they are Thatcherites. This demonstrates that in the post-Thatcher period Conservative MPs are both strongly Thatcherite in matters of economics and with regard to Britain's relationship with its continental neighbours in the European project. The leaderships of Hague, Duncan Smith and Howard were at root leaderships from the Tory right. Cameron is a textbook post-Thatcherite Conservative in economic and European affairs, but not so in social policy. If his move is a move away from certain conservative social policy ideas then it is a move away from the Conservative right – Thatcherism's territory.

Conclusion: a Cameronite Conservative?

What can be said in summary of Cameron's political thought? What type of Conservative is he? Clearly he has a neo-liberal economic outlook inherited from Thatcherism. He also holds to Thatcherite euroscepticism as a matter of principle, but he is too left-wing in social policy to be classed as a New Right or as a Thatcherite Conservative. His desire to move his party leftwards towards the centre ground and to regain the right to debate the public services, the environment and issues such as poverty and deprivation suggest more than a nod towards the tradition of One Nation conservatism. It is clearly here in this arena that his politics has been affected by New Labour. There is, therefore, a tangible 'New Labour effect' on Cameron. His conservatism is also traditional; he values the institutions of marriage, family, monarchy, nation-state and the union of Great Britain and Northern Ireland. This means he cannot be a neo-liberal in the fullest sense of the term as free markets do not respect tradition or institutions and, for Cameron, the institutions aforementioned trump the benefit of the unbridled free market. Cameron's politics are more socially liberal than the previous generation of Conservative politicians and the phrase 'liberal conservative' whilst not entirely accurate in reflecting the totality of his thought is nonetheless, indicative of his social and economic instincts. Cameron is naturally a Conservative, one who is post-Thatcherite not anti-Thatcherite and one who is post-New Labour. New Labour will continue even if Cameron defeats them at the next election but his politics have to an extent been affected and shaped by the ideological battles they have won and the agenda they have set over the last 12 years in government. Cameronite Conservatism is not as yet an identifiable strand of Conservative ideology. However, if it does allude to something more than merely supporting Cameron's leadership it could reasonably depict a British Conservative who is economically neo-liberal, espouses a One Nation approach to social policy, is eurosceptic in a Thatcherite fashion and Tory in his or her regard for tradition and social institutions. In others words, Cameronite Conservatism is a mixed bag of centre-right ideas and values but distinctly and recognisably Conservative.

Notes

1. I am very grateful to Kevin Hickson, Simon Lee and Philip Norton for reading and commenting on earlier drafts of this chapter. Any errors are of course my own.
2. For other classifications of Conservative thought see Norton and Aughey (1981) and Norton (1990).
3. It is important to note that whilst the term One Nation conservative has over time come to be associated with the Tory left and with an active state approach and with the post-war consensus, the actual One Nation group – a dining club founded in 1950 – contained a plethora of Conservative MPs from across the Conservative Party. This point is well analysed in an essay on One Nation conservatism by Seawright (2005).
4. For more on Cameron's theoretical and normative approach to foreign and defence policy see Dodds and Elden (2008) and see Honeyman (2009) and Lonsdale's chapter in this volume.

3
David Cameron and Tory Success: Architect or By-stander?

Philip Norton

It is an accepted psephological truth that Governments lose elections. Opposition do not win them. Had Labour Prime Minister James Callaghan called a general election in late 1978, there was a chance that Labour would have retained power. In the event, he delayed[1] and went down to defeat the following May. What happened in the interim was not some spectacular action by the Opposition leader Margaret Thatcher but instead the 'Winter of Discontent'. The Conservative Party won narrowly the general election of 1992 but then lost spectacularly in 1997. What happened in the interim was 'Black Wednesday' and Britain's withdrawal from the exchange rate mechanism: the Conservatives' reputation for economic management was shattered (Crewe, 1994: 109) and the party suffered a marked slump in its support, from which it failed to recover. The defeat was on a par with that of 1906.

On this line of argument, all that Margaret Thatcher had to do following the winter of 1978–79 was to wait for the general election. The same with whoever was Labour leader following 'Black Wednesday': the Conservatives would have lost whether it was John Smith or Tony Blair leading the Opposition.

The logic of this thesis is that Conservative success under David Cameron is the product of the actions of a Labour Government under Gordon Brown. Labour will lose, or win, depending on Brown's capacity to govern and, in particular, handle the economic affairs of the nation. During 2008, the Tories maintained a lead in the opinion polls, at one point achieving a 20-point lead and at another point seeing that lead almost disappear. The fluctuation, on this thesis, was the result of Brown's failings as Prime Minister and then his capacity to respond to an economic crisis. The Leader of the Opposition was seen primarily as a spectator rather than a central actor. In the event of Tory victory, he would be seen as being fortunate rather than clever: in the right place at the right time – unlike his three predecessors.

In this chapter, I wish to challenge this analysis. I do not take issue with the assertion that for the Opposition to win a majority at a general election, Government unpopularity is a necessary condition. However, is it necessary *and* sufficient? My contention is that it is necessary and sufficient for the Government to lose. It is necessary but not sufficient for the Opposition to win. By win a majority, I refer to an absolute majority. By Opposition, I refer to the official Opposition – opposition with a capital 'O' – in this case, the Conservative Party. My thesis is that for the Opposition to win, it has not only to face an unpopular Government but also has to demonstrate to the electorate that it is electable – or at least that it is not unelectable. Let me begin with the empirical evidence for my thesis.

At the start of the 1980s, the Tory Government under Margaret Thatcher was unpopular. The country was in a recession and the Chancellor was introducing budgets that were unpopular not only with the voters but also with some within his own parliamentary party. According to MORI, Margaret Thatcher was the least popular Prime Minister since it started polling. There was talk of her being challenged for the party leadership in 1981. The Government's support was tumbling in the opinion polls. Given this, one would expect the beneficiary to be the Opposition – opposition with a capital 'O' – the Labour Party.

The problem for Labour in 1981 was that it was not electable. Voters still assessed Labour on a retrospective basis (Whiteley, 1983: ch.4). The party was led by a leader, Michael Foot, who was not seen by the electorate, or by the media, as prime ministerial material. It was badly split. The dilemma for electors was that they faced a Government in trouble but an Opposition that they did not consider was ready to take over. What, then, was the outlet for electors' discontent? The answer lies in the third party or, in this case, third-party alliances. The creation of the SDP and the formation of the SDP-Liberal Alliance offered the electorate another choice. The result was that the United Kingdom experienced briefly not two-party competition but three-party competition. At one point, the Conservative Party was pushed to third place in the opinion polls. Labour, though, had not done enough to establish itself as a credible alternative. Indeed, in November 1981 it was vying with the Conservatives for second place in the opinion polls. A MORI poll recorded 44 per cent support for the Alliance, 27 per cent for Labour and 27 per cent for the Conservatives. A Gallup poll put the Alliance support even higher. The Government recovered its position, as much by default as by an increase in support. The Government's landslide victory in 1983, wrote Peter Riddell, 'was a direct reflection of Opposition divisions' (Riddell, 1985: 4). In the 1983 general election Labour was still vying for second place, this time with the Alliance.

Now let me fast forward to the general election of 2005. Though the Conservatives made gains in the election, the number of Tory MPs returned still fell below 200, fewer than Labour won in the 1983 general election. This is a remarkable contrast given that the Government in 2005 was more vulnerable than the Tory Government in 1983. As Anthony King has shown, the Blair Government in the year-and-a-half prior to the 2005 election rarely achieved an approval rating in excess of 30 per cent; at one point it fell to less than 25 per cent (King, 2006: 153). Satisfaction with Blair as Prime Minister also showed a marked decline in the latter half of the parliament. Between 1997 and 2003, Blair's ratings ranged from 40 per cent to 70 per cent. Between mid-2003 and the 2005 election, it was in the 30–35 per cent range. By the time of the election, his standing was below that of three of his Labour predecessors, Attlee, Wilson and Callaghan (ibid.:153–4). There was no one event, equivalent to the Tories' 1992 'Black Wednesday', but rather a series of policies, including the invasion of Iraq, and events that eroded Labour support. As a result, King was able to conclude:

> Going into the 2005 election campaign, the Labour Party was thus extremely vulnerable, far more vulnerable than it had been in either 1997 or 2001. New Labour no longer looked new. On the contrary, it looked old and scruffy, even a little shifty, like a dog that has been caught raiding the pantry. (Ibid.: 159)

Yet as King goes on to observe, despite its vulnerability, no one seriously though that Labour was going to lose the election. He argues that there were two factors working to ensure that outcome. One was the economy. As he then goes on to write: 'As most readers will already have guessed, the other factor was the Conservative Party. Seldom can an unlucky government have been so lucky in its opposition' (ibid.: 162).

One of the conditions was thus met, but not the other. I shall come on to the reasons in due course. The essential point for the moment is the fact that in 2005 the Conservative Party was not seen as electable.

There were two consequences. One was the return of a less than popular Labour Government on a small percentage of the poll. The other was the return of the largest number of Liberal Democrat MPs since the party was formed and the best result achieved by the third party since 1929.

Let me now move ahead three years to 2008. There are two features that are especially salient. The first is the standing of the parties in the opinion polls. An Ipsos MORI opinion poll, taken on 12–14 September, showed the Conservatives on 52 per cent, Labour on 24 per cent and the Liberal Democrats on 12 per cent (Ipsos MORI, 2008a). As Ipsos MORI recorded: 'This is both the highest Conservative lead ever recorded by Ipsos MORI, and also the largest Conservative share we have ever recorded.'

The focus was on the Tory lead over Labour. That lead reduced later in the year as Gordon Brown accrued some popular support for his handling of the economic crisis that hit the nation in the autumn. There are two features here that are especially salient. The first is that Labour narrowed the gap, at one point – according to one poll – closing it. This undermines the cyclical thesis: namely, that after a number of years the desire for change will deliver victory to the opposition. On this thesis, Cameron was leader at the right time. The poll data suggested that simply standing back and waiting was not sufficient.

The second and arguably the key feature that derived from the lead established in the 12–14 September Ipsos MORI poll was the level of support for the Liberal Democrats. Insofar as electors distrusted Labour, their disaffection did not translate into support for the third party. There was a greater willingness than on the previous occasions cited above to support the Conservative Party. The party might not be elected at the next election, but electors were treating it as electable. In short, it was seen as a credible alternative to the Labour Government. This was reflected in the tactics adopted by the Liberal Democrats. They started playing 'me too' in relation to the Conservatives. They followed the Conservative practice when faltering in the opinion polls of replacing the party leader (replacing Sir Menzies Campbell with Nick Clegg). They changed policies (notably on taxation) as well as switching tactics to target Labour rather than Conservative seats.

The change in Liberal Democrat tactics reflected the elite and popular perception of the Conservative Party that was lacking in the preceding two parliaments. The media, interest groups, and the civil service recognized that the Conservative Party might now form the next government, indeed was considered more likely than not to form the next government. Interest groups and other organizations, having previously deserted it, re-discovered the party. In previous years, the party had difficulty attracting organizations to hire stands at the party conference. In 2008, Tory politicians attending the conference were inundated with invitations to meetings on the conference fringe. The Conservative Party had the air of a party of governance. It was seen as electable. One notable finding of the September Ipsos MORI poll was that 54 per cent of those questioned believed that the Conservatives were ready to form the next Government.

What, then, has brought this about? What did the Conservative Party do to render itself as electable? What did the Conservatives do wrong between 1997 and 2005 (not electable), and what have they apparently done right since 2005 (electable)?

What did the Conservatives do wrong?

The period between 1997 and 2001 was a dismal one for the Conservative Party. As one Conservative MP subsequently conceded: 'Looking back, it is clear that the events of the 1997–2001 parliament were a disaster for the Conservative Party. Far from undergoing a great revival, the party slipped back further' (Taylor, 2003: 229).

Let me summarize the reasons for Conservative failure in 2001.[2] First, there was no fresh thinking that allowed the party to claim the intellectual high ground. There were sporadic forays but nothing that moved the party away from terrain that it had previously occupied. As Seldon and Snowdon observed: 'Much effort was expended trying to find a "narrative" to explain why the electorate should vote Conservative, but none could be found' (Seldon and Snowdon, 2005: 253).

Second, there was a failure to link ideas to policies. Broad principles enunciated by the leadership were not given effect in the policy positions taken by the party. The closest that the leadership came to making that link was in the 2002 document *Leadership with a Purpose: A Better Society*. Though some likened it to the 1975 policy document *The Right Approach*, the comparison, as Lynch and Garnett noted, '… was overstated: though it provided some themes, it did not deliver a particularly distinctive or compelling narrative' (Lynch and Garnett, 2003: 262).

Third, and related, there was an excess of policy proposals. Far from there being a shortage of policies, there was a surfeit of them. The more that were published, the more confused the electorate became. There was an emphasis on detail, lots of it. In 2000, Geoffrey Howe argued the case for fresh policy positions: 'That', he wrote, 'certainly doesn't require another bible of detail on everything under the sun, such as the *Common Sense Revolution* document'.[3] Furthermore, the more that was published, the more ammunition the party handed to its critics. Various policies were rushed out and then, when they attracted serious criticism, were abandoned. Critics could pick and choose which of the many policy pronouncements to emphasize. They were successful especially in characterizing the Tories as 'extreme'. Tory frontbencher Shaun Woodward made such a claim in defecting to Labour. During the 2001 election campaign, two former MPs, John Lee and Tony Nelson, defected, claiming that the party had become too right-wing.

Fourth, many policies appeared to be reactive. Not only were some dropped when they attracted strong opposition, but others were also introduced in response to what was perceived to be popular at the time. Policies were adapted to meet shifting public moods, as over the issue of fuel prices. The effect was to convey that the party was opportunistic rather than principled. As Seldon and Snowdon noted: 'The Party was all too easily lampooned by its critics for peddling "bandwagon politics"' (Seldon and Snowdon, 2005: 253).

Fifthly, the party appeared divided. As I wrote in my analysis of the party in that parliament, 'Not only could the party not convey a consistent message, it could not convey a united message' (Norton, 2002: 81). European integration continued to be a particular bone of contention within the party's ranks and was compounded by divisions over social policy, including immigration, homosexuality, and drugs. What it demonstrated, as I have argued elsewhere, is that Thatcherism was starting to unravel (Norton, 2002: 87).

Against this background, William Hague failed to establish himself as prime ministerial material; in this respect, he was in the mould of Michael Foot and Neil Kinnock. According to MORI polls conducted throughout the parliament, the proportion of those satisfied with his leadership never reached 30 per cent. The party was also hit by continuing scandal, not least in respect of Jeffrey Archer, who had to withdraw as the party's candidate for London mayor.

As the 2001 election approached, and it was obvious the party was heading for defeat, the leadership shifted its approach and adopted a core-vote strategy. The problem with this approach was that it entailed embracing policies that alienated the very voters that the party needed to attract if it was to stand any chance of improving its position, never mind winning. The result was, in effect, a standstill election in terms of parliamentary representation. It was even worse than that in terms of party attachment. The 2001 results meant that former Conservative voters who had voted Labour in 1997 had also abandoned the party in 2001. They had lost the habit of voting Conservative.

The Conservatives would have lost the election in 2001 regardless of the actions of the party leader. The necessary condition for Labour to lose was not in place. Labour was presiding over an apparently sound economy and had done nothing major to dent the support it had garnered in 1997. It was not notably vulnerable. Labour was clearly going to win. The fact that the Conservative Party had not demonstrated that it was electable enhanced the scale of Labour's victory but was not the cause of it. There was no evidence that the electors were looking for a credible alternative. The important point for my thesis is that, in 2001, neither condition for Opposition victory was met.

The short-term approach taken by the party in the parliament of 1997–2001 was adopted in the subsequent one. Hague's successors, Iain Duncan Smith and Michael Howard, effectively repeated the mistakes of the previous parliament. Like Hague, Duncan Smith lacked deep support and was elected more for who he was not than for who he was. He had reached the final ballot in the leadership contest because he wasn't Michael Portillo and he won the final ballot because he wasn't Kenneth Clarke. Duncan Smith looked an older version of William Hague and rather acted like a poorer version. He lacked Hague's oratorical skills and his speeches failed to make an impression. He appeared inconsistent and split the party on a range of issues.[4] A former Maastricht rebel, he accused some in the party of disloyalty. When a number of Tory MPs voted for gay adoption – in defiance of a three-line whip – he read into their action an attempt to destabilize his leadership. He called a snap press conference and said that the party had 'to unite or die!'[5] The *Times* columnist Matthew Parris observed that 'death is a distinct possibility'.[6] MPs began to share Parris' view and during 2003 there was a growing pressure for Duncan Smith to be ousted from the leadership. Just before the party conference in October of that year, a YouGov poll found that 53 per cent of party members felt that the party made a mistake in electing him as leader.[7] When parliament resumed, the requisite number of Tory MPs had written to the chairman of the 1922 Committee requesting a vote of confidence in the leader. The vote took place on 29 October. Probably the best speech Duncan Smith made as leader was his last one, when he addressed the 1922 Committee, but it was too late: he was ousted by 90 votes to 75.

Sensing the dangers of another bruising leadership contest, Tory MPs coalesced behind one leadership contender, Michael Howard.[8] By the time Howard declared his candidature, he had already amassed the support of more than half the parliamentary party.[9] Recognizing the mood of the parliamentary party, no other leadership contender put their name forward. Howard was proclaimed as leader at a meeting of the 1922 Committee. The mood at the meeting, compared with that previously addressed by Duncan Smith, was notably optimistic: Howard was seen as having the potential to take the party to victory or at least seriously dent the Government's majority at the next election.

In the event, Howard failed to deliver. He repeated some of the mistakes of his predecessors. He proclaimed his views, but failed to convey a clear sense of direction. As with both his predecessors, there were inconsistencies. He appeared opportunistic. He led his party in opposition to university top-up fees, even though they were a logical extension of what the party had done in government. He carried the party in the Commons, but Tory peers were more supportive of the proposal. He sought to make an issue of the absence of weapons of mass destruction in Iraq, while stating that he would still have voted for war with Iraq. Not wanting to be outflanked by the government, he decided to support the introduction of identity cards. He argued his case before the 1922 Committee: it was clear that he was having an uphill struggle. Only a little over half the parliamentary party turned up to support him in the division lobbies. There were tensions between some in the party dubbed 'modernizers' and those dubbed 'traditionalists', not least on the issue of gay rights. The modernizers could claim to appeal to the wider electorate and the traditionalists to core Tory supporters, though not to all Tory voters.[10]

The consequence of all this was an extension of what had gone before. In a YouGov poll in September 2004, 68 per cent of those questioned agreed that it was 'hard to know what the Conservatives stand for at the moment'.[11] This figure was higher than the one the previous year under Duncan Smith's leadership. As a general election loomed, Howard followed the approach of Hague and drew the wagons around the party: he adopted a 'core vote' strategy. Whereas Hague had gone for the issue of Europe, Howard took the issue of immigration. Although voters supported the party's stance on immigration, only 9 per cent thought the issue was important. On the economy, Labour enjoyed a lead of 30 points at the start of the campaign, and it increased as the campaign progressed. The result was another Labour victory, despite lacking the confidence of voters. Labour was returned to office because the voters saw no credible alternative. The first condition was met, but not the second.

What has Cameron done right?

David Cameron was the surprise victor of the party's leadership contest in 2005, sweeping aside candidates thought more likely to win, notably

Ken Clarke and David Davis. Cameron started his campaign with a little more than a dozen MPs on his side and finished it by winning 134,446 votes to Davis' 64,398 in the vote of the party membership (Elliott and Hanning, 2007: 256–90). After his election, Cameron adopted an approach, and re-positioned the party, in such a way as to make it electable. The Government succeeded in meeting the first condition. As for the second, Cameron appeared to craft a credible, and hence electable, Opposition. He did so having learned the lessons of earlier periods of Opposition. Fundamentally, he did not engage in the politics of panic and avoided a short-term approach. As I have previously argued (Norton, 2008), Cameron's approach was characterized by five features that stand in contrast to those adopted by his immediate predecessors.

First, he has proved more value-oriented than his predecessors and has recognized that values come first; policies come later in order to give effect to those values. Like Churchill and Thatcher, he has recognized the need to convey a value-driven approach, in essence that the party stands *for* something, other than simply winning elections.

Second, he has identified new areas of concern. He has moved away from the traditional policy areas that have been at the heart of appeals to the party's core voters and instead has raised the environment and other ethical issues that resonate with the electorate. Unlike the Cornerstone group of Conservative MPs, he appears to have read Michael Ashcroft's *Smell the Coffee* (2005), which identified the basis of the public's dissatisfaction with the party's stance and policies, and has taken its findings to heart. He has recognized that the electorate has changed and that the party has to craft its appeal to resonate with electors. At the 2005 Channel 4 Parliamentary Awards ceremony, where he won the award for opposition politician of the year, John Bercow said that MPs who fell out with their party often claimed that they had stayed the same but it was their party that had changed. With him, he said, it was the other way round. He had changed, but his party had not.[12] Cameron has learned the lesson and it is the party that is changing.

A corollary of this change has been emphasizing what the party is for rather than what it is against. The 'extremist' tag attached to the party at the 2001 and 2005 elections was fuelled by the appearance of being, in Theresa May's words, 'the nasty party'. The party was seen as being against things, be it European integration, immigrants, or gay sex. Even if people sympathized with some of its stances, they nonetheless did not want to be associated with it. David Cameron has re-positioned the party, for example, to be *for* the National Health Service – keeping and improving it was identified as a top priority; to be *for* the family (rather than being against, or appearing to be against, certain family units); and to be *for* equality on issues such as gay rights; in doing so, he has proved to be in tune with changing – certainly a more tolerant – popular opinion.[13] 'What we want', Cameron said, 'is for people to be different but to be treated equally, rather than for people to be treated differently' (cited in Jones, 2008: 170). There was an emphasis on those who wanted to do well and improve their position in life: 'There is still that aspirational side to us, because we're on the side of striving people' (cited in Jones, 2008: 106). In the September 2008 Ipsos MORI poll, 49 per cent of those questioned thought that Cameron represented 'modern Britain'; only 36 per cent disagreed (Ipsos MORI, 2008a). Combining these first two points, Cameron has, for example, emphasized what has been termed 'the politics of wellbeing'. Speaking in 2006 he declared:

> Well-being can't be measured by money or traded in markets. It's about the beauty of our surroundings, the quality of our culture, and above all, the strength of our relationships ... It's time we admitted that there's more to life than money, and it's time we focussed not just on GDP but on GWB – general well-being. (Cited in Marshall et al., 2007: 24)

As the authors of the Ipsos MORI report on *Blair's Britain: The Social and Cultural Legacy* record laconically: 'The data suggests he may have a point' (Marshall et al., 2007: 24). Voters were less content than before, despite being richer, and were emphasizing more ethical consumerism and the environment.

Third, he has avoided making too many specific commitments. He has been accused of being 'policy-lite'. That was the charge levelled by Labour Government ministers, but that was an easier charge to live with than the charge of generating excessive, inconsistent and uncosted policies. Specific policy commitments were seen as necessary for an election manifesto, not for the period in between elections. When there was no election in the offing, Cameron could offer the occasional policy – or engage in occasional kite flying – sufficient to show that the Opposition was engaged in serious thought, but nothing that would necessarily stick and nothing that carried a significant price tag. Raising the prospect of a British Bill of Rights, or embracing English votes for English laws, was a means of attracting some attention, showing the party was not somnolent, but not something that would create a headache for the Shadow Chancellor. Instead, media attention focused on Government policy. Only at times of economic crisis and in response to Government actions did the party have to generate or revise policy commitments, adapted in light of the situation a future Tory Government was likely to face. Otherwise, most policy commitments were for the manifesto rather than for the next day's press.

Fourth, he appointed groups to consider policy options. This draws on the practice of previous periods of what may be termed successful periods of opposition. They were not much in evidence in the period from 1997 to 2005. William Hague appointed three commissions – I chaired one of them – and showed what could be done in researching a subject, engaging with people outside the party, and generating considered conclusions; but the practice was not extended. It was the exception rather than the norm. David Cameron made it the norm. This had several benefits. It provided a defence to the claim that the party was not generating policies. Rather, it was ensuring that the policies it would put forward at the next election were fully considered. It was also a means of drawing in people who were not party members but who were prepared to contribute to these arm's-length inquiries. A number of the groups have been advised by high-profile public figures. It also provided a means of allowing new ideas to be given an airing, under the auspices of the groups, without carrying the party's endorsement. If they attracted a bad press, they could be disowned. Throughout the exercise, Cameron made clear that the groups were offering advice to the party. There was no commitment that their recommendations would find their way into the party's election manifesto. The recommendations would need to be considered by the shadow cabinet, with input from the 1922 Committee, before they could make it as policy for a future Conservative Government.

The work of the different policy groups also enabled the party to convey that it was occupying the intellectual high ground, as it did in the late 1970s. It did so against the backdrop of a Government that was lacking new ideas and had moved from being a Government to an administration responding to events.

Fifth, and finally, Cameron directed his appeal to the centre ground of British politics. By this, I refer to the electoral centre rather than the ideological centre, conveying that the party is close to the median position of electors in their ascription of where they stand. Like Blair, his approach has been inclusive, moving away from a narrow partisan appeal to a more broad-based approach. The advantages have been most marked under the Brown premiership. Whereas under Blair, Cameron's approach was dismissed by some as essentially a 'me too' approach at a time when it appeared to be losing its appeal, under Brown it appeared to have borne political capital. As Brown embraced a strident partisan approach, often harking back to previous periods of Tory government, Cameron's softer, inclusive approach served to achieve a resonance that eluded Gordon Brown.

There is one other element of Cameron's leadership that enabled these characteristics to deliver a marked improvement in Tory fortunes. That is Cameron's skills at communication. Hague and Howard were good debaters, but their oratorical skills lacked the softer edge that Cameron employs in reaching out beyond the House of Commons. The position is well summarized by Elliott and Hanning, when they write:

> The 'project' he commands is every bit as much about David Cameron as New Labour was about Tony Blair. Voters are invited to believe that the Tories have changed because he has changed, that they have strong values because he has them and that his party is no longer 'nasty' because he himself is likeable. (Elliott and Hanning, 2007: 291)

Cameron has achieved one notable result denied his predecessors. The Ipsos MORI poll of September 2008 found that Labour was seen as more likely than the Tories to 'promise anything to win votes': 40 per cent thought Labour more likely to make such promises, against 36 per cent giving such a response for the Conservatives. I cite one other feature of the poll that demonstrates that the Conservative Party was seen as being electable. The Conservative Party was considered to be better than Labour (by 39 per cent to 21 per cent) in 'having the best team of leaders' (Ipsos MORI, 2008a). That perception was not necessarily immutable but it was something that set the party apart from how it was viewed in the previous two parliaments.

Conclusion

David Cameron has thus been central to resuscitating the Conservative Party as a party of government: a party recognized by the electorate as being a viable alternative to Labour as a governing party. Government unpopularity remains a necessary condition for a Government to lose an election. However, the Opposition has to be seen as electable if popular dissatisfaction with Government is not to be channelled into support for third parties or even a reluctant retention of the Government in office. There is a difference between being elected and being electable, but without being electable a party is not going to be elected. In the 2005 parliament, the Conservative Party became electable, in a way that it was not in the period between 1997 and 2005. One cannot explain why that is the case without factoring in the leadership of David Cameron. *Quod erat demonstrandum.*

Notes

1. For Callaghan's reluctance to risk an election, see Donoughue (2008: 412).
2. For further information on this failure, see Norton (2002: 68–94).
3. *Independent*, 4 November 2000. Quoted in Norton (2002: 80).
4. For more information, see Norton (2002: 38–40).
5. *Independent*, 6 November 2002.
6. BBC News Online, 6 November 2002.
7. *Daily Telegraph*, 9 October 2003.
8. For more information, see Crick (2005: ch.19).
9. *Daily Telegraph*, 31 October 2003.
10. See, further, Ashcroft (2005: 26–7).
11. *Daily Telegraph*, 4 October 2004.
12. Channel 4 Parliamentary Awards Ceremony, 8 February 2005.
13. Ipsos MORI polls have tapped a marked increase in acceptance of homosexuality. A majority of electors now believe (which they did not do before 2001) that sexual relations between two adults of the same sex is not at all wrong. More remarkably, an unpublished Ipsos MORI poll found that the percentage of people believing gay couples should be allowed to get married increased from 46 per cent in 2000 to 68 per cent in 2007. See Marshall et al. (2007: 39).

4
David Cameron and the Renewal of Policy

Simon Lee

When the Conservative Party lost general elections in 1945 and 1966, it set in train reviews of its ideas and policies which moved it closer to those of the incumbent government. When the Conservative Party lost two general elections during 1974, rather than moving her party closer to the ideas and policies of the Wilson and Callaghan governments, Margaret Thatcher decided to break with the post-war social democratic Keynesian consensus of state-led modernization. Instead she harnessed the Conservative Party to market liberalism, and eventually implemented policies of liberalization, deregulation and privatization that enabled the Conservatives to win the battle of party ideology, and define British politics for a generation. Consequently, when he became party leader in December 2005, David Cameron had to determine the extent to which there would need to be continuity and change in the party's policies. For the Conservative Party to avoid the possibility of a fourth consecutive general election defeat, Cameron had to avoid the mistakes in party ideology and policy which had confined his four immediate predecessors to the opposition benches.

In the event, Cameron decided to follow the example set by Tony Blair following his election as Labour Party leader in June 1994. Despite Labour having already experienced 15 years of opposition, four consecutive general election defeats, and a major review of party policy between 1997 and 2001, Blair had determined that urgent policy reform was still necessary because his party still lacked a credible project that would persuade voters in numbers sufficient to elect a Labour government.

Consequently, Blair had chosen to demonstrate to the public how his party had changed, and was committed to changing the United Kingdom, by drawing up a new Labour Party constitution and creating a 'New Labour' programme for political, economic and social renewal. Rather than opt for Old Labour's state-led social democratic modernization agenda or Thatcherism's market-led, neo-liberal alternative, Blair had chosen a Third Way of modernized social democratic renewal (Lee, 2003).

This chapter will demonstrate how, from the very outset, David Cameron adopted a similar urgency to Blair by seeking to persuade his party of the need for urgent policy reform. However, it will be argued that there are several distinctive features of Cameron's approach to the renewal of Conservative Party policy. First, unlike his predecessors from Heath to Howard, Cameron decided that the focus of his policy review should be upon addressing social decline rather than the United Kingdom's relative economic decline. In short, where Thatcher had 'mended the broken economy in the 1980s, so we want to mend Britain's broken society in the early decades of the twenty-first century' (cited in Jones, 2008: 308–9). This strategy has been adopted because Cameron's thesis has been that the Conservative Party has won the battle of ideas in British politics, as proven by the very existence of the New Labour project. Therefore, in reviewing its policy, the party's challenge has been to come to terms with its triumph, and extend the victorious idea of entrepreneur- and market-driven change and renewal from the realm of the economy to that of society, by creating a new generation of social entrepreneurs.

Second, the development of Conservative Party policy under Cameron can be divided into three distinct phases. During the first phase from December 2005 until September 2007, six policy groups commissioned by Cameron developed detailed recommendations for the future direction of Conservative Party policy. It was assumed throughout this period that the economy was not broken, that the proceeds of continuing economic growth would be available to share between the public services, the taxpayer and the consumer, and that the policy priority was fixing the broken society. During a second phase of Conservative Party policy development from September 2007 until November 2007, triggered by the demise of Northern Rock and a series of bank bailouts and recapitalizations, Conservative Party policy continued to address the broken society, but became increasingly preoccupied with the mounting evidence that the economy was indeed broken. This phase, during which Cameron and Osborne developed a critique of the Brown government's economic policies, is addressed in the next chapter. During the third phase of Conservative Party policy development, from November 2008 onwards, Cameron has abandoned his previous strategy of matching the Blair and Brown governments' planned totals for public spending. Instead, Cameron has orchestrated the publication of a series of Conservative Party policies designed both to highlight the failure of the Labour governments' modernization programme for national renewal since May 1997 to fix the United Kingdom's (allegedly) broken economy, society and polity, and to outline some of the Conservatives' alternative policy proposals.

The chapter will also focus upon a third distinctive feature of Cameron's compassionate conservatism approach to policy renewal which is the separation of the British state from British society. Entrepreneurial initiative and the innovation of individuals, businesses and voluntary organizations operating in civil society have been identified as the principal agencies of social change that will deliver Cameron's agenda for fixing the United Kingdom's broken society. This process, which has drawn heavily upon ideas which inspired the Bush Administration during the first decade of the new century, has entailed a political renaissance for Iain Duncan Smith, Cameron's immediate predecessor but one as Conservative Party leader. The chapter will suggest that Cameron's strategy for policy renewal now confronts some major challenges and serious political risks, not least the prospect of a Conservative government having to take office against the context of the deepest recession since the Great Depression of the 1930s and the weakest public finances since the end of the Second World War. Cameron's objective is to lower public expectations of the state in the longer term but, as the record of past governments has attested, not least those of Thatcher herself, public policy can be a very blunt instrument when seeking to alter the expectations of the British electorate.

Learning the lessons from past Conservative policy renewal

The Conservative Party is not accustomed to Opposition. It held office, either on its own or in coalition, for around 70 years of the twentieth century. As historians of the party have noted, the 'Conservative Century' reflected the overriding importance placed upon securing office and holding on to power (Seldon and Ball, 1994; Davies, 1995). Policy and ideology had been adjusted pragmatically to these ends. This trend came to an abrupt end in May 1997. The Conservative Party's 1997 general election result was its worst defeat since 1906. It had won its fewest votes since 1929 and its lowest share of the vote since 1832. The party had campaigned with the slogan and manifesto title, *You Can Only Be Sure with The Conservatives* (Conservative Party, 1997). The manifesto had reminded voters that Conservative economic policy had delivered a post-war record sixth consecutive year of growth; inflation at below 4 per cent for the longest period for almost half a century; the lowest mortgage rates for 30 years; and the lowest unemployment for six years (Conservative Party, 1997: 6). However, despite this record, the Conservative vote collapsed as people remembered the deep recession of the early 1990s, which had only been ended by the financial trauma and national humiliation of 'Black Wednesday' (16 September 1992). Party ideology and policy appeared to be in such disarray that political obituaries were written for conservatism itself (e.g. Gray, 1997). Some within the party urged new party leader William Hague to 'learn the lessons of 1906 and 1945. We need both renewal of our organisation and a programme to reach out to the electorate with whom we have lost contact' (Willetts, 1998: 116). Others claimed the time was ripe for 'a new statement of principles which brings the party back to the "One Nation" approach of the postwar period' (Garnett and Gilmour, 1998: 130).

In the event, Hague chose to modernize his party's organization, but failed to complete the sort of thorough long-term policy review which had been instrumental between 1945–51, 1965–70 and 1975–79 in regaining power. A policy review was begun under the leadership of Peter Lilley, but effectively abandoned because of the fear that it was failing to identify 'clear blue water' between Conservative policy and New Labour (Seldon and Snowdon, 2001: 11). As Dorey has noted, 'In the context of such uncertainty, Conservative policies often lacked coherence, clarity and consistency' (Dorey, 2005: 125). For example, Hague's own 'Tax Guarantee' flagship policy pledge to the 1999 Conservative Party conference, that taxes would fall as a proportion of national income during the lifetime of a future Conservative government, was abandoned in July 2000 in a joint announcement by Hague and his Shadow Chancellor, Michael Portillo (Dorey, 2005: 129). The Conservative Party's 2001 general election result was little better than 1997. One additional seat was won at Westminster, but 1.2 million fewer people voted for the Conservatives. The party manifesto had claimed it was *time for common sense* (Conservative Party, 2001), but few voters had been attracted by its promise to cut taxation and save the pound.

Under William Hague, the Conservative Party had no answer to the New Labour agenda of economic, social and political renewal. At the same time, it had failed to resolve the dilemma of whether the appropriate response to Tony Blair and New Labour was to move closer to the Labour government ideologically and in policy terms, or to move further to the right to adopt a purer form of Thatcherism. These same problems were to hinder the renewal of Conservative Party policy under both Iain Duncan Smith and Michael Howard. In 2005, under the orchestration of Michael Howard and David Cameron, as chief policy coordinator, the Conservative manifesto had asked the electorate *Are You Thinking What We're Thinking?* (Conservative Party, 2005). Party policy had been simplified and summarized in 11 words: 'More police, cleaner hospitals, lower taxes, school discipline, controlled immigration, accountability', but these policies had yielded only an additional 33 seats.

In the wake of the 2005 general election defeat, Michael Ashcroft's detailed study of public opinion towards the Conservative Party and its policies had served up some important lessons about the policies developed by the Conservative Party under the leadership of Michael Howard and David Cameron, as the party's policy coordinator. It had found that no fewer than 53 per cent of voters concurred with the proposition that 'the Conservative Party doesn't seem to stand for anything anymore'; 70 per cent thought 'the Conservatives just attack the government over whatever happens to be in the news, but never say anything positive'; and only 38 per cent thought the Conservatives 'would do a good job of running the country' (cited in Ashcroft, 2005: 7). When asked, by a majority of 78 per cent, voters wanted the Conservatives to concentrate on the development of policies to improve the National Health Service and other major public services. By a majority of 46 per cent, voters also wanted the party to champion policies that would make government less interfering in how people lived their lives, and by a majority of 44 per cent to involve more women, young people and ethnic minorities in the party 'to make the Conservatives look more like modern Britain'. Intriguingly, no fewer than 81 per cent of 18–24 year olds stated a specific policy commitment to tax cuts would make them more likely to vote Conservative (Ashcroft, 2005: 22–3).

In his own approach as party leader to the renewal of policy, David Cameron has demonstrated that he has learnt some vital lessons from the failure of previous Conservative leaders since 1997. Cameron may be a fan of his Foreign Secretary, William Hague, and has described him as 'a great leader', not least because he thought Hague had initially set out with a modernizing programme. Indeed, Cameron was initially 'very pro-Hague at the time [1997 and 1998], but then he changed tack' (Jones, 2008: 75), and had made the mistake of shoring up the Conservatives' core vote, at the expense of deterring floating voters and defectors from other parties. Thus, Hague's particular value to Cameron as an adviser and confidant in the renewal of policy would be that 'he made all the mistakes the first time round' (ibid.: 112). Following Hague's departure as party leader, Cameron had voted initially for Michael Portillo rather than Iain Duncan Smith 'because he thought the party needed a change', but then voted for Smith in the membership ballot (ibid.: 77). Following Smith's departure, he also supported Michael Howard, because 'the party needed shoring up', but despite Howard's professionalism, organizational skills and performance in the Commons, he too had made the same mistake as William Hague. In Cameron's judgement, 'After making some modernising announcements he lurched to the right' (cited in ibid.: 80).

Of his own candidacy for the party leadership, and that of David Davis, Cameron has stated 'I didn't think he was the obvious choice' (cited in Jones, 2008: 84). The Conservative Party must engage in and win 'the day-to-day battle of the media' because 'If you don't win that battle then you're history' (ibid.: 310). The Conservative Party also needed to broaden its appeal because 'If the Conservative Party cannot appeal to people in the heart of our great cities then we are failing', for the party had become 'too rural and too southern and we need to change that' (ibid.: 137–8). Therefore, it was apparent that under the leadership of David Cameron, the party's renewal of policy would take a very different direction, and one that could find some policy answers to challenge Tony Blair, Gordon Brown and the New Labour modernization project.

The policy groups: the first phase of Cameron's policy renewal

Within a week of becoming party leader, David Cameron had set out his agenda for the renewal of party policy as part of his wider 'change to win' agenda for the renewal of the Conservative Party itself. Announcing the appointment of six policy groups, to respond in turn to the six big 'complex and interconnected' challenges confronting the United Kingdom and the world, Cameron promised the development of policy 'on the basis of hard work and hard thinking, drawing on the best and most creative ideas, wherever they come from'. Moreover, the policy groups would not be 'stuffed with politicians but led by the best thinkers, with a passion for change and a desire to get to grips with these difficult challenges' (Cameron, 2005e). As it happened, these 'best thinkers' happened to include as chairmen, no fewer than five former Conservative cabinet ministers: John Redwood (Economic Competitiveness Policy Group), Peter Lilley (Globalization and Global Poverty), Stephen Dorrell (Public Services Improvement), John Gummer (Quality of Life) and, most notably of all, Iain Duncan Smith (Social Justice). Pauline Neville-Jones, the former Chairman of the Joint Intelligence Committee and chair of the

National and International Security Policy Group, was the only woman and non-politician to chair any of the policy groups.

In identifying these six major challenges and policy areas, Cameron claimed 'This is our agenda for the next four years.' His wish was that the policy groups would be 'the national focus for debate, discussion and free thinking' (Cameron, 2005e). However, in giving the groups 18 months to report, Cameron almost guaranteed that the groups could not possibly be the national focus of debate, particularly when in competition with developments in government policy, and the regular outpourings of influential and media savvy think tanks on the right, notably Policy Exchange and the Centre for Policy Studies, Margaret Thatcher and Sir Keith Joseph's fulcrum for winning the battle of ideas during the late 1970s. What was also conspicuous about the policy groups was that only one was devoted to economic policy, reflecting Cameron's intention to switch the focus of Conservative Party policy towards the United Kingdom's purportedly broken society. At the same time, Cameron specified that their recommendations would not be binding upon the shadow cabinet. None of the groups' work was devoted to any of the policy issues – Europe, crime or immigration – which had previously either created divisions within the party and/or deterred prospective voters. Moreover, given that the Economic Competitiveness Policy Group was being chaired by an unreconstructed and unrepentant disciple of Thatcherism (e.g. Redwood, 2002), it was highly improbable that its likely principal recommendation of sizeable tax cuts would be countenanced by either Cameron or his Shadow Chancellor, George Osborne. They had repeatedly warned that there would be no fiscal policy announcements or spending commitments which had not first been fully costed, had their personal approval, and the subsequent endorsement of the shadow cabinet.

With the exception of the Social Justice Policy Group, which was attached to Iain Duncan Smith's Centre for Social Justice, none of the policy groups attracted much public attention during their research work. By the time the first policy groups reported in July 2007, their work had been largely forgotten. A further problem with the reports was their sheer length and diversity of policy recommendations. For example, the Quality of Life Policy Group's *Blueprint for a Green Economy* weighed in at 540 pages, hardly an environmentally sustainable use of resources. This was, however, positively brief compared with the output of Duncan Smith's Social Justice Policy Group. Following its 3,000 hours of public hearings and submissions from more than 2,000 organizations to its Working Groups, no fewer than six volumes and more than 1,000 pages of policy recommendations were published to set out its 'Breakthrough Britain' agenda for redressing the broken society (Social Justice Policy Group, 2007).

Cameron's policy renewal and Thatcherism: continuity or change?

By the time the final of Cameron's six commissioned policy groups' reports had been published in September 2007, it had become apparent that their policy recommendations were diverse, and apparently lacking any unifying theme (apart from their length) that might, in due course, form the basis of a future Conservative Party manifesto. In a sense, their effect had been basically to reinforce Cameron's control over the policy renewal agenda, since so few of their recommendations appeared likely to attract widespread public support. Given the possibility that Gordon Brown would call a snap general election, this threw the limelight back on to Cameron's own ideology and policy agenda, and whether his thinking would mark essential continuity with or a departure from the legacy of previous Conservative Party leaders, most notably Margaret Thatcher.

Cameron's biographers have noted that 'he was, as university friends confirm, a dyed-in-the-wool Thatcherite himself, and his parents, especially his father, idolised her' (Elliott and Hanning, 2007: 83). Indeed, as one former colleague from Cameron's time as a special adviser to Norman Lamont had reflected, 'He was a twenty-five-year-old natural Tory who had come to help the Conservatives – but to help the Tory Party that Margaret Thatcher had built' (cited in Elliott and Hanning, 2007: 106). That Thatcherism has provided and will continue to provide the blueprint for the Cameron-led Conservative Party's policy renewal has been affirmed in Cameron's statement that 'You can trace very clearly the line between the Thatcher Conservative Party that was about transforming our economy and recognizing the limitations of government in regard to the economy and what I'm saying, which is that we need a similar scale of transformation in terms of our society' (cited in Jones, 2008: 309).

Cameron has acknowledged his personal debt to Thatcher, in making environmental issues a cornerstone of Conservative policy, by claiming he was awakened to such matters by 'the great Thatcher speech of '88, or was it '89' (cited in Jones, 2008: 232). This was Thatcher's 8 November 1989 address to the General Assembly of the United Nations, which actually served as a platform for legitimizing the privatization of the water and electricity supply industries. However, Cameron has also asserted that 'towards the end of the 1980s we had become too much the economics party' (ibid.: 288). The Conservative Party was certainly not insufficiently pro-business or pro-free market or pro-City: 'our problem was no one knew what we thought about the health service, or the environment or society' (ibid.: 290). Therefore, by widening the application of, rather than abandoning, the Thatcherite principles of entrepreneur-led and market-led initiative and innovation, Cameron's prescription for policy renewal has been that 'The centre right have still got some of the best arguments about how we change society, how we improve the economy, how we get people back to work, how we get better results from schools, and a modern generation of Conservatives can make those arguments free of the baggage of the past' (ibid.: 177). In short, there should be both continuity and change in Conservative Party policy.

Compassionate conservatism: the political rebirth of Iain Duncan Smith

In outlining the ideas that have underpinned his agenda for policy renewal, David Cameron has claimed he has always had 'a very liberal conservative outlook – freedom of the individual but believing in a responsible society, too' (cited in Jones, 2008: 32). He has also confessed not to like 'grand plans and grand visions', but to be 'an instinctive Conservative' (ibid.: 43, 78). This approach has been founded upon a belief in the importance of understanding the instincts of those being governed, which is a question 'all about character, and in the end I think that's more important than any one particular policy' (ibid.: 104). The aim of Conservative Party policy must be 'Giving people more power and control over their own lives. Trusting people rather than big government. All else follows from there' (ibid.: 105). The Conservative Party should be aspirational, with 'a very clear set of values, understanding that society is built from the bottom up, it's about individuals and families and neighbourhood organisations and we want to strengthen those ties that bind, that help families and help couples' (ibid.: 106). For these reasons, Cameron has also claimed to enjoy devolving power, because 'the best politicians are the ones with clear principles who are pragmatic' (ibid.: 108; 110).

For Cameron, the big theme for the Conservative Party's policy renewal is 'mending Britain's broken society' (cited in Jones, 2008: 63). Here a key distinction must be drawn between state and society, for 'Labour is about the state and we are about society' (ibid.: 78). For Cameron, 'The big picture is explaining to people that real change is not delivered by government on its own, it's delivered by everyone playing their part in a responsible society', which means the agents of social change are not the institutions of the British state but individuals, families and businesses, acting as social entrepreneurs (ibid.: 308). People should be encouraged to take risks, particularly to be entrepreneurial in the public sector (ibid.: 147).

The ideological inspiration for this approach to policy reform, like so many aspects of Gordon Brown's agenda for economic and social renewal (Lee, 2007b, 2009), has emanated from the United States, in the form of the political ideology and domestic policy agenda of President George W. Bush, and his policy adviser Marvin Olavsky. For Bush, 'Conservatism must be the creed of hope'. That hope would emanate from compassionate conservatism. Bush claimed 'Often the truest kind of compassion is to help citizens build lives of their own. I call my philosophy and approach "compassionate conservatism"' (Bush, 2002: 3). As an 'economic conservative', believing in cutting taxes to stimulate economic growth, Bush contended that prosperity must also have a purpose. That should include everyone in a different form of affluence, that is, the wealth of 'justice and compassion and family love and moral courage' (Bush, 1999: 216). True compassion could not originate from paying taxes or the role of the state, for 'government can spend money, but it can't put hope or a sense of purpose in our lives'. Moreover, Bush insisted that 'Real change in our culture comes from the bottom up, not the top down', necessitating 'a different role for government. A fresh start. A bold approach', in which 'the failed compassion of towering, distant bureaucracies', would be replaced by 'government that both knows its limits and shows its heart' (Bush, 1999: 218–19).

For policy to be effective, resources 'should be devolved, not just to states, but to charities and neighborhood healers'. Social security would be strengthened by tax incentives to encourage 'an outpouring of giving' mobilizing 'the armies of compassion' (Bush, 1999: 223). To achieve this approach to policy, the nation must transcend two narrow mind-sets. First, that 'government provides the only *real* compassion'. Second, that 'if government would only get out of the way, all our problems would be solved' (Bush, 1999: 224–5). Like Thatcherism and Reaganomics before it, compassionate conservatism would not seek to create something new, but merely to restore through policy something held to have been lost, namely a land of social entrepreneurs, and a country whose citizens adhered 'to the habits promoted by any code of morality that emphasizes work, marriage, and family rather than a search for immediate gratification' (Olavsky, 2000: 107).

Bush had outlined a vision of conservatism in which 'the role of government is not to create wealth, but an environment in which the entrepreneurial spirit can flourish' (Bush, 2002: 1). Given his ambition to widen rather than abandon the application of the entrepreneurial spirit, the appeal of compassionate conservatism as the ideological basis for his renewal of Conservative Party policy was evident to David Cameron. However, he was not the first post-Thatcher Conservative Party leader to identify its potential to form the basis of an effective alternative policy agenda to New Labour's modernization programme. Compassionate conservatism's potential had first been identified by Iain Duncan Smith during his tenure as party leader. While Cameron may have learnt important lessons from Duncan Smith in terms of image and style, and how not to communicate the Conservative Party's ideas and policy to the electorate, he has equally derived substantive ideas for his conception of modern conservatism *qua* compassionate conservatism from Duncan Smith.

It was Duncan Smith who first realized that there was little mileage for the Conservatives to focus their policies on attacking New Labour with a thesis of the broken economy or the broken polity. Gordon Brown's tenure as Chancellor of the Exchequer had been marked by continuous growth, and historically low inflation, interest rates and unemployment – continuing the trends established since the final quarter of 1992, under Kenneth Clarke as Chancellor. The Conservative Party could not claim plausibly that the economy was broken, not least because opinion polls demonstrated that the Conservatives were still not trusted to deliver a competent economic policy, as a lasting consequence of their superintendence of the deep domestic recession of the early 1990s. It had ended only with the political and financial humiliation of 'Black Wednesday' (16 September 1992) – a humiliation observed at close quarters by Cameron as special adviser to then Chancellor Norman Lamont. Nor could the Conservatives claim that the political process was broken, when New Labour had implemented measures to redress the sleaze that had marked John Major's ill-starred tenure as Prime Minister.

If the Conservative Party wanted to roll back further the frontiers of the state, it would have to challenge popular expectations of state-financed welfare provision. In this society, a myriad of social problems could be attributed to the failure of New Labour's extensive social policy reform agenda. Compassionate conservatism could juxtapose the unprecedented levels of material prosperity and public spending on the welfare state with the widespread examples of societal breakdown, be it binge drinking, drug dependency, anti-social behaviour or violent crime.

The key task for compassionate conservatism would be the separation of state and society, and in particular the separation of state from civil society. On the one hand, New Labour's tax-and-spend welfare state could be portrayed as centralized, sclerotic, not joined-up, expensive, obsessed with auditing, targets and indicators, and the source of perpetual dependency and misery for a significant minority of the population. On the other, the Conservatives could offer the alternative of a society composed of individuals, families, great professions, and voluntary, charitable and community-based organizations, in which individuals would possess the freedom to enjoy 'the dignity of discretion, the freedom of standing on our own two feet', and families would come first (Streeter, 2003b: 6). The Conservatives must address directly the issue of the quality of life, and the work–life balance in modern Britain. In short, they 'must not stand for social liberalism, but social justice'. Moreover, the party must 'champion the interests of the poor in every part of Britain. Only then will the Conservative Party deserve the people's respect again' (Streeter, 2003b: 9).

For Duncan Smith himself, the challenge for the Conservative Party was nothing less than the very renewal of British society. The new central battleground in British politics between New Labour and compassionate conservatism would be 'the state–society faultline', namely Labour 'centralism versus localism; uniformity above diversity; control instead of innovation; bureaucracy rather than democracy' (Duncan Smith, 2003: 32). The project for the next Conservative government would be to extend 'the environment that fostered economic entrepreneurship' to 'a parallel project: the encouragement of social entrepreneurship and support for the people-sized institutions of society' (ibid.: 36). This in turn would require the Conservative Party 'to dig deep into the one nation heritage of our party' (ibid.: 37), but critically not to revive the technocratic pragmatism of the social democratic 'middle way' fostered by the one nation conservatism of Harold Macmillan and R.A. Butler. Furthermore, the renewal of society would require government to become 'the servant of society – not its master' (ibid.: 37), a phrase that was to resonate four years later, not in David Cameron's policies, but in the language of Prime Minister Gordon Brown's 'servant state' (Brown and Straw, 2007 cited in Lee, 2007b: 234).

The principles of compassionate conservatism were set out in a landmark publication, *There Is Such a Thing as Society*, which for the first time clarified, if it did not actually refute, Margaret Thatcher's (in)famous remark from October 1987, 'And you know, there's no such thing as society. There are individual men and women, there are families' (Thatcher, 1987). As Oliver Letwin explained, rather than being an actual denial of the existence of society, Thatcher had been pointing towards 'a more enduring vision of society – a society composed of active citizens and strong families' (Letwin, 2003: 39). In this vision, any taxpayer-funded collective provision of welfare would be a charge upon the community. Thus, the reform of local government finance in England and Wales was termed the 'community charge', rather than the poll tax, because Thatcher regarded it as a charge upon the community. That the inspiration for this Conservative renewal of society would be the compassionate conservatism of George W. Bush was comfirmed not only by the editor of *There Is Such a Thing as Society* having drawn upon the advice of Marvin Olavsky, the intellectual inspiration for the concept of compassionate conservatism (Olavsky, 2000), but also by the inclusion in the book of an essay from Rick Santorum, the Republican Senator for Pennsylvania, who pointed towards the insights of Bush's 22 July 1999 'Duty of Hope' speech, in which Bush had promised 'a government that both knows its limits, and shows its heart' (Bush, 1999, cited in Santorum, 2003: 67).

The broken economy: from critique to clear blue water

Iain Duncan Smith had identified an agenda for the Conservative renewal of policy that could be advanced as an alternative to New Labour's economic, political and social renewal proposals. The problem for Duncan Smith was that he could never develop a political narrative or transmit it persuasively to convince either his own party or the broader electorate. However, once liberated from the leadership of his party, Duncan Smith was able to use his own think tank, the Centre for Social Justice, to provide Michael Howard and David Cameron with a series of detailed case studies of the broken society and some equally detailed policy recommendations to repair it. These recommendations tended to reinforce Cameron's own agenda for the mobilization of a new generation of social entrepreneurs to reduce the burden upon the state. However, by the time Duncan Smith's Social Justice Policy Group reported in September 2007, Cameron found himself confronting a very different political scenario than when he had commissioned the six policy groups' reports 18 months earlier.

The fact that Gordon Brown had developed an opinion poll lead of between eight and ten percentage points for the Labour Party by early September 2008 (the so-called 'Brown Bounce') fuelled intense media speculation that an autumn general election would be called. David Cameron found himself confronted with a scenario where his six policy groups had reported at great length and in considerable detail, but none of them had delivered any new eye-catching or potentially vote-winning policies, to supplement his own broken society focus. In effect, an early general election would have left Cameron and Osborne to write a manifesto from scratch, a scenario which Cameron had already faced with disastrous electoral consequences in 2005. At the time, the influential Tory historian Anthony Seldon had reflected that 'Whatever the Tories do, they're doomed'. Seldon had concluded, 'The painful truth for the Tories to swallow is that, as long as Blair remains in office, backed by the Murdoch press and with the economy doing well and interest rates low, and as long as he is able to keep Labour in the centre, Howard's room for manoeuvre will be severely constrained' (Seldon, 2004).

Tony Blair is no longer in office. Gordon Brown did not call the autumn 2007 election, and missed his opportunity to expose the fact that, after two years as leader, Cameron had made little progress in developing the policies that could form the basis of a credible Conservative general election manifesto and programme for government. The collapse of Northern Rock, subsequent repeated taxpayer-funded bailouts and recapitalizations of major United Kingdom banks, allied to the onset of the deepest recession since the 1930s, have lifted some of the constraints that operated upon Michael Howard, and provided Cameron greater room for manoeuvre to develop broader and more detailed policy proposals. These have capitalized on the increasing evidence that both the British economy and British politics are broken (Lee, 2009). The Conservative Party has developed its vision for policy through the three themes of an opportunity agenda, a security agenda, and a responsibility agenda (Conservative Party, 2008a). The latter theme in particular has enabled party policy to reconnect with the aims and values first set out by Cameron's Conservatives in *Built to Last* (Conservative Party, 2006). Cameron has not neglected areas of traditional concern for core Conservative voters, notably crime and immigration, but these have been addressed within the compass of the Conservative Party's plans for social reform (e.g. Conservative Party, 2008b), rather than with the negative language that had fuelled the 'nasty party' image of the late 1990s.

Between September 2007 and November 2008, the major thrust of Conservative Party policy was a growing critique of the policies of the Brown government (e.g. Conservative Party, 2008c, 2008d). However, in the week prior to the publication of the Brown government's 2008 pre-budget report, Cameron's policy renewal entered its third phase. Cameron announced the abandonment of his party's longstanding commitment to match the government's future planned totals for public spending. As an alternative, the Conservative Party would place a greater emphasis upon fiscal responsibility by cutting future planned public spending growth. This would begin with a cut from 3.4 per cent to 2.6 per cent in real terms in planned growth for 2009–10 to finance a £5 billion package of tax cuts for savers. This policy would enhance the Conservative Party's strategy of personalizing the responsibility for the broken economy with the Prime Minister, and portraying it as Brown's 'debt crisis' (Conservative Party, 2009a).

Conclusion

When David Cameron initiated a review of Conservative Party policy in the weeks following his election as party leader, his approach was guided by two assumptions. First, because the Conservatives had won the battle of ideas, especially in political economy over the virtues of capitalism, entrepreneurship and open, liberalized markets, they simply needed to come to terms with their triumph. Tony Blair and New Labour had occupied that very same ideological common ground as the Conservatives, so the task confronting the Conservative Party now would be to develop policies, and a shadow cabinet team to implement them, which would eventually be regarded as more competent to deliver than a tired, third term Labour government. Second, because the United Kingdom economy had been growing for more than a decade, there was little political capital to be made in challenging the Blair government's economic policy record. By the same token, there was little need for an urgent review of Conservative economic policy – since the assumption was that Gordon Brown's British model was based upon a political economy that owed its origins to Adam Smith and other proponents of limited government and a moral defence of capitalism.

As an alternative to a thesis of the broken economy, David Cameron's policy review has throughout his tenure, focused upon the thesis of the broken society, and how it can be joined up to parallel debates about the reform of the public services, crime, and the quality of life. Underpinning this thesis has been the desire to separate society from state, and to extend the Thatcherite insight of individual entrepreneurial initiative as the prime agency of social change from the economy to society. Conservative Party policy under Cameron has sought to diminish the popular expectations of the state by mobilizing individuals, corporations and, above all, civil society organizations to launch a new era of social entrepreneurship. This strategy has enabled the Conservative Party to address issues of popular concern such as crime, alcohol and drug abuse, anti-social behaviour and immigration but without recourse to the sort of language redolent of the Major 'back-to-basics' and Hague 'foreign land' eras. This 'nasty party' language, as Michael Ashcroft's research had shown, had been a major deterrent to the attraction of votes from other political parties and the mobilization of the Conservative Party's core vote among middle-class professionals.

With the onset of the credit crunch and domestic recession, from the summer of 2008, Conservative Party policy has broadened to embrace the further theses of the 'broken economy' and the 'broken polity'. However, the suspicion remains that Cameron's approach to policy renewal has been too opportunistic and essentially reactive to the Brown government's failures, rather than principled and proactive in asserting a convincing political vision for the future of the United Kingdom. In giving key roles to Iain Duncan Smith and William Hague, Cameron is also open to the critique that his policy review is too backward looking, and risks repeating the errors of past failed Conservative Party leaderships. The calculated political risk of the return of Kenneth Clarke to the shadow cabinet, at the age of 68 and after three failed attempts for the party leadership, which have only served to demonstrate his proclivity for dividing the Conservative Party over the question of the European Union, has suggested that Cameron is still struggling to communicate a clear policy agenda for a future Conservative government. The chapters which follow now offer the reader the opportunity to explore and evaluate that agenda.

5
Convergence, Critique and Divergence: The Development of Economic Policy under David Cameron

Simon Lee

By the time David Cameron was elected as Conservative Party leader on 6 December 2005, the UK economy had experienced uninterrupted economic growth for almost 13 years, nearly five of which had occurred under the Major government. Consequently, unlike previous Conservative oppositions in the late 1940s, 1960s and 1970s, it did not appear at that particular juncture that Cameron's Conservatives would be able to base their forthcoming general election strategy upon a Labour government's record of failure in economic policy. Moreover, despite more than eight years of opposition, Cameron's predecessors as party leader and their Shadow Chancellors had failed to construct an effective critique to tarnish Gordon Brown's reputation as the prudential 'Iron Chancellor'.

The manifesto promises of £8 billion of tax cuts in 2001 and £4 billion in 2005 had neither returned disillusioned Conservative voters to the fold in significant numbers, nor restored the party's previous and longstanding reputation for economic competence, which had been so severely damaged by the recession of the early 1990s, and the humiliation of 'Black Wednesday' (16 September 1992). In 2005, the party's general election manifesto question to voters – 'Are You Thinking What We're Thinking?' – had been met with a resounding 'No' or sheer indifference.

These were not promising foundations upon which to reconstruct a credible modern Conservative economic policy, built to last. Cameron's own competence to lead the process of reconstruction was highly questionable. First, he had witnessed at close quarters the economic and political trauma of 'Black Wednesday', when serving as Chancellor of the Exchequer Norman Lamont's special adviser in September 1992. Second, he had been a principal architect of the ineffectual 2005 general election manifesto. However, Cameron did at least enjoy one significant asset. His close personal friend and campaign manager during the Conservative Party leadership contest, George Osborne, had already served six months as Shadow Chancellor, having been appointed by Michael Howard on 5 May 2005. Even before Cameron's election, Osborne had laid out the four principles of a future Conservative economic policy – macroeconomic stability, increased productivity, a reduction in the long-term demands on the state, and lower taxation (Osborne, 2005) – with which Cameron agreed wholeheartedly. Indeed, as he later admitted, he and Osborne possessed 'a very clear, shared analysis of what's wrong with the country and what the Conservative Party ought to be doing, and what a Conservative government would do'. They believed in a low-tax economy not only for economic reasons, but also for moral reasons (Jones, 2008: 48, 280).

This chapter seeks to analyse the development of economic policy since December 2005, and to show how policy has evolved through three phases. During the first phase of convergence and consolidation, and in the 18 months following David Cameron's election as Conservative Party leader, Conservative economic policy was dictated by a simple political calculation. This was that, of New Labour's three objectives of political renewal, economic renewal and social renewal, the least political capital was to be made from the Blair governments' economic record of macroeconomic stability (Lee, 2008). It had delivered a decade of unbroken growth, low inflation, high levels of employment and rising prosperity. The assumption made was that the economy was not broken, or rather that it would be very difficult for the Conservatives to convince the electorate that this was indeed the case – as the results of the 2001 and 2005 general elections attested. Better to converge with Gordon Brown's British model of political economy and to consolidate the party's economic policy by emphasizing its own commitment to economic stability and fiscal prudence. Moreover, the very electoral and economic success of New Labour could be attributed to modern conservatism's victory in the battle of ideas (Cameron, 2006b), and the acceptance by Blair and Brown of the fundamental tenets of the Thatcherite counter-revolution in political economy (Lee, 2008).

As an alternative political and electoral strategy, David Cameron's thesis of Britain as a 'broken society' would focus instead upon the purported failures of New Labour's social renewal. As a defensive strategy, to defuse the government's previous critique that the election of a Conservative government would mean major cuts in public services, both Cameron and his Shadow Chancellor of the Exchequer, George Osborne, pledged repeatedly that they would match the government's planned public spending. The proceeds of growth would be shared between higher public spending on essential public services, on the one hand, and the pockets of ordinary consumers and voters on the other. However, this meant that Conservative Party policy at this stage was, to a large extent, reactionary rather than proactive, in that it was being shaped by the Blair governments' fiscal policies.

A second distinct phase in the development of Conservative Party economic policy under David Cameron only began with the onset of the problems of Northern Rock in the late spring of 2007, and the growing realization that economic policy and Brown's British model of political economy was broken after all. During this phase, which marked a transition from economic policy convergence to burgeoning critique, the Conservative Party sought to personalize the responsibility for the UK's faltering economic performance by attributing it to the imprudence of Gordon Brown. As an alternative, Cameron and Osborne began to emphasize the importance of fiscal conservatism and 'living within our means'. However, the commitment to match planned public spending remained, and to share the proceeds of growth, even though those proceeds were beginning to diminish. Conservative Party economic policy was still essentially reactive, and being dictated by the planned spending totals announced in the Brown government's 2007 Comprehensive Spending Review. The economic policy proposals developed during this phase were duly published in *Reconstruction: A Plan for a Strong Economy* (Conservative Party, 2008d).

The third phase of policy divergence in the evolution of Conservative economic policy under Cameron, which would be of central importance for the outcome of the next general election, began in the week prior to the publication of the Brown government's pre-budget report. This was marked by David Cameron's announcement of the Conservative Party's abandonment of its pledge to match the Brown government's planned public spending totals from 2010 to 2011. While continuing to match Labour's spending on health, education, defence and international development, the Conservative Party pledged to cut spending elsewhere, including £5 billion of cuts during 2009–10 to cut taxes for savers and businesses, and to restore fiscal prudence and macroeconomic stability through a series of policy innovations. This third phase was marked by a concerted attempt to define a Conservative alternative to the Brown government's measures to tackle the credit crunch and recession. This strategy left the Conservative Party not only in danger of political isolation from the prescriptions for economic recovery advocated by the Brown government, the Obama administration, and the International Monetary Fund, but also open to the charge that, while the Brown government had invested (albeit with taxpayers' and borrowed money) to promote economic recovery, it was the 'do nothing' party, committed only to spending cuts which would do nothing for the growing numbers of unemployed.

Economic policy Phase 1: convergence and consolidation

In British politics, a political party's reputation for competence in economic policy can take years to build, but only hours to wreck. By the time of the 1997 general election, the United Kingdom economy had been growing for 19 consecutive quarters. In other words, there had been growth ever since 'Black Wednesday' – 16 September 1992 – and the departure of sterling from the European Exchange Rate Mechanism. In his foreword to the 1997 Conservative Party manifesto, John Major was able to claim '*We have turned around our economic fortunes. We* have fewer people out of work and more in work than any other major European economy' (Conservative Party, 1997). Indeed, the UK was 'on course to grow faster than both France and Germany for the sixth consecutive year in 1998 – a post-war record'; inflation had been below 4 per cent for over four years, 'the longest period of low inflation for almost half a century'; unemployment had fallen 'to its lowest level for 6 years' – lower, and with a higher proportion of people in work than any other major European economy; and the UK was 'the favourite location for inward investment into Europe', with 'the lowest tax burden of any major European economy' (Conservative Party, 1997: 1, 6).

None of this was sufficient to persuade the electorate that the Conservative Party was still better qualified to manage the economy, and therefore to secure a fifth consecutive general election victory. The Conservatives' hard-won reputation for competent economic management, once lost, would not be easily regained. For example, prior to the 1992 general election Norman Lamont had recorded a negative net satisfaction rating (i.e. dissatisfaction) with both his own performance (–13 per cent) and his government's policies (–4 per cent). However, following 'Black Wednesday', that negative net satisfaction soared by March 1993 to –52 per cent for Lamont's personal performance and –31 per cent for the Major government's policies. Under Kenneth Clarke, Lamont's successor, the Conservative Party would never again record net satisfaction before its May 1997 general election landslide defeat. Net satisfaction with Clarke's own performance ranged between –53 per cent (December 1994) and –4 per cent (November 1996). Net satisfaction with the Major government's economic policies ranged from between –18 per cent in November 1996 and –41 per cent in November 1995 (Ipsos MORI, 2008b).

Paradoxically, in April 1997, the Conservative Party was still regarded as having the best policies to manage the economy by more people (33 per cent) than the Labour Party (26 per cent). However, a year after Gordon Brown had replaced Kenneth Clarke as Chancellor of the Exchequer, the Labour Party was trusted by more people to manage the economy (40 per cent, compared to the Conservative Party's 19 per cent in May 1998) (Ipsos MORI, 2008c). Similarly, whereas the Conservative Party had been thought by more people to have the better policy on taxation in April 1997 (41 per cent compared to Labour's 26 per cent), a year later more people preferred Labour's policies (36 per cent, compared to 32 per cent support for Conservative taxation policies) (Ipsos MORI, 2008d).

By the time David Cameron became Conservative Party leader, public opinion had turned against New Labour's economic policies, offering Conservative strategists an electoral advantage, if they could identify a credible alternative economic policy. While Gordon Brown's personal net satisfaction rating as Chancellor had remained steadfastly positive throughout his decade at the Treasury, until the final six months following the delivery of his final pre-budget and budget reports (reaching a nadir of –13 per cent in April 2007), public dissatisfaction with the Blair government's economic policies had been evident from March 2002, and remained almost continually disgruntled thereafter. While there was a positive +3 per cent rating for the Blair government's economic policies in May 2007, shortly before Brown left the Treasury, subsequently net public satisfaction had turned significantly negative (–7 per cent in November 2007, and –14 per cent in March 2008) (Ipsos MORI, 2008b). Moreover, the Ipsos MORI Economic Optimism Index (i.e. the calculation of the percentage of respondents expecting economic improvement minus those expecting things to get worse) had remained almost continually negative since June 1998, immediately prior to the inaugural Comprehensive Spending Review. Indeed, from the time that Brown departed the Treasury, when net economic optimism stood at

–20 per cent, public pessimism has increased so that by January 2008, it had reached –51 per cent, and by March 2008 –60 per cent, a level of pessimism not witnessed since the recession of spring 1980 (Ipsos MORI, 2008b).

Paradoxically, despite this level of dissatisfaction, the Labour Party had continued to be regarded as the political party with the best economic policies to manage the economy, recording, for example, an average lead of 16 per cent over the Conservative Party between September 2006 and September 2007 (Ipsos MORI, 2008c). Therefore, as with other areas of Conservative Party policy since 1997, the central dilemma confronting economic policy reformers had been whether to regard electoral defeat as indicative of the need for substantive policy change, or whether to continue with the ideological and policy 'common ground' that had delivered four consecutive general election victories from 1979 to 1992.

During the late 1940s, Conservative modernizers, notably Harold Macmillan and R.A. Butler had redefined Conservative economic policy to create an all-party consensus around full employment, the welfare state, and state-led modernization of key industries (Lee, 1996). During the late 1960s, the party had continued to occupy the same middle ground of state-led modernization when Edward Heath had followed the Wilson government's technocratic National Plan with his own managerialist agenda for a 'Quiet Revolution'. However, in the late 1970s, Margaret Thatcher and Sir Keith Joseph had seen the need to abandon the collectivist 'middle ground' of being 'over-governed, over-spent, over-taxed, over-borrowed and over-manned' (Joseph, 1976b: 19), to relocate economic policy on the alternative 'common ground' of an entrepreneur-driven enterprise culture.

In the late 1970s, Thatcher and Joseph had been able to call upon a groundswell of academic and political commentators prepared to challenge the core assumptions of the post-war social democratic Keynesian consensus, and to identify both the causes of and the remedies for British decline (Lee, 1997). Sir Keith Joseph had himself asserted boldly, 'Proclaim The Message! Keynes is Dead!' (Joseph, 1978: 99). Convinced that monetarism would not be enough, Joseph identified the equal importance, beyond reforming economic policy to reverse the trend of 'the mis-application of the work of Keynes and Beveridge' in the erroneous pursuit of full employment and equality, of addressing 'psychological and social factors' if an entrepreneur-driven enterprise culture was to be restored (Joseph, 1978: 99–100). Joseph was adamant that salvation did not reside in further technocratic social engineering where 'if the right levers are pulled, the right results must come up' (Joseph, 1978: 99). Nothing less than the reversing of the trend towards socialism by the restoration of an entrepreneur-led enterprise culture would suffice.

David Cameron and George Osborne were not able to draw upon the sort of powerful critique of the orthodox political economy assembled by the Centre for Policy Studies and the Institute of Economic Affairs during the late 1970s. Nor did they see the need for change rather than continuity in economic policy since, in their analysis, New Labour had occupied the common ground. They opted instead for an incremental strategy of decontaminating the Conservative economic policy brand from the toxic legacy of 'Black Wednesday', and three consecutive general election defeats. They would pursue a pragmatic strategy of 'sharing the proceeds of growth'. As the economy grew, the revenue arising from growth would be divided between improved public services, reduced borrowing and lower taxes. Over the economic cycle, the state would consume a smaller share of national income (Osborne, 2006a, 2006b).

Important lessons had been learnt from the economic policy failures under the leaderships of William Hague, Iain Duncan Smith and Michael Howard. Under Hague's leadership, for example, the party had found it difficult to launch an effective critique of Gordon Brown's 'British model of political economy' (Lee, 2007b, 2008), following its messianic conversion to entrepreneurship, competition and enterprise; its manifesto commitment not to raise income tax during the lifetime of the parliament; and its actual delivery of four further years of low inflation, rising employment, prudent public finances and unbroken economic growth. Indeed, the most salient feature of Conservative economic policy during this period had followed Michael Portillo's appointment as Shadow Chancellor in February 2000. He had pragmatically facilitated the convergence of Conservative Party economic policy towards Gordon Brown's British model by abandoning Conservative opposition to the independence of the Bank of England, full employment as a policy objective, and the national minimum wage (Dorey, 2003: 128).

Nor had the Conservative Party managed to restore its (post-'Black Wednesday') diminished reputation for economic competence. On the contrary, Hague's campaign strategy of a 'Sterling Guarantee' to save the pound from European Monetary Union singularly failed to resonate with the electorate in general, and Conservative voters in particular. They ranked it 11th of 11 electoral issues (Travis, 2001). Rather than articulating a clear policy on government spending and taxation, Hague's Conservatives repeated the same mistake of a confused and inconsistent fiscal policy made by the Labour Party at consecutive general elections from 1983 to 1992. Having pledged tax cuts of £8 billion in its manifesto, the party's macroeconomic credibility was undermined by the claim made by Oliver Letwin, the Shadow Chief Secretary to the Treasury, that the true figure for tax cuts might be nearer to £20 billion (Dorey, 2003: 130). A £12 billion 'black hole' was duly identified in the Conservatives' fiscal policy.

To avoid the possibility of a repetition of such electorally damaging uncertainty or inconsistency in Conservative fiscal policy, the party would adhere to New Labour's planned totals for public spending on health and education. The proceeds of growth would be divided between more resources for the public services and higher private incomes for individual consumers and taxpayers. However, over the economic cycle, the Conservatives would ensure that the average growth rate of spending would be set below the trend rate of economic growth. This in turn would guarantee that tax revenues would increase faster than spending over the economic cycle, borrowing would be reduced, and headroom would be created for sustainable tax cuts.

The Conservative Party would be wedded to the same principles of macroeconomic stability and fiscal prudence as championed by Gordon Brown. Consequently, confronted by this ideological and policy convergence, the electorate would be presented with a future choice on the basis of competence. If the Brown Boom came to an end, or there were divisions within New Labour over whether the pound should participate in economic and monetary union, the Conservatives would be in prime position to offer themselves as the competent alternative. In the interim, the shadow cabinet and parliamentary party would avoid the political hostage of any unfunded public spending commitments, and would content themselves with a pragmatic opposition strategy of embarrassing the government at every opportunity. Osborne himself would attempt to build his reputation by developing a critique of Gordon Brown's economic record in office, and in particular his rapidly receding record of fiscal prudence.

During this phase of the development of economic policy, the principal ideological challenge from within the ranks of the Conservative Party and its supporters came from the Thatcherite right, led by the Centre for Policy Studies (e.g. Lea, 2006, 2007). The demand was for a clear commitment to major cuts in taxation, public expenditure and regulation. At the forefront of such demands was John Redwood, who Cameron appointed to be co-chairman of the Economic Competitiveness Policy Group (together with Simon Wolfson, the Chief Executive Officer of Next plc).

When the Group reported to the shadow cabinet in August 2007, Redwood's foreword noted that the report was based 'on the strong evidence from around the world that countries which choose the lowest tax rates, and which have the least oppressive but effective regulatory regimes, are the ones that grow the fastest and become the richest'. Therefore, the Group believed that 'any Conservative Chancellor should set business free to compete, by creating a simpler and more competitive tax and regulatory framework for enterprises based in Britain'. Where the nineteenth century had seen the expansion of the right of many to vote, and the twentieth century the expansion of home ownership, the twenty-first should see 'decisive steps' to expand share ownership, rekindle a 'savings culture', and promote 'a more enterprising Britain' (Economic Competitiveness Policy Group, 2007: 4–5).

The Group had also endorsed in turn the recommendations of the Tax Reform Commission, initiated by George Osborne, for a 2p cut in the basic rate of income tax, and a total package of fiscal reforms costing £21 billion over the lifetime of a parliament (in terms of expenditure cuts to finance them) (Tax Reform Commission, 2006: 9–10). However, whenever confronted by such recommendations, Cameron and Osborne's consistent retort was to reiterate their respective commitments to macroeconomic stability ahead of up-front tax cuts, and the matching of the Labour government's spending levels throughout the duration of the 2007 Comprehensive Spending Review, i.e. until the end of financial year 2010–11. In future, macroeconomic stability would be entrenched through the commitment to the triple lock of 'an independent Bank of England, independent national statistics and independent fiscal rules' (Osborne, 2006b).

Economic policy Phase 2: from convergence to critique

If the first phase of the development of economic policy under David Cameron's leadership was marked by cautious and pragmatic evolution, it reflected Cameron and Osborne's assumption that their party had won the battle of ideas in political economy, and that there would continue to be dividends from growth to share. The phase of convergence and consolidation also reflected a desire to instil discipline within and Cameron's personal and political authority over the shadow cabinet by avoiding any politically damaging policy commitments. With the onset of the demise of Northern Rock, as the first of a series of major financial crises in the United Kingdom's banking sector, the second phase of policy development was characterized by a much harsher political assault upon Gordon Brown and the Brown government, and a greater willingness to roll out policy innovations. This reflected the growing realization that Conservative Party strategy had been based on a central flawed assumption – that the British economy was not broken, when its huge levels of imprudent private debt, over-inflated property market, and rapidly rising government debt demonstrated that it was (Lee, 2007b, 2008).

As Gordon Brown's British model of political economy faltered, and the sheer scale of the domestic implications of the sub-prime mortgage market-led credit crunch became apparent for United Kingdom-based banks, the Conservative Party's economic policy critique became ever more strident. In particular, it focused upon the personal failings of Gordon Brown, both as the purported cause of the crisis during his tenure as Chancellor of the Exchequer, and as the obstacle to a more hasty resolution of the crisis – on account of his dithering and erroneous policy choices as Prime Minister. The Brown government was lambasted for its 'borrowing binge', 'borrowing splurge' and for having 'maxed out our nation's credit card' (Cameron, 2008c, 2008d).

In this analysis, an imprudent Brown had allowed 'an unsustainable debt-fuelled bubble' to develop through irresponsible fiscal policies which had meant that New Labour 'didn't fix the roof when the sun was shining' (Osborne, 2008). Responsible economic management, and Brown's own fiscal rules, had been abandoned 'in favour of good old-fashioned Keynesian demand management' (Osborne, 2008). Osborne and Cameron had lost few opportunities to remind Brown of his past statements on prudence and stability. For example, in more affluent times, Brown had claimed 'unfunded promises are empty and hollow promises'. Furthermore, his party had 'learned from past mistakes … you cannot spend your way out of recession'; and that 'To make unfunded promises, to play fast and loose with stability (indeed to play politics with stability) is … something I will never do and the British people will not accept' (Brown cited in Cameron, 2008c). Now, these words returned to haunt the Prime Minister.

Brown was further accused of adopting 'the Keynesian approach', but 'Simple Keynesian economics and the active demand management that it recommended were comprehensively discredited in the stagflation of the 1970s.' These 'big state solutions' had failed (Osborne, 2008). Moreover, Labour's programme of 'new, unfunded tax cuts and new, unfunded spending' was 'reckless and wrong', and should be rejected because it was not affordable in 'Brown's age of irresponsibility'; had been attempted in Japan during the 1990s and resulted in 'crippling debt'; and could be counter-productive, by compromising investor confidence, and forcing up interest rates (Cameron, 2008c). In short, 'The Brown Boom has burst', signifying nothing less than 'the failure of an entire economic approach', an approach based upon 'the unstable foundations of public and private debt', with a housing and finance boom 'ending in the bust of a recession' (Cameron and Osborne, 2008: 1).

The solution for economic policy would be to move 'from Gordon Brown's age of irresponsibility to a new age of responsibility' by deploying the Conservative Party's economic policy agenda specified in *Reconstruction: Plan for a Strong Economy* (Cameron and Osborne, 2008: 1). This plan incorporated a number of significant policy and institutional innovations. First, to institutionalize 'a totally different approach' to fiscal responsibility, and to enable government to live within its means, a new Office for Budget Responsibility (OBR) would be created. It would 'assess independently the sustainability of the public finances and hold the Government to account', and be charged with providing 'a full, independent audit of the nation's debts, including all the liabilities hidden off balance sheet' (Conservative Party, 2008d: 3).

In the Conservative plan, this new quango would be purely advisory. The Conservative plan was categorical that 'The OBR's recommendation will not be a substitute for the annual Budget judgement' (Conservative Party, 2008d: 11). The major aspects of fiscal policy, namely 'the level and composition of government spending, tax rates and the structure of the tax system' would continue to be regarded as 'rightly political issues' which would remain 'the exclusive responsibility of democratically elected politicians' (ibid.: 7). Consequently, the evolution in fiscal policy-making from Gordon Brown's British model would be through incremental institutional change rather than radical innovation. The Conservative fiscal policy commitment to share the proceeds of growth remained 'At the core of our strategy' (ibid.: 20).

To avoid repeating the same mistakes, what was needed was 'a totally different approach that will tackle the causes of bubbles before they emerge, provide proper supervision of the financial system, and give the authorities the powers they need to stop individual failures threatening the whole economy' (Conservative Party, 2008d: 18). This would be accomplished through the establishment of 'a new Debt Responsibility Mechanism', wherein the Bank of England would be given 'a broader responsibility for debt in our banking system and our economy, the risks it poses'. The Bank in turn would pen a regular open letter to the Financial Services Authority (FSA), in which it would set out its assessment of 'market-wide risks'. The FSA would then be required to set out how it would respond to the Bank's recommendations, including using new powers 'to take pre-emptive action to control banks' lending when there is danger of an asset boom' (Conservative Party, 2008d: 18, 20). This signified a remarkable U-turn in Cameron's own perspective on regulation of financial services. He had previously championed the City of London as 'a great UK success story' built upon Conservative tax reforms, and the 'Big Bang' of market deregulation and liberalization. He had also asserted that, to maintain the City's status as the largest international financial centre on earth, the key to success would be 'Low tax. Low regulation. Meritocracy. Openness. Innovation' (Cameron, 2006b).

The Conservative economic plan was also adamant that, in order to create 'a broad-based, dynamic economy that can withstand global shocks', laissez-faire would not be enough. Therefore, the plan would seek 'a more balanced economy' by lessening the UK's dependency upon financial services, housing and other service industries. There was an urgent need for both supply-side reforms, notably 'Bottom-up reform of our education, skills and welfare systems', and major infrastructure plans to be delivered 'on time and on budget' (Conservative Party, 2008d: 34, 36). However, the plan offered few clues as to how a greater role for competition and the private sector in skills provision would surmount the long-term market failure of under-investment in skills which had led to state provision in the first place. Nor did the plan explain how, under the Private Finance Initiative (PFI), a future Conservative government would ensure that the private sector would actually bear the risk for infrastructure projects, when the previous market failure and insolvency of private sector contractors such as Metronet on the London Underground, had left the Brown government with little alternative but to burden the taxpayer with £2 billion of additional expenditure and risk.

Economic policy Phase 3: from critique to policy divergence

The third phase in the development of Conservative Party economic policy under David Cameron emerged during the autumn of 2008, when the full extent of the UK's slump into recession, and its rapidly deteriorating public finances, would become apparent with the publication of the 2008 pre-budget report. Alistair Darling's announcement of dramatically higher public borrowing, not just in the immediate short-term, but for the foreseeable future, provided Cameron with the opportunity to establish clear blue water between the two major political parties on economic policy. Cameron prefaced his major economic policy announcement by reaffirming his belief that 'free enterprise, open economies are best for creating the prosperity we need', to be achieved through low inflation and a fiscal surplus during good years, to enable people to be assisted during bad years. However, as a 'practical man, not an ideologue', Cameron recognized that politicians should not cling to beliefs 'if circumstances render them obsolete' (Cameron, 2008e).

Alistair Darling should not replicate the Japanese policy, between 1992 and 2002, of additional borrowing to combat recession, which had resulted in government net debt increasing by 58 per cent of GDP and 'a "lost decade" of stagnation'. On the contrary, the solution lay in practising both the politics and economics of fiscal responsibility, which meant in turn recognizing that Labour's economic mismanagement had necessitated 'a new path for restraining the growth of spending'. Therefore, the Conservative Party would abandon its previous policy of adhering to the Brown government's planned public spending totals, in the interests of 'sharing the proceeds of growth'. From fiscal year 2010–11, if elected, a future Conservative government would increase spending below Labour's 'unsustainably high' planned totals. This would avoid 'a borrowing bombshell' being dropped on Britain (Cameron, 2008e).

With the possibility that Gordon Brown might yet call a spring 2009 general election, to capitalize upon his own recovery in the opinion polls during the latter half of 2008, and in an attempt to accentuate the divergence in economic policy choices between the two major parties, Cameron made his bid to portray the Conservative Party as the party of prudence for 'Britain's economic future'. To redress the 'Debt Crisis' and help transform Britain 'from a spend, spend, spend society into a save, save, save society', Cameron proposed the abolition of income tax on savings for basic rate taxpayers, but with top rate taxpayers continuing to pay the same tax, and a raising of the tax allowance for pensioners by £2,000. More significantly, rather than waiting until financial year 2010–11, as the Brown government had proposed, before cutting the rate of planned increases in public expenditure, the Conservative Party would fund its £5 billion of tax cuts for savers by cutting the planned public spending growth for 2009–10 from 3.4 per cent to 2.6 per cent in real terms. While spending plans for the National Health Service, education, defence and international development would be honoured, spending growth elsewhere would be restricted to a 1 per cent increase in real terms. This would establish 'A culture of thrift at the heart of government, and a culture of savings at the heart of the economy' (Cameron, 2009b).

In its campaign for the Labour Party and Gordon Brown to be held responsible by voters for the onset of recession in the UK, but also for prolonging the downturn's duration and severity, the Conservative Party published a compilation of debt statistics. In claiming that 'Britain's economy is in a debt crisis: Labour's Debt Crisis', the Conservatives noted that net government debt in 2013–14 was now projected to reach £1.084 trillion, or £17,031 per person. The Brown government's projected borrowing of £77.6 billion during 2008–09 would mean £1,254 in extra debt per person. Moreover, these official statistics had disguised the true extent of debt, for if the liabilities of the state-rescued Royal Bank of Scotland (equivalent to 125 per cent of GDP) were to be added to the national balance sheet, along with Private Finance Initiative liabilities of 5 per cent of GDP, and public sector pension liabilities of 84 per cent of GDP, the United Kingdom's gross liabilities would exceed 275 per cent of GDP (Conservative Party, 2009a: 4–8).

The responsibility for the growth in private debt to £1,456 billion by the end of November 2009 (Credit Action, 2009) should lie with Gordon Brown. He had made a 'catastrophic regulatory mistake' in 1997 when removing 'the Bank of England's historic ability to ensure that banking credit was kept within responsible limits'. This error had then been compounded by Brown's having allowed an unsustainable boom to go on too long, while ignoring the many warnings between 2002 and 2007 from reputable sources, i.e. the Bank of England, the International Monetary Fund, the Bank of International Settlements, and the Conservative Party itself, about the dangers posed to macroeconomic stability by growing private imprudence and indebtedness. This had meant the United Kingdom had entered the credit crunch with not only the biggest housing bubble (arising from average 9.2 per cent real house price inflation between 1997 and 2007) and more personal debt (186 per cent of disposable income in 2007) than any other major economy, but also one of the lowest savings ratios (at 13.7 per cent of GDP in 2007) in the developed world (Conservative Party, 2009a: 10–15). Brown should also be blamed for the government debt crisis, because he had borrowed massively during a decade of economic growth, to enter the recession with 'a larger budget deficit than 104 other countries', including developing economies such as Chad, Kazakhstan and Guatemala (Conservative Party, 2009a: 16).

There were several problems with this analysis of public and private debt in the UK. First, on an international comparative basis, and despite the significant increases since 2001 (from a low point of 40.4 per cent of GDP in 2001), at 58.7 per cent of GDP in 2008, the stock of public debt in the UK remained one of the lowest in the G7. It was, for example, not only below Germany's 64.8 per cent, the United States' 73.2 per cent and Japan's 173.0 per cent, but also below both the average in the euro area (70.7 per cent of GDP) and in the OECD area (79.7 per cent) (OECD, 2008). Second, during the recession of the early 1990s under the Major government, the stock of general government gross liabilities had risen from 32.8 per cent of GDP in 1991 to 52.0 per cent in 1997 by the time the Major government had left office (OECD, 2008). It would therefore not be unexpected for the level of government liabilities to increase by a similar 20 per cent of GDP during the tenure of the Brown government, as it came to grips with the credit crunch and recession during 2008. Third, and perhaps most importantly, the attribution of responsibility for the public and private 'debt crisis' to Gordon Brown and New Labour ignored the already substantial build-up of debt prior to May 1997, made possible by the processes of deregulation, liberalization and demutualization enacted and championed by the Thatcher government. If blame was to be attributed, the Conservative Party could not legitimately escape its own substantial culpability without an extraordinary act of political and historical amnesia.

To be sure of winning the economic argument, the third phase of Conservative economic policy witnessed the portrayal of Gordon Brown and the Labour Party's policy failures as the obstacles to economic recovery. Cameron's thesis was that 'The longer Labour are in, the worse it gets. The worse it gets for the economy – with Labour's Debt Crisis and extra borrowing making the recession longer and deeper.' It was 'Labour's Debt Crisis', contributing to 'Labour's Broken Britain' (Cameron, 2009b). Labour was portrayed as having failed in the past and the present. Its past failure was to allow the accumulation of 'too much debt – too much government debt; too much corporate debt; too much personal debt' (ibid.). Labour's contemporary failure was the 'absolutely criminal waste of public money' of squandering £12 billion on a temporary cut in Value Added Tax (VAT), which Cameron claimed had 'undermined confidence and actually made things worse with the promise of painful tax rises needed to pay it back' (ibid.).

The Conservatives' alternative long-term economic future for the UK envisaged by Cameron was 'an economy where government and its citizens live within their means, save for a rainy day, waste not and want not'. This modern economy would not only provide the opportunity for wider home ownership, a better quality of life and work–life balance ('where we work to live, not live to work'), but also be more productive and better balanced. Ownership and opportunity would be spread 'throughout Britain, so it's not just concentrated in the hands of the few in one corner of the country' (Cameron, 2009b). This vision reflected the modern Conservative Party's belief in 'responsible business and ethical capitalism – an economy with rules'. However, he asserted that those rules 'completely broke down under Gordon Brown', but they could be recreated 'without chucking free markets and their benefits overboard'. Indeed, tying his economic vision in with his broader ambition of social and environmental renewal to mend 'Broken Britain', Cameron boldly claimed that his vision of a good future was of 'a less materialistic country, more concerned with people and our relationships; a contributor society not a consumer society' (ibid.). In short, Cameron's modern conservatism would be nothing less than 'more green, more local, more family-friendly, less arrogant about what central government can do for us and more optimistic about what we can all do for ourselves if we all work together – individuals, communities, businesses – in a spirit of social responsibility' (ibid.).

To achieve Cameron's nirvana of a prospering and productive, but simultaneously green, decentralized and social responsible economy, he proposed to construct a hybrid model based upon a combination of 'the best of these islands' and six components from 'the best of some of the places in the world that I most admire'. First, from overseas he would draw upon 'the progressive, family-friendly culture of Scandinavia', but had nothing to say about the particular set of political, historical, institutional and social factors which had fostered that culture, not least a markedly higher level of taxation than would be compatible with Cameron and Osborne's fiscal conservatism. Second, Cameron would draw upon 'the creativity and dynamism of Silicon Valley', but provided no clues how this unique global focal point for high-technology innovation and entrepreneurship was to be replicated in the United Kingom. Third, Cameron would draw upon 'the savings culture of Japan', but failed to acknowledge that this was the product of a unique political and institutional history, including a very different welfare state tradition and willingness to defer gratification in a manner largely alien to debt-laden Britain.

Fourth, Cameron would seek to replicate 'Germany's apprenticeships and manufacturing strength', itself the product of a unique history and political economy, which had entailed the past willingness of employers and bankers to engage in a model of social partnership anathema to the Anglo-American model of capitalism. Fifth, Cameron looked to 'France's high-speed rail system', but didn't acknowledge that it had been the product of the very dirigiste centralized interventions for which he had lambasted the Brown government, and from which he had promised to depart. Finally, Cameron would draw upon 'America's strong mayors giving their cities real economic leadership', but failed to mention that, in the recent history of New Orleans and Detroit, that leadership had been powerless to act, in the face respectively of hurricanes and major flooding, and the collapse of the American domestic car manufacturers, and had instead looked to the federal government to rescue their cities' fortunes (Cameron, 2009b).

The third phase of economic policy development had seen the Conservative Party commit itself to a further range of short-term and long-term policy commitments. These included the freezing of council taxes for two years; a £2.6 billion package of tax cuts for employers to be paid £2,500 for each long-term unemployed person taken back into work; a cut in the main rate of corporation tax to 25 per cent, and the small companies' rate to 20p; a £50 billion National Loan Guarantee Scheme to underwrite bank lending and ease the credit crunch; a six-month Value Added tax holiday (funded by a 7.5 per cent interest rate on delayed payments); and a temporary, six month cut in National Insurance payments by 1 per cent for firms with fewer than five employees (Conservative Party, 2009b).

Cameron justified the abandonment of the past caution on policy and spending commitments, which had characterized the first phase of his economic policies, by arguing that 'It's a mistake to think you should keep your best policies up your sleeve until the election' (cited in Eaglesham and Parker, 2009). However, there were at least three attendant political risks with this strategy. The first danger arose because New Labour had a longstanding track record of taking opposition party policies and adopting them as its own. Once more, imitation might soon become the most sincere form of flattery. Indeed, on consecutive January days, the Brown government adopted Conservative policies, initially by announcing that it was going to offer £2,500 to employers for each unemployed person hired, who had been on the dole for more than three months; and then by detailing how it would implement a national loan guarantee scheme, providing up to £20 billion of loan guarantees for small and medium-sized enterprises.

A second political danger for Cameron's economic recovery plan, with its emphasis on thrift and prudence, through curtailed government borrowing and spending, would be that the Brown government's strategy of public investment would be contrasted with the Conservatives' plan for cuts in public spending. An even greater political danger confronting

Cameron's economic recovery plan, particularly in the run-up to the next general election, arose not from divergence in economic policy, but potential isolation. Since the start of the recession in the United States, estimated to have begun in December 2007, unemployment had risen by 11.1 million or 7.2 per cent of the working population, an increase of 3.6 million or 2.3 per cent of the working population, and the largest number of jobs lost in a year since 1945. In December 2008 alone, payroll employment had fallen by 524,000, and by 1.9 million in the final four months of 2008 (Bureau of Labor Statistics, 2009: 1–2). In the face of such major job losses, which he warned could see the United States' economy fall $1 trillion short of its full capacity and cost every family of four more than $12,000 of lost income, President-elect Barack Obama had outlined his $775 billion American Recovery and Reinvestment Plan to tackle 'a crisis unlike any we have seen in our lifetime' (Obama, 2009). However, even this scale of fiscal activism had been portrayed as 'unlikely to promote a lasting recovery unless they are accompanied by strong measures to further stabilize and strengthen the financial system' (Bernanke, 2009: 15). With the Chairman of the Board of Governors of the United States' Federal Reserve, the International Monetary Fund, the Organization for Economic Co-operation and Development, and the German government all advocating and/or implementing a major fiscal stimulus to restore investor confidence to global markets, the Conservative Party would be vulnerable to Gordon Brown's repeated taunt of being the 'do nothing' party, with nothing to offer to the UK's growing ranks of jobless, and invoking politically damaging memories among the electorate of the social upheaval the last time a Conservative government had presided over 3 million unemployed.

Conclusion

Under David Cameron's leadership, Conservative economic policy has evolved through three phases: convergence; critique; and divergence. It initially converged towards New Labour and Gordon Brown's British model of political economy, on the assumption that neither the economy nor the model was broken. When that core assumption was proven to be mistaken, an increasingly strident critique was deployed in a concerted attempt to personalize responsibility for the domestic recession, attributing it to Gordon Brown, economic mismanagement during his tenure at the Treasury, and dithering and imprudence during his tenure as Prime Minister. Finally, the onset of recession and deteriorating public finances were mobilized during November 2008 as political weapons to justify the abandonment of the core economic policy commitment to share the proceeds of growth, in favour of thrift through cuts in planned public spending and borrowing.

Throughout its three phases, Conservative economic policy under David Cameron's leadership has remained wedded to Thatcherism's core assumptions about the respective roles of the state and market. In particular, both Cameron and Osborne have shown in their rhetoric and actions to be adherents to a political economy and economic policy agenda which continues to identify individual entrepreneurial initiative as the prime agency of economic and social change. Indeed, as demonstrated elsewhere in this volume, that entrepreneurial innovation is to be extended to social policy and the reform of the welfare state by enhancing the role of social entrepreneurs in the voluntary sector.

Despite the huge market failures, attested to by the magnitude of the global credit crunch, open, deregulated markets have continued to be esteemed as the location wherein the necessary information, knowledge and competition will be found to take risks and discover profitable innovations in goods and services.

David Cameron has stated his desire to 'rebalance' the Conservative Party because 'towards the end of the 1980s we did become too much the economics party' (cited in Jones, 2008: 288). He felt able to do so because of his conviction that his party has won the battle of ideas in political economy, and that New Labour's success was the very proof of that. However, by January 2009, the recession had not provided Cameron's Conservatives with the decisive opinion poll advantage to guarantee victory at the next general election. On the contrary, a YouGov poll in early January 2009 gave the Conservatives (41 per cent), a lead of only 7 percentage points over the Labour Party (34 per cent). This would be sufficient only to make the Conservatives the largest party in a hung parliament (Pascoe-Watson, 2009).

While YouGov found that only 28 per cent of respondents thought Brown had sensible economic policies for tackling Britain's problems (compared to 52 per cent who didn't), no fewer than 40 per cent disagreed that Cameron had sensible economic policies, with only 26 per cent in agreement (Pascoe-Watson, 2009). A subsequent Populus poll, while giving the Conservatives an overall 10 percentage point lead (43 per cent to Labour's 33 per cent), also saw Brown and Cameron tied upon 37 per cent, in terms of their being regarded as the right leader to deal with the recession. Moreover, voter trust in Brown and Darling's handling of the economy, at 38 per cent, was still 3 per cent higher than for Cameron and Osborne's alternative (Riddell, 2009). Cameron's economic policy calculation remained that the onset of recession and rising unemployment would eventually reverse this trend, to help deliver for his party an unassailable opinion poll lead, and a Westminster majority built to last.

6
'Fixing Our Broken Society': David Cameron's Post-Thatcherite Social Policy

Stephen Driver

In July 2008, the Conservative leader David Cameron made a speech launching his party's campaign in the Glasgow East by-election. The theme of the speech was 'the broken society': 'the social breakdown you see here [in Glasgow Gallowgate] is just an extreme version of what you can see everywhere', the Conservative leader said (Cameron, 2008f). British society was broken. The Labour government was to blame; and the Tories were just the party to fix it. A year earlier, Cameron had first talked in these terms ahead of the report from the party's Social Justice Policy Group, one of a series of policy groups established by the new Tory leader. Cameron gave welfare reform to former party leader Iain Duncan Smith and his Centre for Social Justice. Under Duncan Smith between September 2001 and October 2003, the Tories had failed to make any headway in the polls, despite his attempts to find a more compassionate side to modern British conservatism. Now, under Cameron, the idea of the 'broken society' was being used to help to dispel the impression that the Conservative Party, by its own admission, was the 'nasty party' of British politics.

But what substance is there to the Conservative analysis of the 'broken society'? Have the Cameron Conservatives, as Gordon Brown claimed during his 2008 speech to the Labour Party conference, 'changed their tune' but 'not their minds'? To answer these questions, this chapter will first look at the Conservative Party's relationship with the post-war welfare state as it turned from consensus to critique in the 1970s and 1980s. The chapter then examines how the Conservatives have sought to build a social reform agenda in the long years of opposition to Labour since 1997.

The Conservative Party and the welfare state

Post-war Conservative politics were shaped by those 'one nation' Tories, notably Harold Macmillan and R.A. Butler, who believed the role of the party was to manage the welfare state and the mixed economy in such a way that had desirable outcomes for economic growth and social cohesion. The Conservatives shared in a post-war consensus spanning all three major political parties. By the late 1960s, with Britain's economic position deteriorating, this consensus was being called into question. Within the Conservative Party there was a growing weight of opinion that Tory politics had to change. But if many in the party believed change was necessary, there was no agreement about what this should amount to. Some, like Edward Heath, believed the party and the country had to modernize, in particular, through membership of the European Community. Others on the Right favoured a more aggressive free market approach that tackled head on the logic of the social democratic state.

Most notably, Sir Keith Joseph, a central figure in the subsequent development of Thatcherism and Secretary of State for Health and Social Services in the Heath government elected in 1970, made a series of speeches in which he acknowledged that poverty persisted in modern Britain; and that the very poorest in society were caught in a 'cycle of deprivation' that transmitted poverty from generation to generation creating a permanent underclass of British families. Joseph established a joint working group between the Department for Health and Social Services and the Social Science Research Council to fund research in the field. By 1974, the disillusioned Joseph set up the free market think tank the Centre for Policy Studies. And with the Tories defeated in a second general election in October 1974, Joseph challenged Heath for the leadership of the party. But social policy was to be the undoing of Joseph and his leadership ambitions. In a speech made in Birmingham on 10 October 1974, Joseph's suggestion that 'the balance of our population, our human stock, is threatened' by high birth rates among the underclass; and that greater birth control was needed, smacked of a compulsory sterilization programme for the poor (Macnicol, 1987). The speech, rightly or not, was harshly criticized and he stood down as a candidate. His close supporter Margaret Thatcher took his place.

Under Mrs Thatcher's leadership a New Right view grew within the Conservative Party that challenged the basic assumptions of the social democratic welfare state: wealth creation should come before welfare provision; individuals should be self-reliant rather than dependent on collective state services; freedom and choice should take priority over equality and social justice; and, wherever possible, markets rather than hierarchies should be deployed to allocate resources, whether or not assets were privatized or not. This was all controversial stuff – and most of Mrs Thatcher's senior colleagues in the party did not share her views. Once elected, divisions within the party continued to dominate debates around political economy – in particular, between 'one nation' conservatives ('wets') and neo-liberals ('dries'). This divide had deep roots in the history of the Conservative Party and British conservatism, stretching as far back at least to Disraeli and Salisbury in the late nineteenth century (see Gamble, 1994). The one nation view within the party, represented by MP Sir Ian Gilmour, was that the welfare state was a public good underpinning freedom in the society by addressing poverty and enlarging security (Gilmour, 1992). Budding Thatcherites demurred.

So what did the Conservative Party do with the welfare state in its 18 years in power? Three broad themes emerge: first, the control of public spending; second, welfare to work; and third, market/private sector governance. The control of public spending was a totem of Thatcherite Conservative politics in the 1980s. During the 18 years of Conservative government, public spending under Margaret Thatcher grew in real terms by 1.1 per cent per year on average; and under John Major by 2.4 per cent (Emmerson and Frayne, 2005). The growth in spending in the early 1980s and early 1990s was, in part, fuelled by increases in social security spending (which accounts for around a third of total public spending) as unemployment shot up. During 18 years of Conservative government, spending on social security increased in real terms by 3.5 per cent per year – a shade under the long-term trend rate of 3.7 per cent. Attempts to control spending on welfare by switching from earnings-related increases to prices-related increases (earnings generally rise faster than prices) did little to dent state spending on social security. Public spending on other areas of the welfare state, notably health and education, were squeezed. Spending on the NHS increased in real terms by 3.1 per cent per year under the Conservatives (and much of this was during the 1990s under John Major) – under the trend rate of 3.7 per cent. On education, Conservative spending increased by only 1.5 per cent per year, well under the trend rate of 4 per cent. This under-funding on public services was one of the key legacies of Conservative social policy in the 1980s and 1990s.

The second major theme in Conservative social policy was the idea that work was better than welfare; and that the welfare state should be reconfigured in such a way as to promote employment rather than welfare dependency. Critics called it the 'workfare state'. For most of the 1980s, Conservative governments took the approach that work could be made a more attractive option for those on welfare by cutting the value of social security. However, the expansion of means-tested health and disability benefits meant that reform led to welfare to welfare rather than welfare to work – and this produced a legacy of economic inactivity that persists today. But Conservative governments did begin a policy shift that would lead to the Labour government's reforms of tax and benefits and the New Deal programme. In 1986 the Conservative government introduced Family Credit, a form of social security that could be claimed in-work; and in 1996 with Project Work, the Conservatives piloted a welfare-to-work programme that acknowledged that simply changing incentives to take employment was not enough; and that government needed to enhance the capacity of individuals to find work. Such 'active labour market strategies' would become a central feature of welfare capitalism around the world.

The third main theme in Conservative social policy – and where the Tories perhaps had most success in reforming the post-war welfare state – was altering the supply and delivery of services by government. The new public management (or as some have called it, the 'managerial state') advocated market solutions and private sector governance to public policy questions. In 1980 the sale of local authority housing stock started under the right-to-buy policy. In a series of education reform acts in the 1980s and early 1990s, 'quasi markets' were introduced into schooling that attempted to bring greater choice and diversity into the supply of education, as well as the competitive rigours of the market place. Following the 1983 report from Sainsbury's supermarket boss Roy Griffiths, a similar internal market was attempted in the National Health Service through the division of providers and purchasers and giving greater autonomy to hospitals (the main health providers) and the general practitioners (the main purchasers).

While many of the policies, in particular in health, struggled to deliver on their promises in terms of more efficient and effective public services, their legacy was significant. While reform of the welfare state remained unfinished business for the incoming Labour government when it took office in 1997, the broad contours of policy-making had been established by the Conservatives. Welfare to work and public sector reform would become the leitmotivs of New Labour social policy.

Conservative divisions in opposition

The Conservative Party's defeat to 'New Labour' in the 1997 election exposed deep divisions within Tory politics. Thatcherism's uneasy alliance of free market liberals and more traditional conservatives was already by the mid-1990s showing signs of strain. The party of community and one nation had, to some, become the slave to individualism and the free market (e.g. Gray, 1993; Scruton, 1996). In opposition it was clear that Conservative politics was divided over the character of modern society. Thatcherism was unravelling as modernists and traditionalists (or 'mods' and 'rockers') took sides. In Phillip Norton's terms, the 'neo-liberal Thatcherites' were on one side; the 'pure Thatcherites' and the 'Tory right' were on the other (Norton, 1996a). Michael Portillo led the mods; Iain Duncan Smith was a leading rocker. Other frontbench figures fell between the two camps, notably David Willetts.

The source of conflict was one of the great unanswered questions of Thatcherism: the limits of freedom. Most of the time, Conservative governments in the 1980s and 1990s had championed *economic* freedom in the market place. Where this concerned social policy, the emphasis was on individual responsibility for welfare; and the introduction of markets and the private sector into the governance and delivery of public goods such as health, education and housing. Thatcherism had very little to say on *social* freedom. Indeed, where it did take a view, for example in clause 28 of the 1988 Local Government Act that prohibited local authorities promoting homosexuality as a 'pretended family relationship', it took a distinctly conservative one. Thatcherism's 'strong state' was generally on the side of traditional society, not just the rule of law.

But many Thatcherites were not only economic liberals but social ones as well. One strand in New Right thinking toyed with the liberalization not just of the market place but social relations as well. This view was sympathetic to the legalization of drugs and to other social questions which were, they believed, ones of individual responsibility and choice. These Thatcherite mods believed it was possible to be economically and socially liberal (Duncan and Hobson, 1995, 1999). By contrast, Thatcherite rockers were gung-ho on economic freedom, but drew sharp lines in the sand on a whole host of social questions that touched, they believed, on traditional sources of authority in society.

The battle of ideas inside the Conservative Party was, then, also a cultural war about questions of identity and patterns of social change. While both sides acknowledged the party needed a social agenda, including support for the public services (and the rocker David Davis was prominent in this respect), there were important divisions about the substance of that social agenda. The mods in the party felt more in tune with modern society: with progressive social developments and even with changes in family living arrangements. The traditionalists, by contrast, regarded such change as a modern malaise that, in particular regarding marriage, was the root cause of the social problems facing modern society.

The election of William Hague as Conservative Party leader in 1997 did little to bring to an end the internecine warfare inside the party. The election, dominated by the question of the European Union, saw the centre-right of the Conservative Party get behind Hague against the centre-left Ken Clarke. Hague, a politician embracing the Thatcherite economic legacy, was supported by some leading mods inside the party, including Alan Duncan who acted as his campaign manager. King of the mods, Michael Portillo, did not stand. Initially Hague appeared to draw inspiration from the revival of centre-right politics in the US under the banner of 'compassionate conservatism'. Republican state governors such as George W. Bush in Texas advocated a strong social message, in particular, on education and poverty. Bush went on to make this appeal a central element of his 2000 presidential campaign. Hague attempted something similar in the UK. He appointed Portillo as shadow chancellor – and U-turns were performed on the minimum wage, among other things. But with little movement in the opinion polls, the Hague Conservatives turned to 'common sense conservatism' and, when all else failed, to 'saving the pound'. But nothing could save the Conservative Party going down to a heavy defeat in the 2001 general election. It was the end of Hague as party leader; and the lurch to the right looked set to continue with a new leader, Iain Duncan Smith.

Iain Duncan Smith: 'There is such a thing as society'

The selection of Iain Duncan Smith was viewed by many as a consolidation of the Thatcherite revolution inside the Conservative Party. The rockers had defeated the mods supporting Michael Portillo, who quit politics. Duncan Smith's background is important. He was a Tory on the right wing of the Conservative Party (a member of the Thatcherite No Turning Back Group); the man who filled Norman Tebbit's shoes as MP of Chingford in north-east London; and a representative of that tough brand of conservatism that went down well with lower middle and working class voters. Duncan Smith was a traditional Tory who blended Thatcherite free market economics with a deep commitment to the nation state, national sovereignty (he was an original Maastricht rebel) and traditional institutions such as the family, church and the armed forces. He even had problems early on with links to the far right British National Party (one of his campaign team for the leadership turned out to be the father of the BNP leader Nick Griffin).

But as leader of his party, Duncan Smith played a different hand to the one many expected. While his leadership left the party more or less where it started in the polls – and he was unceremoniously sacked in 2003 – under Duncan Smith, a signal went out that the Tories should govern for 'the whole country', in particular, by shifting attention to social issues under the banner of a 'A fair deal for everyone' (Cowley and Green, 2005). One indication of change was the appointment by Duncan Smith of a leading mod, Theresa May, as party chairman in 2002. In this post, May famously delivered the Tories some home truths: 'Our base is too narrow and so, occasionally, are our sympathies', May told delegates to the annual conference. 'You know what some people call us: the nasty party.' Much of the focus of May's speech was on questions of representation – and how the party, accurately or not, 'demonized minorities'. To have any future, May argued, the Conservatives had to develop a more inclusive politics in tune with modern society (May, 2002).

This included talking about poverty. Much has been made of Duncan Smith's Damascene conversion on the rundown housing estate Easterhouse in Glasgow in April 2002. In interviews, Duncan Smith suggested the visit simply brought into sharp focus ideas he already had (see Anthony, 2008). The point was that Duncan Smith as party leader attempted to reposition the party in such a way that it had something to say beyond free markets and defence of the nation state – about the poverty and deprivation that many communities across the United Kingdom continued to suffer despite the general prosperity of the country. The search for a new Conservative social agenda was led by one of the party's key intellectuals, David Willetts. In a series of speeches and articles in 2002 (and after a night on the streets with homeless Londoners) (e.g. BBC, 2002; see also Willetts, 2005), Willetts as shadow welfare minister got the Conservative Party thinking about poverty and what a Tory government might do about it in power. Conservatives, Willetts insisted, did believe in society (and always had done) and had policy ideas to prove it (Streeter, 2003b).

However, talking about poverty and social change was far from straightforward for the Conservative leadership. The culture wars still raged inside the party, in particular, over the Labour government's Adoption and Children Bill, which included a clause allowing 'gay adoption'. The bill divided mods from rockers; and Duncan Smith made the question of the vote on the bill in the House of Commons into one of confidence in his own leadership – which proved to be in short supply. The party turned to the old stalwart of the Thatcher/Major years Michael Howard to limit the damage at the next election by digging up some old favourites of the core Tory vote, immigration and crime.

Smelling the coffee: David Cameron

In the aftermath of the Conservative Party's defeat in the 2005 general election, Tory treasurer Lord Ashcroft urged Conservatives to 'smell the coffee' (Ashcroft, 2005). With this in mind, they chose David Cameron, not David Davis, as party leader in December 2005. David Cameron was very much a mod, not a rocker. 'I am a child of my time', he told the party's annual conference in 2008 (Cameron, 2008a). Pushed by his adviser Steve Hilton, the new Conservative leader set about 'decontaminating the Tory brand'. Broad political canvases, not detailed policies, were painted to give a sense of what Cameron Conservatism stood for. These images included a splash of green (and a great big oak as the new party insignia), as Cameron sought to display his party's environmentalist credentials. There was also a hint of pink as the new leadership attempted to draw a line under old battle grounds with Labour on, in particular, funding for public services. The Cameron Conservatives would stick to Labour's spending plans (an echo of Labour's pre-1997 pledge to do the same with Tory ones); and the NHS, Cameron could almost have said, really was safe in his hands (the passport out of the NHS idea, a policy Cameron had written into the 2005 manifesto under Howard, was quietly dropped).

But if the Cameron Conservatives were to win the next election, large canvases needed more detailed studies. These came in the form of six policy groups, set up and reporting to the party leadership. In the field of social policy, welfare reform was handed to Iain Duncan Smith and his Centre for Social Justice, established in 2004 to 'develop new and innovative poverty-fighting solutions'. In December 2006 and July 2007, the Social Justice Policy Group published two reports: *Breakdown Britain* and *Breakthrough Britain* (Social Justice Policy Group, 2006, 2007). The Public Services Improvement Group, chaired by MP Stephen Dorrell and Conservative peer Baroness Perry, published *Restoring Pride in Our Public Services* in September 2007 (Public Services Improvement Group, 2007). These reports were followed up by a series of policy papers on schools, welfare reform, health, education and training and the voluntary sector.

The broken society ...

David Cameron's pitch is that British society is broken, not just parts of it; and that the underlying causes are cultural not economic (Cameron, 2008f). Taking his cue from the Social Justice Policy Group, the Conservative leader argues that British society is broken because of what he terms the decline in 'responsibility' and 'social virtue'. Civil society has become a lot less civil. By extending the powers and reach of the state, and taking responsibility away from individuals and communities, the Labour government has added to this social fracture, the Conservatives have claimed.

Many of the indicators of the 'broken society' will be familiar to observers of the Labour government's own measures of social exclusion (see Department for Work and Pensions, 2008). British society is broken, the Conservatives argue, by poverty, low incomes, economic inactivity, teenage pregnancy, drug use, crime and disorder, ill health, poor housing and low standards in schools. The picture can look pretty bleak. 'The thread that links it all together', David Cameron argues, 'passes, yes, through family breakdown, welfare dependency, debt, drugs, poverty, poor policing, inadequate housing and failing schools but it is a thread that goes deeper, as we see society that is in danger of losing its sense of personal responsibility, social responsibility, common decency and, yes, even public morality' (Cameron 2008f).

Social circumstances, Cameron acknowledges, matter. They help to shape people's lives. 'But social problems are often the consequence of the choices that people make', the Conservative leader insists. Too many people are making the wrong choices for themselves, their families and their communities because society is not telling them they should do otherwise:

> We as a society have been far too sensitive. In order to avoid injury to people's feelings, in order to avoid appearing judgemental, we have failed to say what needs to be said. We have seen a decades-long erosion of responsibility, of social virtue, of self-discipline, respect for other ... Instead we prefer moral neutrality, a refusal to make judgements about what is good and bad behaviour, right and wrong behaviour. Bad. Good. Right. Wrong. These are words that our political system and our public sector scarcely dare use any more. (Cameron 2008f)

It's not the economy, stupid, but the 'national culture'. No Conservative politician has got so 'back to basics' since John Major.

So, what does David Cameron think can be done to fix the broken society? 'Our central mission', he writes in the foreword to the party's *Repair Plan for Social Reform* (Conservative Party, 2008b), 'is to repair our broken society'. To this end, the Conservatives have put forward plans in four main areas: education and training; welfare reform; crime and rehabilitation; and families. First, on education reform, the Conservatives promise their reform plans reflect 'our profound commitment to social justice – a society made more equal by dispensing opportunity more widely, and more fairly' (Conservative Party, 2008b: 8). Alongside proposals to improve school discipline, expand academic streaming and cut the 'testing bureaucracy', the main feature of the Conservatives' education proposals is to expand school places through a 'supply-side revolution': allowing parents, charities and other voluntary organizations to establish new schools in the state sector (Conservative Party, 2008e). On training, the Conservatives propose reforming and expanding apprenticeship schemes; and expanding (and deregulating) the supply of further education (Conservative Party, 2008f).

Second, on welfare reform, the Conservative message is work not welfare – except for those on incapacity benefit who really can't. Otherwise, Conservative proposals include 'a comprehensive package of support for job seekers' (with a greater involvement from the private and voluntary sectors); quicker assessments procedures; and time limits and other penalties for non-compliance (Conservative Party, 2008g).

Third, the Conservatives' plans for the criminal justice system include more police on the streets, more powers to stop and search, tougher sentencing for knife crime (and for crime in general), directly elected police commissioners, and a payment by results scheme to improve rehabilitation and reoffending rates.

Finally, on families, the Conservatives promise to 'give families the support, flexibility and financial help they need': this includes proposals to reform tax and benefits to end the 'couple penalty' (whereby couples with children receive higher social security if they live apart) and 'recognize marriage'; increase 'flexible' parental leave; introduce a 'universal home health visiting service'; and promote relationship counselling (Conservative Party, 2008b).

The overarching theme of all these social policy proposals is to 'roll society forward', for 'Changing our culture is not easy or quick. You cannot pull a lever. You cannot do it top-down. But you can give a lead. You can give a nudge. You can make a difference if you are clear where you stand.' Government can help to fix the broken society, Cameron says, 'but in the end, the state cannot do it all' (Cameron,

2008f). To do this, the Conservatives propose 'to expand the role and the influence of charities, social enterprises and voluntary bodies in our society' by supporting volunteering, the voluntary sector and by working with voluntary and community providers to deliver public services (Conservative Party, 2008b).

... Or broken communities?

The first concern with the broken society thesis is that the Conservative leader is in danger of exaggerating the social problems facing Britain today. Few would deny that there are *parts* of British society that are broken, but the sum of these parts does not make a broken society. While popular opinion might be behind the idea that society is shot to pieces, as the Conservatives claim (see Centre for Social Justice, 2008), this perception flies in the face of social trends since the mid-1990s that point in the other direction.

Taking key social indicators, it is clear that Britain may have broken communities, but is not a broken society. These figures highlight the deep social problems some local communities face: the entrenched and interlocking problems of poverty, crime, ill health, drug and alcohol abuse, low educational attainment, family breakdown and anti-social behaviour. But taken as a whole, many social trends since the mid-1990s are positive in terms of incomes, opportunities, employment, poverty, education attainment and even crime (Department for Work and Pensions, 2008). The figures on ill health and drug abuse and family breakdown are less encouraging; and trends on employment and poverty have reversed since 2005. None the less, while the economic downturn will make it an awful lot harder for individuals and families across the country to make ends meet, much of British society, to use Harold Macmillan's well-worn phrase, has never had it so good. So, the first problem with the 'broken society' thesis is that it is something of an exaggeration.

Leading Tories acknowledge this. London Mayor, Boris Johnson, dismissed the 'broken society' as 'piffle' (Johnson, 2008). Chris Grayling, who took over the welfare brief from David Willetts, has also been at pains to contrast British success stories alongside 'the serious pockets' of deprivation that persist (Grayling, 2008). Even David Cameron, when pushed on the Andrew Marr Show, acknowledged that 'parts of our society are badly broken ... and in parts of Britain, our community and our organisations are extremely strong' (Cameron, 2008g).

The debate on the scale and scope of the social problems in British society needs a sense of proportion. The actual numbers of individuals and families making up the 'broken society' are small – something like 100,000 problem families, of which a fifth are 'hard core', according to government figures. These families may, as government and opposition agree, have a disproportionate impact on their communities and the welfare state; and there are larger problems of economic inactivity and educational under-performance, in particular, that policy-makers on all sides acknowledge must be tackled. But at worst, Britain has broken communities. To bundle all of the social policy issues together under the umbrella of the 'broken society' may be good politics for Conservatives seeking to establish themselves as a party of 'radical social reform', but it may not make for clear thinking on future social policy-making.

British social policy: continuity or change?

To what extent would Conservative social policy mark a break with current Labour social policy? Behind the rhetoric of change, has something of a consensus emerged on the reform of the welfare state? The potential continuities between the Labour government and a future Conservative government under David Cameron are striking. First, on education reform, the Conservatives' 'supply-side revolution' is a logical extension of Labour's reforms to the provision of schooling. In particular, its academic schools programme and the focus of attention on disadvantaged areas. Old Conservative education policies to expand selective education (a key policy divide with Labour in 1997) have gone. The Conservatives might pursue the policy of making it easier to set up new schools more rigorously – though it would face the same old entrenched interests Labour has faced in government. In other areas of public sector reform, notably health policy, the Conservatives promise to cut bureaucracy and central targets, and devolve decision-making to frontline professionals and the users of public services (Conservative Party, 2008h). While the Labour government has been guilty of an overly centralized approach to public sector reform, it has also promoted a policy of greater choice and diversity (including the private sector) in the delivery of public services. Just as New Labour embraced the new public management in 1997, so the Conservatives would further embed this central feature of post-Thatcherite public policy-making.

Second, on welfare reform, Conservative policies would reform Labour reforms to government welfare-to-work programmes, not abolish them (just as many Labour reforms did with Conservative policies from the 1980s and 1990s). The broad thrust of welfare reform under Gordon Brown following David Freud's report focusing on the economically inactive and a greater role for the private and voluntary sectors in delivering the government's active labour strategies would continue. The Conservatives can, with some justification, claim to have got there first; and, as with schooling, they might take reform further and faster. But proactive welfare-to-work programmes would continue to be a central feature of British social policy under the Conservatives.

Third, on crime policy, the Conservatives promise to get tougher on crime and punishment than Labour. The rise in the prison population over the past decade hardly suggests that Labour has been a soft touch. But behind all this tough talking, there is in Conservative thinking on the criminal justice system a shift in focus to the significance of rehabilitation and the social factors driving crime and disorder rates. If David Cameron promises to be tough on crime, tough on the causes of crime, it won't come as too much of a shock.

Finally, on the family, the suggestion that a Conservative government would support marriage in the tax and benefit system has brought accusations of the same old Tory social policy. However, beyond this one commitment, it is clear that just as with New Labour, the Cameron Conservatives would support families not the family. The distinction is important, recognizing that in modern society, families come in all shapes and forms; and that public policy should support, wherever possible, the stability of all families in bringing up children.

But would a Cameron Conservative government give poverty the same priority in social policy-making as Labour? The pledge to cut child poverty became a central element of the Labour Party's welfare reforms once in power. Since 1997, the government has had some success in cutting child poverty rates – at least until economic growth slowed in 2005. Redistributive fiscal policies via tax credits and child benefit have increased the incomes of the working poor, especially those with children. The Tories may talk about poverty, but what would a Cameron Conservative government do? There is a clear policy consensus that work is the best way out of poverty for those that can. The Conservatives have been harsh critics of Labour's fiscal policies, in particular, the system of tax credits. But while relative poverty – i.e. the income of individuals below 60 per cent of the median incomes – does not figure prominently in current Conservative welfare reforms, the party *is* committed to boosting the incomes of poor families via the tax credit system to cut poverty rates (Conservative Party, 2008b). Times have changed.

There are, then, important continuities between current Labour social policies and a future Cameron Conservative government. There are, of course, differences as well – and these shouldn't be discounted, notably

Conservative plans for locally elected police commissioners. Moreover, the fact that there are continuities between Labour and the Conservatives on social policy doesn't mean that a Cameron administration wouldn't do a better job of managing change in the welfare state. It might – or it might not. But what is clear, a Cameron Conservative government would not mark a sea-change in British social policy.

The problem of agency – and the role of the state

This broad consensus on the reform of the welfare state raises a third concern with David Cameron's broken society thesis. For the Cameron Conservatives, the idea of 'rolling society forward' has been central to the critique of Labour's 'statist' social policies. But what does 'rolling society forward' mean in practice; and what would be the role of the state under a new Conservative government?

'Rolling society forward' is used in two senses in Cameron Conservatism. First, it is about the voluntary, community and private sectors doing more as part of a 'post-bureaucratic state' in terms of the delivery of social policy and coming up with services to fix the broken society. Whether it is in welfare reform or in the provision of new schools, social entre-preneurialism and corporate social responsibility, these sectors are key elements of the Cameron Conservative social policy brief. Second, rolling society forward has a more explicitly moral agenda in the sense that communities – whether these are community organizations or just families – are best placed, Conservatives insist, to put pressure on individuals to alter their behaviour in ways that have desirable social outcomes (so-called 'nudges'). Social values are best changed by communities not by government. Cameron Conservatism stands for 'libertarian paternalism', not the nanny state.

In the first area, while there may be some important points of disagreement between Labour and the Conservatives on levels of public spending before and after the next general election, current Tory thinking on harnessing the voluntary and private sectors into the broader reform of the welfare state shows a marked continuity with New Labour thinking and practice (e.g. HM Treasury, 2007a). Both Labour modernizers and their Conservative counterparts have hitched their political projects to a post-modern version of the state. But government under any new Tory administration is not about to be swept away by the onward march of society. The Cameron Conservatives may be right that under Labour, the state has grown too much and has become too centralized. Simply talking about 'rolling society forward', however, is not a clear answer to what the size and scope of the state might be under a Cameron Conservative government. Certainly the voluntary and private sectors would continue, as they have done under Labour, to play a greater role in the delivery (though not in any significant way, the funding) of public services, including core parts of the welfare state. But there are, as some Conservative modernizers acknowledge, limits in terms of capacity to this US-style emphasis on voluntary action. Britain is not America; and government will continue to be the main agent of social reform in the United Kingdom (O'Hara, 2007). As shadow welfare minister Chris Grayling has emphasized, fixing the broken society is about a 'big change in government' (Grayling, 2008) – not getting rid of it.

How then to change behaviour in ways that benefit the individual and the rest of society? Traditional levers of power are poor instruments in this respect. Incentives are often not enough to get to the bottom of the problems facing broken communities. The demand for labour, for example, has expanded since the mid-1990s; but rates of economic inactivity have barely changed. Voluntary action may well be vital for providing some of the 'nudges' individuals, families and communities need to get back on track. But if 'libertarian paternalism' is going to have any hope of working – in schools, on the streets, in homes – it will need some 'big government' conservatism to back it up (Mead, 1992) – not least to fund it and set the framework of welfare rights and responsibilities. Indeed, for all the talk of rolling out society, there remains a significant role for the state as the agent of social reform in Cameron Conservatism.

Post-Thatcherite Conservatism

Gordon Brown says the Conservatives have changed their tune, but not their minds. Is he right? Do current Tory proposals for reform of the welfare state mark a new direction for the party?

New Labour shifted the political and policy landscape just as much as Thatcherism did (Driver and Martell, 2006). And the continuities between Labour and Conservative social policies would suggest that Cameron Conservatism is anything but a re-run of Thatcherism. First, there is in current Conservative social policy a positive commitment to public service and the public services. These services need to be supported financially by taxpayers, but they also need to be reformed (and there is something of the Major Conservatives in this respect). The degree to which the Cameron Conservatives have nailed their colours to the public sector concerns come Tories – and not just unreconstructed

Thatcherites. Think tanks such as Reform and Policy Exchange that have underpinned the party's modernization worry that David Cameron has conceded too much ground to an unreformed welfare state by ruling out alternative models of public sector reform, in particular on health (e.g. Bosanquet, Haldenby and Rainbow, 2008). Second, whatever talk there is of a post-bureaucratic state, under a future Cameron government, voters would see an activist state and not a return to old style safety net welfare policies that, rhetorically at least, dominated the politics of Thatcherism. State action, not limited government, is necessary because there is recognition that however important market-led growth is to fixing the broken society, it is not enough. There are real problems of poverty and social breakdown that a political economy based on the incentives of market forces cannot fix. Governments, working with other agencies of collective action, have a role. Finally, the conservative (with a small 'c') social agenda of Thatcherism has been replaced with a recognition that modern society is diverse and that modern Conservative politics has to work with contemporary social relations not against them. A Cameron Conservative administration would be a government largely of mods not rockers.

Conclusion: the politics of welfare in hard times

Fixing the broken society won't be easy if the Conservative Party does win the next general election. Whatever social policies are in a Tory manifesto presented to voters in 2009 or 2010, reform of the welfare state will prove tough going for Cameron. Tackling poverty and social breakdown was hard enough when the going was good. More than a decade of non-inflationary growth cut unemployment, drove up incomes, helped reduce poverty and provided the resources to pay for large increases in spending on core public services. But still key indicators of social exclusion, such as economic inactivity, remained stubbornly high. By 2009, recession has seen unemployment rise and poverty levels increase. Welfare to work will be challenging; spending on core public services (and the NHS is the Conservatives' 'number one priority') will be difficult as tax revenues fall. All governments and oppositions promise to cut the fat from the public sector. The decision to abandon the commitment to match Labour's spending plans in the face of the government's fiscal stimulus package may create more room for manoeuvre. But the politics of the welfare state has been changed by the economic downturn. As a *Times* leader put it, 'Compassionate conservatism is a more difficult proposition in a recession' (*The Times*, 2008).

The political pressures on the Cameron Conservative Party and a Cameron Conservative government will be intense. Even if the public are receptive to the idea of a broken society, the brutal truth is there aren't many votes for the Conservatives on rundown council estates in places like Glasgow Gallowgate. Even if voters buy into the broken society thesis, they may not think that fixing it is something best left to Conservative politicians. As times get even harder, will Tory voters continue to support the high levels of funding in Britain's (Labour supporting) inner-cities where society is most broken?

These pressures will also be felt inside the Conservative Party. Just as New Labour was ahead of its party, so the Cameron Conservatives are leading a Tory Party that will tolerate them only so long as they bring the prospect of electoral victory closer. The lines of division are clear: the balance between tax and spend; the distribution of costs and benefits; and modern social relations versus traditional ones. The lingering doubts over whether the Conservative Party really believes in Cameron's social policy fixes is reflected in Tories' own doubts on whether they believe them. Since the late 1970s, as we have seen, the Conservative Party has worked with an anti-state default setting. Changing this in the area of social policy hasn't been easy. When the proverbial hard choices have to be made in government, and Conservative MPs, activists and core voters are all voicing their opinions, the pressure on a Cameron government to fall back on traditional Conservative ways of doings things will be intense. The Cameron Conservatives may well be serious about doing something about Britain's broken communities. The question remains whether they can deliver in power.

7
Cameron's Conservatives and the Public Services

Simon Griffiths

The journalist Andrew Rawnsley has written that the 'enduring question of British politics is about our public services. How do we make them responsive to those who use them and accountable to those who pay for them?' (Rawnsley, 2008). The dramatic economic downturn in mid-2008 adds another question: how much are we prepared to spend on them? With a general election by May 2010, the answers to these questions are likely to provide some of the main points of conflict between the main political parties and represent a significant strand of ideological and policy debate. To Rawnsley, 'The outcome of that election may well depend on who offers the most plausible answers' to the questions set out above. The public agree. In a recent poll 71 per cent of people thought that government policy on running public services would be important in deciding their vote at the next election (Ipsos MORI, 2008e). In this chapter, I attempt to summarize where the Conservative Party stands on the reform of the public services – in terms of both policy and ideology – and what, if anything, differentiates them from the other main parties.

The rise of the Conservative 'modernizers'

Labour won the 2005 election with a reduced majority of 66. That was not success enough for the Conservatives to keep Michael Howard in his post; he declared his intention to step down the morning after the election to 'allow a younger leader' (BBC, 2005a). Howard was the fourth Leader of the Opposition that Tony Blair had faced during his time as

Prime Minister (after John Major, William Hague and Iain Duncan Smith) – a remarkable testament to his electoral abilities. After a long election – which worked in favour of the relatively unknown eventual winner – David Cameron became leader of the Conservative Party in December 2005 after a ballot of the party's members.

Cameron's success was a surprise to many. The front runner to win the leadership election had been David Davis, the Shadow Home Secretary, and a 'traditionalist', seen as on the right of the party. Davis was 'in the same mould' as the three unsuccessful previous party leaders (Gamble, 2006: 97). However, his campaign faltered after what was perceived to be a lacklustre performance at the autumn party conference (Tempest, 2005). Cameron and his team, by contrast, had run an almost flawless campaign (the notable defect being rumours of past drug use – BBC, 2005b) and he was elected as a modernizer, on the promise of 'change'. Change, it was hoped, that would revive the party's moribund electoral performance since 1992 (Cameron, 2005f).

Between the Conservative general election victory of 1992 (in which they gained 42 per cent of the vote) and 2005, the party's poll rating rarely climbed above 32 per cent, and for long periods stayed well below that, sinking as low as 20 per cent in December 1994. For 13 years from the general election of 1992, despite four leaders, the Conservatives' poll rating remained stubbornly low. They lost the general election of 1997 to a Labour landslide, but – unlike any other time in the party's modern history – they failed to recover. The party had suffered severe electoral losses before – in 1906, in 1945, in 1966 and in 1974 – and had always bounced back, either narrowly losing the next general election (as they did in 1910 and 1950) or winning the subsequent general election outright (as they did in 1970 and 1979) (Gamble, 2006: 94–5).

Since 2005, the Conservatives' fortunes have steadily improved. The Conservative Party has certainly had some success: polls showed the party leading Labour by 28 points in September 2008, although it fell back steadily throughout autumn of that year as voters doubted its response to the economic crisis (Ipsos MORI, 2008f). Both the arrival of Cameron as leader in 2005 and Labour's own (eventual) electoral problems from around that date help to explain the Conservative revival. By 2005, it was already clear that the Labour government was failing to motivate its core constituency and had lost much of the support it had on entering office among floating voters. Although Labour won the 2005 general election, the victory was underwhelming. It was elected with one of the lowest percentage of votes that any government had ever secured. As Gamble has commented, 'In any other election such a performance would probably have spelled defeat: their victory was a result of the Conservatives being even more unpopular than the government' (Gamble, 2006: 94).

David Cameron's election as leader must be seen as a response to historic failure of the Conservatives to turn around Labour's electoral majority. There had been earlier 'modernizers' in the party's recent past – notably Michael Portillo (after something of a reinvention in the late 1990s) – but it was the sustained electoral losses of 1997, 2001 and 2005 that resulted in a modernizer succeeding as leader. In Gamble's words, the modernizing group realized that the party 'needed to draw on its rich and ambiguous tradition to reinvent itself, by downplaying certain aspects of the party's heritage and accentuating others' (Gamble, 2006: 97). It was this message that Cameron heard once he became leader of the party.

From the moment he announced his leadership bid, Cameron made major attempts to distance the Conservatives from their image as the 'nasty' or 'uncaring' party – or as several commentators noted, to 'decontaminate' the brand (Stelzer, 2007). He announced his candidature with the words that 'This Party has got to look and feel and talk and sound like a completely different organisation' (S. Evans, 2008). Cameron warned the party that they 'face irrelevance, defeat and failure', unless they reclaimed the centre ground (Branigan, 2006: 11). After Cameron's first 100 days as leader, the political commentator George Jones noted that, 'Rarely a week goes by without Mr Cameron ditching a piece of traditional Tory policy or shamelessly pinching an idea from New Labour' (BBC, 2007). Cameron also distanced himself from his party's past by apologizing for the Conservatives' introduction of the 'poll tax' in Scotland, its failure to impose sanctions on apartheid South Africa, and for rail privatization (S. Evans, 2008). Cameron and his team also worked hard to present a new image. He was pictured, for example, pursuing a series of 'green' activities – notably, sledging with huskies on a Norwegian glacier (to focus on global warming) and cycling to work through London (although, it was later revealed to Conservative embarrassment, that he was followed by a car carrying his briefcase).

All this led to severe criticism from some on the right of his own party, such as Norman Tebbit, who compared Cameron to Pol Pot for, what he saw as, Cameron's neglect of Thatcher's role in the party's history (Helm and Rennie, 2006). Former *Daily Telegraph* and *Evening Standard* editor Max Hastings, noted that, 'Plenty of party activists and MPs harbour private misgivings. They were appalled when Cameron publicly renounced school selection, appeared to rule out radical reform of the NHS and downgraded tax cutting as a priority ... Nor do they much care for the idea that the party's Central Office will impose candidate quotas of women and gays' (BBC, 2007). All of this demonstrates what appears to be a radical departure for the Conservative Party. The rest of the chapter largely focuses on whether Cameron's claim, that 'This Party has got to look and feel and talk and sound like a completely different organisation' (quoted above), applies when it comes to the Conservative approach to public service reform. First, however, some warnings need to be given about the dangers of this examination.

Warnings

In this chapter I look at the main ideas informing Conservative proposals for public service reform under Cameron. Before doing this, several provisos need to be made. First, although this chapter focuses on the political ideas that shape the policy of the contemporary Conservative Party, there can be a significant gap between ideology and the eventual policy pursued. Ideas shape policy, but they do so only as part of a mix of other factors, including deals struck with vested interests, 'events' and electoral politics. Yet, although the importance of political ideas as a guide to policy formation should not be overstated, it should not be neglected either. Political ideas are crucial in the formation of policy: amongst other things, they provide a framework for development and help differentiate political parties and actors.

Second, any account of the political ideas of a group of people – even a fairly small one, such as those people who shape policy in the upper echelons of the Conservative Party – will contain abstraction and simplification. Differences of opinion exist between individuals within that loose group, within the wider Conservative Party, between the Conservative Party and its wider membership, and between members of the Conservative and rival parties. These differences are made more obvious by devolution, where parties are pursuing their own national agenda in the devolved parliaments of Scotland, Wales and Northern Ireland. The chapter also simplifies differences between the public services. It focuses largely on health and education – two of the largest services. However, social care, transport and the police, for example, are all different and raise unique challenges. To take an example, ideas around the desirability of 'individual budgets' (a policy discussed in more detail later) are more appropriate in social care than in the reform of the police. In any discussion of changing policy ideas, abstraction and simplification are unavoidable.

A third set of warnings surrounds what we know – and can know – about Cameron himself. In writing about Cameron and the contemporary Conservative Party one must recognize that we know very little about him and less about what he is likely to do in office, if he gets there. First, this uncertainty is because the future is inherently unknowable. As Gamble has commented, 'Like many opposition Leaders in the post, the real nature of Cameron's Conservatism is unlikely to emerge until he is forced to define it by the nature of the choices he makes in office' (Gamble, 2009). Thatcherism, for example, did not emerge as a 'public philosophy' during her period in opposition from 1975 to 1979; it took the privatizations of the early 1980s and the Falklands War for 'Thatcherism', as we now know it, to develop.

Second, we know little about Cameron and the Conservatives because they are keeping their policy cards close to their chests, avoiding detailed policy announcements. The main exception to this is the unilateral policy pronouncement – copied from Blair and New Labour – in which, without any formal consultation with the party, the Cameron team would announce an eye-catching policy designed to keep Cameron newsworthy and continually in the public eye.

Third, we know little of Cameron because he is relatively young (he became leader at just 39), with no experience in office and little as MP. As such it is difficult to predict his future ideological and policy direction from his past. Cameron was only elected as an MP in 2001, four years before being elected party leader. This stands him in stark contrast to Brown, who was elected to parliament in 1983 and became party leader 24 years later – a period that included the longest chancellorship in modern history. Adding to this uncertainty about Cameron, there seems to be a disjuncture between Cameron's early career, behind the scenes for the Conservative Party, where he was seen as on the right of the party, and his image since then. Stephen Evans has questioned whether it will be the case that Cameron's '"inner Thatcherite" could yet triumph over his reforming self' (Evans, 2008).

The public services then: older debates between left and right

To compare and contrast Conservative thinking on the public services with that of the other main parties was, in some ways, easier before the 'modernization' of the Labour Party and the arrival of New Labour, when the differences between the two parties were starker. Before examining Cameron's views on public service reform in more detail, in this section I briefly set out the context for these debates by introducing several interrelated themes in public service reform in recent decades, including the role of public service professionals; the market in public service provision; user choice; and public service spending.

For much of the post-war period, many on the Left, including many amongst the leadership of the parliamentary Labour Party, argued that public services should be delivered by professionals – such as doctors and teachers – directed by Whitehall, who, it was assumed, were straight-forwardly altruistic, acting selflessly on behalf of society and guided by a 'public service ethos' (Barber, 1963). This view has increasingly been rejected over the last 30 years. Scepticism has come from both Right and Left. From the Left, critics argued that professionalism is a strategy used by particular occupations – teachers, doctors and so on – to manipulate the labour market for their own ends (Parry and Parry, 1976). With this view, the professions can be seen as effectively having a veto on reform. In practice, for the Left this argument led to a call for more participatory public services, in which users had a much greater voice in reshaping the bureaucracies in which public servants worked.

This critique was mirrored by the Right, and gained greater prominence under the governments of Margaret Thatcher after 1979. Advocates of 'New Public Management' saw public services as institutions run by bureaucrats (whether they were doctors, teachers, social workers, refuse collectors or the police) intent on maximizing their own utility. On the Right, this led to calls for market mechanisms and private sector practices to be applied to the public services. In general, this would involve the contracting out of services by measures such as compulsory competitive tendering (CCT). Under CCT, frontline staff would be employed by a contractor who would be accountable to those public bodies that had commissioned service provision. As Thompson notes, 'In short, public service providers would be subject to the disciplines of the market: a view which also privileged the needs of the service user as consumer' (Thompson, 2009). As consumers, democratic mechanisms of 'voice' were to be strengthened by 'choice' – notably the right to exit public services. (The introduction of 'choice' / exit mechanisms into the public services is discussed further below.)

The distinction between altruistic views of public services, which dominated the immediate post-war period, and the idea that such workers are self-seeking, was recently popularized by the economist Julian Le Grand, a senior policy adviser to Blair, who labelled the division as being · one between 'knights' and 'knaves' – the former motivated by altruism or a public service ethos, the latter by self interest (Le Grand, 2003).

Contemporary policy discussion often implies that public services need to shift from domination by the interests of producers to domination by users. Cameron, for example, has noted that 'you often hear that public services suffer "producer capture" – that they work according to the convenience of the producers, not the users they actually exist for. And in a sense ... that's true' (Cameron, 2007b). At the heart of much of the contemporary debate on public services is the desire to put the user at the heart of the public services. As Pauline Perry and Stephen Dorrell note in their Conservative Party Public Services Improvement Group report, 'Nothing ... can be more important for a government than to offer public services which are responsive to the needs of those who use them' (Public Services Improvement Group, 2007: 1). Although the main political parties agree on this, the Conservatives differ in what this means and how it can be achieved, as I discuss below.

One of the main mechanisms for putting the user in control is the introduction of greater choice into the public services. Under the governments of Tony Blair there were significant increases in the use of 'choice' systems, particularly in the health service. First, this entailed choice for the citizen. For example, patients were given the right to choose between hospitals if they were moving from primary to secondary care – although early indications showed that there was limited take-up of this offer (Page and Byrom, 2005). Second, in order to make choice meaningful, there was a diversification of providers. For example, Independent Sector Treatment Centres (ISTCs, which use private health organizations to deliver NHS care), foundation hospitals (in which NHS hospitals are given more autonomy over management), trust schools (where schools are given similar autonomy) and City Academies (which use private sponsorship to fund secondary education).

At the same time, the internal structures of the public service bureaucracies were restructured to open them to competition – or at least 'contestability'. (The latter term denotes the argument that monopoly providers do not need to be exposed to actual competition in order to act competitively, but only the threat of competition – Baumol, Panzar and Willis, 1982; Ham, 1996.) The most obvious example was the re-introduction of quasi-markets in the NHS. Quasi-markets are designed to capture the efficiency-gains of free market systems whilst maintaining the equitable outcomes of traditional systems of financing and public administration.

In this context, the most obvious example was the NHS Internal Market, first introduced by the Conservatives in 1991. It created a split between purchasers (health authorities) and independent service providers in the form of newly created hospital trusts. District health authorities became 'purchasers' (later 'commissioners') of healthcare, alongside those GP practices which opted to become fund holders. From then on, healthcare was to be delivered by contracts established between purchasers and (in theory at least) newly established provider trusts competing with one another for the work.

Although abolished by New Labour when it came to power in 1997, a form of market-based healthcare delivery has since been reintroduced. This version of the quasi-market is based on patient choice of provider and a system of 'payment by results', in which hospitals and other providers are paid according to the treatments they actually provide. Provision, by NHS trusts and foundation trusts, is supplemented by ISTCs (Furness et al., 2008).

Alongside the introduction of greater choice, Labour also made substantial investments in the public services after 1997. For example, between 1997 and 2006, public spending on health increased from 5.4 per cent to around 7.3 per cent of gross domestic product (GDP). In 2007/08, spending on the NHS will be approximately £92 billion as compared with £33 billion in 1996/97. Between 1997 and 2006, government spending on education rose from 4.5 per cent of GDP to roughly 5.5 per cent of GDP (Cabinet Office, 2007; Prabhakar, 2009). Yet by late 2008 the tightening economy was clarifying differences between the main political parties.

Evoking New Labour's promise to stick to Conservative spending plans during its first two years in office, Cameron and his Shadow Chancellor, George Osborne, had previously committed to keep to Labour's spending plans if they were to win the forthcoming general election. This was seen as part of the 'decontamination' strategy, as the Conservatives sought to distance themselves from the under-investment in public services of the 1979–97 period. In November 2008, this pledge was dropped in response to the economic slowdown, one consequence of which was to force politicians to prioritize spending plans more acutely. To Nick Clegg, leader of the Liberal Democrats, this was a return to the Conservatism of the Thatcher era. Clegg commented that, 'David Cameron has learned nothing. It's exactly what the Conservatives did in the 1980s ... To simply slash public spending when we are heading into a recession – there's no case for it whatsoever' (BBC, 2008a). It seems that as of late-2008, the old divides on public services and spending were reopening.

Cameron's Conservatives and the public services

Many contemporary writers have noted the seeming emergence of a new consensus – particularly before the Conservatives jettisoned their policy of matching Labour's spending plans in late 2008. However, as Ben Pimlott and more recently Peter Kerr have argued, 'any attempt to identify a consensus merely provides us with a mirage which distracts attention away from what should be the key concern; that is, the areas of conflict and disagreement between the parties. It is the conflict over ideas which, arguably, provides the main dynamic for change ...' (Kerr, 2007). If it is the differences between the parties which are important (and given the warnings set out in the earlier section about the limits of what we can know so far about Cameron), what are the main differences between the post-2005 Conservatives and their main rivals when it comes to public services reform?

In this section, drawing on the work of Rajiv Prabhakar, I focus on three main differences between the Conservatives under Cameron and Labour: Conservative support for greater professional autonomy; their support for greater user choice in the public services; and their scepticism about the role of the state in public service provision (Prabhakar, 2009). First, the Conservatives have made great play out of their support for the autonomy of professional groups, such as doctors and teachers. Cameron has argued that, the 'design of our public services is out of date ... they disempower the professionals whose vocation is all that makes public services work' (Cameron, 2007b). For some, such as the Shadow Minister for Innovation, Universities and Skills, David Willetts, this is part of a rediscovered pluralism that was neglected by free-market conservatism (Willetts, 2009) in which a plurality of bodies, including professional bodies and social enterprises, take on much of the running of the public services – a move which to some degree evokes the guild socialism of the early twentieth century (see for example Hirst, 1989). Yet, this move towards empowering professionals and their representative organizations should not be seen as a return to a simple view of public service workers as 'knights', motivated by a public service ethos, and trusted blindly (along the lines discussed in the previous section). For the Conservatives, the professionals would be held in check by powerful users, exercising their rights as consumers to choose and exit public services as they see fit, in much the same way they do as consumers of private services.

Yet, one can overstate the differences between the main parties here. The argument goes that Conservatives trust professionals to do their job, whilst Labour gives them top-down targets. Brown argued that, although a period of top-down target setting was necessary in 1997 in order to 'remedy decades of neglect and to establish a basic level of standards below which no school or hospital would fall', this period is now over (Brown, 2008). By the time Cameron was elected many of the main targets had been met – particularly those concerning waiting times (Appleby and Harrison, 2005). As Thompson has noted, as the target regime which alienated many professionals recedes into the past, there is broad agreement and '[b]oth Conservatives and New Labour are therefore thinking in terms of a quasi-market model' (Thompson, 2009).

A second difference is over the extent to which user choice can be introduced into the public services. All of the main political parties now pay lip service to the introduction of greater choice in the public services as a way of moving from a one-size-fits-all approach. For many in the Conservative (and Labour) Party this does not just mean the choice between state provided institutions, notably choice of hospital, but between private and third sector providers too. The introduction of greater choice into the public services is seen by many as a Blairite agenda (Griffiths, 2009). In a bid for the middle ground, senior Conservatives have attempted to claim the 'choice agenda', whilst arguing that Brown is either a sceptic or that he does not have the support in the Labour Party to carry on with Blair's choice-based reforms of the public services. Pursuing this tactic, George Osborne risked alienating the right of the party by declaring in 2007 that David Cameron is the true heir to Tony Blair, whilst Brown was 'Old Labour' (C. Brown, 2007). The tactic has some purchase, as there is certainly a highly sceptical strand on the Left, active in both the Labour and the Liberal Democratic Parties, about increased choice and use of non-public sector provision in the public services (see for example Crouch, 2003).

Again the differences between the parties must not be exaggerated. Under Cameron, the Conservatives have revised some of the more radical right-wing proposals for increased choice in the public services. In particular, under the leadership of Michael Howard the party proposed a 'patient passport'. Under this scheme, patients would have been free to choose where they had an operation. The money needed to pay for their treatment would follow them. If they opted to be treated in the private sector, the state would pay some of the bill. The patient passport was dropped by Cameron in early 2006 after criticism that it would undermine public provision.

Whilst the Conservatives have dropped one of their most radical proposals to extend choice, Brown has continued to push the choice agenda in the public services since becoming Prime Minister (despite Osborne's claims and indications during Brown's chancellorship). Brown recently argued that it was time to 'further enhance choice' (Brown, 2008). Meanwhile, the Darzi Review on the future of the NHS – an interim version on the back of which the Prime Minister had nearly rushed into an autumn election in 2007 – argued for greater choice in its very first line, with Darzi calling for 'an NHS that gives patients and the public more information and choice, works in partnership and has quality of care at its heart' (Department of Health, 2008: 7).

A final difference between the two main parties concerns the role of the state. If, as I noted above, it is the aim of all the main parties to create more responsive, tailored public services, the state is increasingly no longer seen as the means to achieve this – particularly in the Conservative Party. This is often couched in terms of a rejection of post-war Labour minister Douglas Jay's claim, that 'in the case of nutrition and health, just as in the case of education, the gentleman in Whitehall really does know better what is good for people than the people know themselves' (Jay, 1937: ch.30) (although, the phrase perhaps unfairly dogged Jay as a summary of his views for much of his career – Toye, 2002). For critics of New Labour, such as the Shadow Chancellor, George Osborne, Labour's attempts to deliver choice in the public services are flawed because they are dominated by a statist approach. Speaking during Brown's 2007 leadership election, Osborne argued, 'Each public service is different. Each person who uses that service is different too. How can the gentleman in Whitehall know what is best for them? How can personalization of public services mean anything if you take the "personal" out of them? Yet that is the route Gordon Brown appears to be about to embark on. Public services that are only provided by the state' (Osborne, 2007). The Conservatives are keen to depict Brown as a statist socialist in the Fabian mould, who equates the public services with the public sector. Although this is far from the case, it is true that the Labour Party as a whole would still see a more extensive role for the state than the Conservatives in the provision of public services and elsewhere. The ease with which the Labour Party accepted the part-nationalizations of the banking sector in late 2008 is perhaps evidence of their acceptance of this.

Conclusions

Despite many similarities, and an undoubted narrowing of political debate over the last twenty years, there are notable differences between the ideas and those policies that have so far been announced by Cameron's Conservatives and the other main political parties in Westminster. It is early to predict how Cameron's future will unfold. However, several areas of difference have been highlighted in this chapter. The Conservatives have a greater scepticism of the state than Labour or the Liberal Democrats. As the economy tightens they are likely to look at increased private provision of public services, making the argument on efficiency grounds. Whilst Labour have wrestled with the potential trade-offs between choice and equity in the public services, the Conservatives have seen choice itself as enough to improve those services. Similarly, the Conservatives have a greater desire for competition within the public services. Whilst, as I have argued elsewhere (Griffiths, 2009), Brown is comfortable with the introduction of private money in the public services, he does not appear to have quite the same belief as Blair in injecting greater competition into those services (although this difference can be overstated). Cameron's Conservatives, by and large, have an intuitive belief in the benefit of greater competition in the public services, largely through quasi-markets. Last, Cameron's Conservatives are far more comfortable with greater devolution to professional groups. Whilst Blair in particular constrained those groups through a serious of top-down targets, the Conservatives have been sceptical of this strategy. (Whether they can maintain this hands-off approach whilst in office in their dealings with doctors, teachers and so on, remains to be seen.) It is unclear whether, if Cameron leads his party to victory at the next general election, and these intimations take form in policy, they will be enough to meld into a 'public philosophy' or 'narrative' of the type that Thatcher created. What has become clearer by late 2008 is a chink of light between the two main parties as they grapple with the role of the state and priorities in public spending in tighter financial times.

8
Cameron's Competition State

Mark Evans

> We on the centre-left must try to put ourselves at the forefront of those who are trying to manage social change in the global economy. The old left resisted that change. The new right did not want to manage it. We have to manage that change to produce social solidarity and prosperity.
>
> > (Tony Blair, speech, Washington, 6 February 1998)

> We face a new world in so many different ways and the old politics is failing and change is required. New world, old politics failing, change is required. That is what we have got to be about today. And you know there has been quite a lot of talk of lurching and I can tell you we are not going to be lurching to the left, we are not going to be lurching to the right. We are just going to provide the good solid leadership that this country needs.
>
> > (David Cameron, speech to the 2007 Conservative
> > Party conference, Bournemouth, 2 October 2007)[1]

The arguments in this chapter proceed from the grounded empirical observation that over the past three decades the character of the British State has transformed from an industrial-welfare state into a competition state. Successive British governments, regardless of their traditional ideological complexion, have increasingly assumed the characteristics and the policies of enterprise associations. The core concern of government is no longer seen purely in terms of traditional conceptions of social justice but in adjusting to, sustaining, and expanding an open global economy in order to capture its perceived benefits. This historic shift from an industrial-welfare state to a competition state reflects political elite perceptions of global realities and informs state strategies for navigating and mediating processes of globalization.[2]

In modernization terms this has been articulated in: leadership rhetoric and discourse; the changing architecture of the state; the nature of political agency in which politicians and bureaucrats have become entrepreneurial agents of globalization promoting 'Great Britain Plc' in the global economy; the decline of ideological differences between political parties and the gravitation of party politics to the electoral centre ground; and, the internationalization of the policy agenda. As Gordon Brown himself has put it, the role of the competition state project is to take 'the hard edges off capitalism without losing its essential wealth creating drive'. It fosters job market flexibility, but 'ensures that those displaced by it are continually retrained so that they remain employable, and it shies away from stiflingly big government, while rejecting the minimalist state favoured by some British Tories and the Republican right'.[3]

This observation, prima facie, appears a bald claim when one considers the package of interventionary reforms recently adopted by Gordon Brown in an attempt to arrest the 2008 global financial crisis. Will Brown's rescue package lead to the emergence of a new economic policy paradigm characterized by the demise of neo-liberalism and the revival of old forms of state intervention in the economy? It is argued here that Brown's flirtation with Keynesianism will be short-lived and is best understood as crisis management rather than as a paradigm shift. A return to neo-liberalism but practised within a stricter regulatory framework appears to be the more likely new orthodoxy of the competition state. Indeed David Cameron's Conservatives look set to continue this trend if they win the next general election. A Conservative government under Cameron is likely to follow the trajectory of the competition state fostered under New Labour in an attempt to adapt state action to cope more effectively with what political elites perceive to be global imperatives. Moreover, the principles of the competition state are more in keeping with the traditional pragmatism of Conservative statecraft (Bulpitt, 1986: 20–3), its 'acceptance of change' and 'strong but limited government' (Norton, 1996b: 72) and its understanding that the art of winning elections is about creating the public perception that Conservatism is synonymous with wealth creation and governing competence.

The discussion which follows is organized into six sections. In the first section a brief account of the transformation of the industrial-welfare state into a competition state is presented. The next section outlines the key features of New Labour's British competition state and generates a series of propositions that are subject to a brief empirical investigation. The third section then explores the evidence that the competition state form exists in practice, and uses comparison with competition states elsewhere in the OECD to establish the extent to which the competition state project has become embedded in British governance. In the fourth section, the dilemmas confronting the British competition state in dealing with the 2008 global financial crisis are addressed. In the next section, Cameron's project is compared with New Labour's competition state to identify continuities and discontinuities. In the sixth section, the chapter concludes by considering whether Cameron can be considered to be Tony Blair's heir apparent.

The rise of the competition state

The main challenge facing governments all over the world is their capacity to adapt to the exogenous constraints and opportunities brought about by different processes of globalization while maintaining a relatively progressive domestic policy programme. These political strategies have depended historically upon the capacity of states to make domestic policy in ways that preserve key spheres of autonomy for policy-makers vis-à-vis domestic and international capital. However, such autonomy is increasingly being constrained by processes of globalization. Some theorists of globalization suggest that all states are losing power and coherence (Reich, 1991), while others maintain that governments are able to adapt state structures in ways that alter, but do not undermine, state capacity (Hirst and Thompson, 1996).

The theory of the competition state provides an alternative understanding of this problematic, which, while accepting that the state is changing its functions due to processes of globalization, argues that the competition state has become the engine room and the steering mechanism of a political globalization process which will further drive and shape economic, social and cultural globalization (see Cerny, 1990; Cerny and Evans, 2004).

The concept of the competition state refers to the transformation of the state from within with regard to the reform of political institutions, functions and processes, in the face of processes of globalization. It is argued that the state does not merely adapt to exogenous structural constraints, domestic political actors take a proactive lead in the process through policy entrepreneurship and coalition-building across traditional ideological boundaries.

The competition state is the successor to the industrial-welfare state, incorporating many of its features but reshaping them, sometimes quite dramatically, to fit a globalizing world. The defining feature of the post-war industrial-welfare state lay in the capacity which state actors and institutions gained, especially since the Great Depression of the 1930s, to insulate key elements of economic life from market forces while at the same time promoting other aspects of the market. This combination, called the 'mixed economy', was seen to maximize conditions for pursuing redistributive policies while protecting national forms of capitalism from market failure. This did not merely mean protecting the poor and powerless from poverty and pursuing welfare goals such as full employment or public health, but also regulating business in the public interest, integrating labour movements into neo-corporatist processes to promote wage stability and labour discipline, reducing barriers to international trade and imposing controls on 'speculative' international movements of capital. All of these forms of intervention-ism have one thing in common: they take for granted a fundamental division of labour between the market, which is seen as the only really dynamic, wealth-creating mechanism in capitalist society, and the state, which is seen as a hierarchical and essentially static mechanism, unable to impart a dynamic impetus to production and exchange except in wartime. The state is thus characterized by a mode of operation which undermines market discipline, substitutes 'arbitrary prices' for 'efficiency prices' and distorts efficient market exchange. When understood from a neo-liberal perspective the state is at best a necessary evil, at worst inherently parasitic on the market.

For neo-liberals then, the welfare state was based on a paradox. Although it was there to save the market from its own dysfunctional tendencies it carried within itself the potential to undermine the market in turn. In the context of the international recession of the 1970s and early 1980s these tendencies would come to have dramatic consequences for the economic policies of advanced industrial states in general.

Chronic deficit financing by governments in a slump period – widely attributed to the rigidities and virtually automatic ratcheting upwards of welfare expenditure in such periods – was seen to soak up resources which might otherwise be available for investment, to raise the cost of capital, and to channel resources into both consumption (increasing inflationary pressures and import penetration) and non-productive financial outlets. Nationalized industry and tripartite wage bargaining were blamed for putting further wage-push pressure on inflation, while at the same time preventing rises in productivity thus lowering profitability through rigidities in the labour market. Attempts to maintain overall levels of economic activity through reflation and industrial policy were seen to lock state interventionism into a 'lame duck' syndrome in which the state takes responsibility for ever wider, and increasingly unprofitable, sectors of the economy. And finally, all of these rigidities, in an open international economy, were increasingly believed to have significant negative consequences for the balance of payments, the balance and composition of trade, the exchange rate and therefore the government's capacity to hold the ring in the first place.

In attempting to overcome these wicked problems, the neo-liberal approach in economic policy turned welfare state policy prescriptions on their heads. Priority in macro-economic policy would be given to fighting inflation over employment and welfare policies; in particular, monetary policy was privileged over fiscal policy – attempting to reduce deficits and lower taxes at the same time, thus squeezing government expenditure. Deregulation was high on the agenda too, to give businesses more freedom to adapt to global market conditions. Capital controls and financial markets were deregulated first, while more pro-market regulatory structures were designed in a number of economic sectors. More rigorous financial management systems and financially led programmes of privatization in the public sector were adopted too. From the beginning, then, the impetus behind the emergence of the competition state was to adjust the economic policies, practices, and institutions of the state to conform to the anti-inflationary norms of the international financial markets in order to prevent capital flight and to make domestic investment conditions attractive to internationally mobile capital.

A new, loosely-knit neo-liberal consensus on the state's role in a global capitalist economy was the product of these changes. Political entrepreneurs like Margaret Thatcher in Britain and Ronald Reagan in the US used the triptych of the 'overloaded state', neo-liberal ideology and globalization as a powerful strategic weapon in public discourse, enabling them to appeal to publics as well as to a new breed of politicians and bureaucrats and in so doing created the Competition State, Mark I.

In this brave new world, globalization became the hegemonic discourse of domestic as well as international politics. As the world recovered in the 1980s and boomed in the 1990s, traditional approaches to economic and social policy were left behind because they didn't fit into the new ideological, social and political realities that kept governments in power. Margaret Thatcher said of her statecraft that 'There is no alternative'. However, the Left increasingly looked to design a political as well as a policy strategy that created an alternative that retained certain traditional welfare ideals of the old left but recast within an alternative vision of globalization. Thus a start was made at creating the Competition State, Mark II.

In the 1990s, the British Labour Party and the Democratic Party in the United States both moved decisively to the right in order to recapture the electoral centre ground and developed competition state projects with labels such as 'New Labour', the 'New Democrats', and the 'Third Way'. Indeed, the Clinton and Blair governments both adopted a policy agenda which in its most crucial aspects reflected the transformation of the industrial-welfare state (although of very different types) into a competition state to cope more effectively with what they defined as global 'realities'. Other states have moved more incrementally towards the competition state model. The failure of much of the 'socialist' (i.e., state capitalist) programme of French President François Mitterrand, elected in 1981, to pull France out of the slump led to his administration adopting the neo-liberal dimensions of the competition state model, although much of French statism remained in a diluted form. Germany and Japan are still in the midst of a transformation from the industrial-welfare state (although of very different types) to the competition state model. The European Union has also acted as a driving force of neo-liberalism and a champion of the competition state model, especially in terms of competition policy and the development of the single market after 1985. While developing states such as Chile and Mexico have become converts to the competition state model (see Soederberg, Menz and Cerny, 2005).

New Labour's competition state

New Labour's Competition State has five key dimensions: the restructuring of the state; policy entrepreneurship; ideological cohesion; a competition policy agenda; and, international policy transfer. Each of these dimensions of the competition state will now be considered in turn.

1. The restructuring of the state

The competition state involves the restructuring of the state in the face of processes of globalization. It may also lead to the empowering of the state in certain areas. In Britain these processes have been associated with a constitutional reformation, the shift from government to governance and traditional public administration to new public management.

It is well documented that constitutions structure domestic economic systems and pattern social relationships and politics (Dearlove, 1989). Constitutional reform may partly be understood as an attempt to reform the constitutional order in line with the economic order, and, most significantly, to alter pre-existing patterns of social relationships and politics in order to allow the state to deal better with the imperatives of globalization (see Evans, 2004). One of the most crucial lessons that the New Labour project learned from 18 years of Tory rule was that the Westminster model of parliamentary government was an obstacle to successful adjustment to the imperatives of globalization (see Hutton, 1995). For New Labour, the constitutional reform project represents a means for reconstituting the relationship between government and the people through constitutional method rather than economic regulation; an ideal replacement for public ownership as an instrument of political modernization.

The constitutional reform project was also introduced to enhance the government's capacity to steer the competition state. For it constitutes a strategy of integration; a process through which new and old political communities are either defined or redefined, created or discarded in both institutional and attitudinal terms. Indeed, historically devolution has been used as a policy instrument by British governments to assimilate the demands of nationalist movements within the 'nations' seeking greater autonomy. Its main aim is to secure elite attachment to the UK system of governance through the forging of a consensus on national policy goals (M. Evans, 2008).

If constitutional reform is about changing the institutional framework according to which the UK is governed, then the New Governance signifies a change in the processes by which society is governed. Box 1 depicts a multi-actored (governmental and non-governmental), multi-level (global, international, transnational, European, national, regional, local) differentiated polity based upon power dependence (Smith and Richards, 2001).

The process of 'hollowing-out' the state that underpins the emergence of the New Governance reveals a further source of pressure from the forces of globalization and a profound challenge to the competition state. Rhodes (1997) has observed that there are four key interrelated trends which illustrate the reach of this process: privatization and limiting the scope and forms of public intervention; the loss of functions by central government departments to alternative service delivery systems (such as Next Steps Agencies) and through market testing; the loss of functions from the British government to European Union institutions; and, the

---

Box 1 **Multi-level governance in a differentiated polity**

Level of governance	*Key representative institutions*
Global, international, transnational	United Nations, World Trade Organization, World Bank, International Monetary Fund, Organization for Economic Co-operation and Development, GATT, G8 including third sector organizations, multi-national corporations and organized interest groups.
European	EU political institutions, processes and civil society including third sector organizations, multi-national corporations and organized interest groups.
State	UK political institutions, processes and civil society including third sector organizations, multi-national corporations and domestic firms and organized interest groups.
Devolved nations	National political institutions (e.g. assemblies, parliaments and executives), processes and civil societies including third sector organizations, multi-national corporations and domestic firms and organized interest groups.
Regions	Regional political institutions (e.g. Regional Development Agencies and Chambers), processes and civil societies including third sector organizations, domestic firms and organized interest groups.
Local (county)	County councils and civil societies including third sector organizations, private firms and organized interest groups.
Local (district)	District councils and civil societies including third sector organizations, private firms and organized interest groups.
Local (community)	Parish and neighbourhood councils, third sector organizations, private firms and organized interest groups.
Coordinating mechanisms	Joint Ministerial Committees, the Ministry of Justice, the Supreme Court.

---

emergence of limits to the discretion of public servants through the new public management (NPM), with its emphasis on managerial accountability and clearer political control created by a sharp distinction between politics and administration.

The process of administrative modernization in the UK has spanned three decades of reform. It was initially galvanized by the need to arrest processes of relative economic decline and the belief within the Thatcher government in the public choice precept that an inefficient public sector was largely to blame for inflation. The reform process has been driven by the desire to increase the capacity of government to govern and management to manage. In practical terms this has meant devolving greater responsibility for initiative and leadership to all levels of public administration to ensure 'economy', 'efficiency' and 'effectiveness' and control public sector costs.

What was initially a relatively parochial modernization process confined to Anglo-American liberal democracies in general and Westminster model parliamentary democracies in particular, became an international movement due to the facilitating role of the OECD, the IMF and the World Bank (Common, 2001; Hood, 1995). For the apostles all assumed that institution-building NPM-style was a necessary condition for economic development despite the self-evident fact that NPM remained a loose-knit collection of ideas for improving performance rather than a coherent governing ideology (see Burnham and Pyper, 2008: 53). These global trends can be organized into four main categories of NPM-inspired administrative reform (market, regulatory/deregulatory, governance and competence reforms) that relate to two main factors: the adoption of certain private sector organizational methods and the move towards governance and away from government. This process of change constitutes a shift from traditional public administration and government to NPM and governance. This endogenous process of 'hollowing-out' leads to the loss not just of the state's previous interventionist role, but also obviates much of its traditional *raison d'être*.

2. Policy entrepreneurship

Rather than attempting to insulate states from key international market pressures, as state actors in the national industrial-welfare state sought to do, political actors in competition states embrace openness and marketization.

State actors and institutions promote new forms of complex globalization in the attempt to adapt state action to cope more effectively with what they see as global 'realities'. Hence they seek to make the domestic economy more prosperous and competitive in international terms while accepting the loss of key traditional social and economic state functions, which were central to the development of the industrial-welfare state. However, in attempting to meet the challenges of globalization, domestic political and bureaucratic actors increasingly transform the domestic political system into a terrain of conflict underpinned with profound policy debates around alternative responses to globalization (e.g. in Britain the issue of the single European currency). There has emerged out of this process of domestic rearticulation, a particular range of policy options that have come to represent a restructured, loosely knit consensus. First on the right (many of whose 'neo-liberal' members have always believed deeply in the disarming of the economic state) and then on the left, as traditional alternatives are incrementally eroded. This increasingly familiar consensus involves both an extensive process of deregulation, liberalization, and flexibilization not only of public policy but also of the state apparatus itself and a refocusing of the state on supporting, maintaining and even promoting transnational and international market processes and governance structures at home. The latter manifests itself in a moral emphasis on personal responsibility, an economic and political acceptance of the correctness of market outcomes, and, paradoxically, an increase in pro-market regulation and intervention (Vogel, 1996).

Thus the rationale for state intervention is aimed not only at sustaining the domestic economy but also at promoting its further integration into an increasingly open global economy in the acceptance that the imperatives of international competitiveness and consumer choice have a higher ideological status than issues of domestic social solidarity.

3. Ideological cohesion

As a result of these changes, some consensual, some coercive, the ideological divide between left and right loses its traditional landmarks.

Social democratic and other centre-left parties begin to search for policies, which, while adapting to the new constraints, are intended to promote a diluted form of neo-liberalism, or a Third Way (Giddens, 1998). In Britain this represents the outcome of the war of ideas between the forces of social democracy and neo-liberalism. Policy initiatives such as: the rejection of Keynsian demand management; the emphasis on promoting economic growth through the introduction of supply-side policies aimed at freeing up markets and expanding choice; close attention to financial management and control of public expenditure; the defeat of inflation; and ensuring the conditions for stability in the private sector's planning environment, have all represented common themes in contemporary British economic discourse. Indeed up until the 2008 global financial crisis, New Labour's economic project was more noteworthy for its similarities rather than its differences with Thatcherism.

4. A competition policy agenda

The creation of a competition state involves a policy agenda, which seeks to provide the conditions that will help the state to adapt state action to cope more effectively with what they perceive as global 'realities'.

In terms of the key elements of economic policy transformation, transnational factors have interacted with domestic politics to bring five specific types of policy change to the top of the political agenda. First, an emphasis on the control of inflation and general neo-liberal monetarism (hopefully translating into non-inflationary growth) has become the touchstone of state economic management and interventionism, reflected in a wider embedded financial orthodoxy. Secondly, a shift from macro-economic to micro-economic interventionism, has been reflected in *both* deregulation and industrial policy and in new social initiatives such as 'New Deal' schemes. Thirdly, a shift in the focus of interventionism at the international level away from maintaining a range of 'strategic' or 'basic' economic activities in order to retain minimal economic self-sufficiency in key sectors to a policy of flexible response to competitive conditions in a range of diversified and rapidly evolving international market places. Fourthly, new regulatory structures have been designed to enforce global market-rational economic and political behaviour on rigid and inflexible private sector actors as well as on state actors and agencies. Indeed, the rapid rise of the competition state, in an increasingly crowded and heterogeneous world economy, has given rise to a further paradox. As states and state actors have attempted to promote competitiveness in this way, they have seemingly voluntarily given up a range of crucial policy instruments. A heated debate rages over whether, for example, capital controls can be reintroduced or whether states are still able to choose to pursue more inflationary policies without disastrous consequences. Finally, a shift has occurred in the focal point of party and governmental politics away from the general maximization of welfare within a nation (full employment, redistributive transfer payments and social service provision) to the promotion of enterprise, innovation and profitability in both private and public sectors. This may be termed the post-welfare contracting state (see Evans and Cerny, 2003).

5. International policy transfer

Policy transfer has become a key mechanism for delivering the policy agenda of the competition state through elite structures of governance.

The ascent of the Blair government to power in the UK in July 1997 led to a proliferation of policy transfer activity between Britain and the United States. The close relationship which developed between the Blair and Clinton administrations was reflected in a long list of common policy initiatives that included: education (reduction of class sizes), crime (zero-tolerance, anti-truancy drives), and welfare (active labour market programmes such as 'Welfare to Work') reform. In addition, the UK's then Chancellor of the Exchequer, Gordon Brown, became convinced of the need for Bank of England independence after discussions with Alan Greenspan, Chair of the independent US Federal Reserve Board (Central Bank), and Robert Rubin, Clinton's Treasury Secretary. Many of these items may be viewed as part of an international policy agenda for the centre-left which was forged by Blair, Clinton, and their advisers. On 6 February 1998 Blair addressed the US State Department outlining what he termed the 'five clear principles of the centre-left' common to both New Labour and the New Democrats:

1. stable management and economic prudence in order to cope with the global economy;
2. a change in the emphasis of government intervention so that it dealt with education, training, and infrastructure and not things like industrial intervention or 'tax and spend';
3. reform of the welfare state;
4. reinventing government, decentralization, opening-up government; and,
5. internationalism in opposition to the right's isolationism.

It is within this international agenda for the centre-left that we are most likely to find examples of policy transfer between the British and American competition states, for example, in public management (Common, 2001), urban (Wolman, 1992) or welfare (Dolowitz et al., 2000) policies.

This policy agenda is spreading internationally primarily as a consequence of two key developments. First, processes of globalization both external to the nation state (e.g. through changes in the nature of geopolitics, political integration, the internationalization of financial markets and global communications) and the 'hollowing-out' of the nation state itself, have created new opportunity structures for policy transfer. Secondly, policy transfer is more likely to occur in an era of New Governance. The shift from traditional government to collaborative governance has increased the range of non-state actors involved in delivering public goods and has created an opportunity structure for cross-sector policy learning. In times of uncertainty policy-makers at the heart of policy networks will look to the 'quick fix' solution to public policy problems that policy transfer can provide (see Evans, 2005).

Comparing competition states

In the previous section, five key dimensions of the British Competition State project were identified but what grounded empirical evidence can we present to demonstrate the existence of this state form in practice? How far has the competition state project become embedded in the institutions, norms and values of British governance?

Box 2 presents 11 hypotheses which capture the key dimensions of the competition state. These hypotheses can be evaluated empirically through the interrogation of OECD data.[4] This provides us with both a measure of the degree to which New Labour has embraced the competition state model

---

Box 2 **Anticipated qualities of competition states**

1. New Public Management and the shift from government to governance
Hypothesis 1: Competition states are leaders in the marketization of public service production

2. Post-welfare contracting state
Hypothesis 2: Social expenditure is lower in competition states than in more traditional welfare states

Hypothesis 3: Competition states make use of Active Labour Market Programmes (ALMPs) as an alternative to social assistance

Hypothesis 4: Competition states are featured by low levels of pension generosity

Hypothesis 5: Competition states are featured by low levels of passive unemployment spending

3. Government regulation of industry
Hypothesis 6: Competition states are featured by low levels of product market regulation

Hypothesis 7: Competition states are featured by low levels of Employment Protection Legislation

4. Taxation
Hypothesis 8: Competition states have lower average rates of income tax

Hypothesis 9: Competition states have lower average top-rates of income tax

Hypothesis 10: Competition states have lower average top-rates of corporate tax

5. International policy transfer
Hypothesis 11: Competition states actively engage in international policy transfer both as policy exporters and importers

---

and a benchmark against which to gauge the extent to which Cameron is the natural successor to Blair. The hypotheses suggest qualities which we should expect to be present within competition states. They are clustered around five sets of variables – NPM and the shift from government to governance; the post-welfare contracting state; government regulation of industry; taxation; and, international policy transfer.

It is important to note at the outset what can and what can't be measured in terms of 'competition stateness'. Hypotheses 1 to 10 can be measured using OECD data. For example, in regard to the claim that competition states are leaders in the marketization of public service production, Guy Peters uses OECD data to demonstrate that Anglo-American countries (Australia, Britain, Canada, New Zealand and the United States) have been the leaders in NPM-type market and governance reform (Peters and Savoie, 1998). He argues that policy learning is a common activity in governments around the world, but that there are differences in the rates at which countries are able to learn and adapt. He attributes these differences to structural factors such as economic, ideological, cultural and institutional similarities. Those states that share common features are more likely to engage in policy transfer with one another. He concludes that cultural variables play an extremely important role in the transfer of policy innovations among countries, particularly in relation to geographical proximity and political similarity. However, another set of policy ideas, those associated with political parties and ideologies, appear to have much less of a relationship with the spread of management reforms.

Horsfall (2009, forthcoming) interrogates hypotheses 2 to 10 using OECD SOCX data. He indexes 25 countries in terms of their 'competition stateness' using a similar method to Esping-Andersen's *Three Worlds of Welfare Capitalism* (1990) which focused on the degree to which the citizens of those countries were protected from the commodifying pressures of the market.[5] Table 1 shows that those countries that were characterized by Esping-Andersen as liberal regimes conform to the competition state thesis particularly in areas relating to welfare expenditure and generosity. Britain is particularly 'competitive' on measures relating to the post-welfare contracting state and government regulation of industry.

It is, however, much more difficult to investigate the observation that competition states actively engage in international policy transfer both as policy exporters and importers due to the absence of base-line data. Although the secondary literature is prone to making claims about the proliferation of policy transfer activity amongst competition states (see Dolowitz and Marsh, 2000; Evans, 2005; and Rose, 2005), the evidence

Table 1   The competition state index (ZBA), shown in rank order of total score, displaying weighted dimension scores, and total weighted index score

Country	Dimension of the competition state index					
	Overall welfare effort	Post-welfare contracting state	Traditional welfare responsibilities	Government regulation of industry	Taxation	Total Score
Ireland	0.872	1.037	1.129	1.592	3.139	7.768
Korea	2.616	−0.813	2.864	−0.535	2.562	6.694
UK	0.070	0.222	1.480	2.530	0.763	5.065
Australia	0.698	−0.310	1.447	2.313	0.653	4.801
New Zealand	0.365	−0.123	0.532	1.102	1.584	3.456
Switzerland	0.193	0.457	−0.066	0.209	2.293	3.085
Canada	0.730	−0.211	1.522	2.052	−1.021	3.072
USA	0.752	−1.031	0.869	2.979	−0.781	2.789
Slovak Rep	0.453	−0.137	0.586	0.538	1.176	2.616
Czech Rep	0.015	−1.008	0.167	−0.871	1.574	−0.123
Japan	0.528	−0.571	0.691	0.261	−1.289	−0.381
Denmark	−1.096	4.352	−3.29	1.167	−1.628	−0.495
Finland	−0.265	1.279	0.155	−0.140	−1.630	−0.600
Sweden	−1.708	3.865	−0.695	0.133	−1.934	−0.606
Norway	−0.698	0.872	0.352	−1.141	−0.307	−0.922
Netherlands	0.1075	2.001	−1.618	−0.317	−1.527	−1.353
Italy	−0.567	0.614	0.160	−1.272	−1.453	−2.518
Spain	0.052	0.949	−0.127	−2.074	−1.350	−2.550
Portugal	−0.279	0.524	−0.109	−2.475	−0.379	−2.718
Greece	−0.136	−0.807	−0.251	−2.317	0.203	−3.308
France	−1.278	2.186	−0.964	−2.287	−1.580	−3.922
Germany	−1.113	2.461	−1.276	−0.575	−3.493	−3.996
Austria	−0.910	0.332	−2.302	0.066	−1.251	−4.065
Belgium	−0.973	2.046	−1.182	−0.215	−3.791	−4.115
Poland	−0.431	−1.172	−1.516	−3.126	1.421	−4.824

Source: Horsfall (2009, forthcoming).

tends to be confined to particular policy arenas within the international agenda for the centre-left.

The question remains, therefore, as to how seriously British public organizations as a whole take international policy learning. Following publication of the *Modernising Government* White Paper (Cabinet Office, 1999), the Centre for Management and Policy Studies was established with a clear mandate both to establish more productive relations between government and academia in order to generate high quality evidence-based research to inform practice and to consider the broader training needs of the civil service (Cabinet Office/CMPS, 2002). Moreover, the Cabinet Office's (2005) Professional Skills for government programme aimed at dealing with the skills and training requirements of the civil service.[6] The importance of international lesson-drawing, however, has never been effectively integrated into research, training and development activities civil service-wide despite the growing concern that the capacity of the UK central government to engage in innovative policy development has been seriously eroded. This could be a reflection of the absence of political leadership or service-wide leadership on international matters or merely a product of cost containment or the legacy of the colonial era when the British civil service led the world in public service innovation and thus few lessons from abroad were deemed worthy of serious consideration. It is therefore difficult to refute the argument that the British civil service believes itself to be a net exporter rather than importer of policy ideas.

In those areas where Britain has imported ideas it has hardly been an unmitigated success (e.g. the Child Support Agency, New Deal for Communities, the action zone experiments, amongst others).[7] This has mainly been due to the rather misguided notion that Britain can only draw progressive lessons from the United States despite significant differences in political culture, systems and public policy belief systems.

The twist in the tale – the competition state project under stress

The 2008 global financial crisis has demonstrated the structural vulnerability of the neo-liberal model particularly in economies such as Britain which had become so dependent on the services sector in the preceding two decades. The ramifications of the crisis for Cameron's Conservatives are deftly dealt with by Simon Lee in Chapter 5 of this volume. It remains here to identify the core governing dilemmas which have confronted the British Competition State and to assess Brown's response.

It was stated earlier in this chapter that the main challenge facing governments all over the world is their capacity to adapt to the exogenous constraints and opportunities brought about by different processes of globalization while maintaining a relatively progressive domestic policy programme. Within this context, the challenges faced by social democratic parties and governments are particularly problematic as for much of the twentieth century they believed that it was their duty to intervene in economy and society to tame capitalism to ensure economic growth and social justice through economic regulation. The neo-liberal model, however, ties the hands of the state in ensuring that it privileges the role of the market by providing the conditions for innovation, opportunity and competition in an attempt to maintain competitive advantage. In policy terms Brown has always vacillated between the competition state model and nostalgia for the industrial-welfare state without fully understanding the tensions that this creates. The 2008 global financial crisis, however, has fully exposed both the tensions between the industrial-welfare state model and the competition state model and Brown's inner struggle for clarity of purpose.

Brown is currently performing the part of an international agent of policy transfer and is being lauded as the saviour of global capitalism by finance ministers around the world and even the Nobel Prize winning economist Paul Krugman. Brown's rescue plan has now been adopted by other governments in need of a quick fix to get them out of the financial crisis. The plan involved the British government taking a stake in three British banks (Royal Bank of Scotland, Lloyds and HBOS) and giving them £37 billion in finance to recapitalize to allow them to cope with current market volatility and the ongoing liquidity crisis. The package was received exceptionally well by the world's markets. In contrast, the US government's bailout package of $700 billion, which was originally intended just to buy off bad debts from failed banks, was badly received by the markets earlier in October 2008 and failed to stem the tide. In consequence, the US government has adopted the Brown plan and recapitalized nine banks (amongst them Goldmans and Morgan Stanley) at the cost of $250 billion. Gordon Brown's newly found role as the saviour of global capitalism is, of course, rich in irony. Brown did not anticipate the global credit crunch despite being in a uniquely privileged position in the capacity of Chairman of the International Monetary and Financial Committee since September 1999 (the IMF's most important advisory committee).

Will this period of crisis management lead to the emergence of a new policy paradigm characterized by the demise of neo-liberalism and the revival of old forms of state intervention in the economy? Although the present financial crisis demonstrates the clear limits to the neo-liberal mantra it also reveals that politics matter in times of uncertainty. The minimal statism and anti-state rhetoric of the competition state is difficult to square in times of recession when state intervention to address the basic needs of the citizenry becomes expected. This of course creates the space for the emergence of new national varieties of capitalism; a likely corollary of the present crisis. In the medium-term, however, a return to a more restrained form of neo-liberalism is inevitable because elite perceptions of global economic fundamentals will remain the same: capital markets can only be subject to light-touch regulation in order to attract capital investment; capital has to be global to achieve maximum return on investment; labour markets have to be flexible in order to compete and retain jobs; trade policy has to be free if state goods are to penetrate foreign markets; government spending has to be closely managed to ensure ongoing investment in infrastructure and to generate greater private savings; and, tax policy has to provide incentives for growth to stimulate enterprise and innovation. These economic fundamentals remain at the heart of the competition state project and sit more easily with Cameron's Conservatives than Brown's New Labour government, particularly in times of economic crisis.

Cameron's competition state – continuities and discontinuities

> Even if Blair and Brown are right and globalisation is the only game in town, the move from a welfare to a market state makes politics a lot more interesting. Why? Because there is only one party in Britain that is really at ease with the slimmed-down, consumer-driven, free market model of the state. And that's the one, despite the cuddly new image, led by David Cameron.
>
> (L. Elliott, 'It's the Tories who will gain from Labour's market state', *Guardian*, 9 June 2006)

An evaluation of this kind is inevitably complicated by the need to deconstruct opposition rhetoric and identify substantive policy pledges. Cameron-speak is littered with rhetoric sometimes rediscovered from the past ('welfare dependency') or combining old with new ('rolling forward society', rather than 'rolling back the state') or attempts at articulating something new such as the concept of the 'broken society' now supplanted by the 'broken economy'. Moreover, a further complication is added by Gordon Brown's policy response to the fiscal crisis. Should we compare Cameron's competition state project with New Labour's pre-crisis or post crisis project? Or of equal concern should we focus on Cameron's pre-crisis or post crisis project? This section presents an overview of the continuities and discontinuities between the two projects which cross-cuts both sets of considerations. There are two main sources of available information to help us identify the competition policy agenda under Cameron. The first sources of information are those few areas of official policy outlined on the party's website and in official documentation.[8] The second, less reliable sources of information can be found in the debates and policy papers surrounding the Conservative Party policy review. In December

2005, Cameron established a wide-ranging policy review by setting-up six policy groups, each chaired by a Tory grandee, charged with thinking 'the unthinkable'. Although he made it clear at the outset that the recommendations from the review would not necessarily be adopted as Tory policy, they provide strong clues as to whether a Cameron government would represent a break with the New Labour competition state project. A brief commentary on each area of policy development follows, beginning with the principles underpinning the policy agenda.

Principles

The principles of the competition state are in keeping with: the traditional pragmatism of Conservative statecraft (Bulpitt, 1986: 20–3); its 'acceptance of change' and 'strong but limited government' (Norton, 1996b: 72); the understanding that the art of winning elections is about creating the public perception that Conservatism is synonymous with wealth creation and governing competence; and, the belief in the notion of the active rather than interventionist state. However, the neo-liberal dimensions of the competition state project are tempered by Cameron's recognition that Thatcherism had failed to provide for balanced social and economic development and had become synonymous with social fragmentation (Scruton, 2006; Elliott and Hanning, 2007). These principles of statecraft explain both the economic liberal and liberal conservative dimensions of Cameron-speak. Indeed, Cameron now shares New Labour's and other social democrats' struggle with balancing market and social concerns. This is reflected in Cameron's and Brown's similar views on the opportunities and dangers of globalization. Indeed Brown's notion of 'Globalization with a Human Face' was expressed in similar terms by Cameron in his speech to the Conservative Party conference in Bournemouth on 2 October 2007:

> In this new world, the winds of change, can sometimes be quite harsh rather than just invigorating. Globalisation will help poorer countries become richer, it will help them close the gap with the richer world, but sometimes globalisation can increase inequalities within a country. And I think we all know that while our economy is getting richer, our society in many ways is getting poorer.[9]

Of course Cameron is not the first and certainly won't be the last Conservative leader to struggle with these issues. Harold Macmillan, for example, was a modernizer, a liberal conservative who was often at odds with the right of his party due to his acceptance of nationalization,

Keynesianism and decolonization. He once wrote that 'John Maynard Keynes ... became the inspiration for much of my political thinking in the Thirties' (cited in Dudley Edwards, 1983: 44).

The restructuring of the state

The incremental restructuring of the state would continue under Cameron, including the constitutional reformation and the shift from government to governance and traditional public administration to new public management. Despite Conservative claims that 'Labour's constitutional vandalism has weakened parliament, undermined democracy and brought the integrity of the ballot into question – and its unbalanced devolution settlement has caused resentment in England and rising nationalism in Scotland and Wales', nothing of a substantial nature has been advanced to redress the imbalance.[10] Cameron's solution to constitutional anomie would be to: 'restore the integrity of the ballot' by introducing individual voter registration and addressing the disparities that exist between constituency populations; 'address the West Lothian question' by giving English MPs a decisive say on laws that affect only England; and, replacing the Human Rights Act with a British Bill of Rights to reassert the power of the executive in the self-proclaimed 'war against terrorism'.[11] Most significantly, however, the democratization project that underpins the New Labour competition state project would be extended to local government with the introduction of directly-elected police commissioners and powers to enable local residents to veto excessive council tax rises.[12]

Cameron also pledges to extend the reach of NPM by enhancing the role of third sector organizations in public service provision and reintroducing cost containment and efficiency drives to tackle 'government waste'. Moreover, New Labour's penchant for partnerships and the marketization of public service production would continue with the creation of more Foundation Hospitals and City Academies and the expansion of the independent school sector with the aim of: freeing up the system whereby new schools are established, to allow charities, livery companies, existing school federations, not-for-profit trusts, co-operatives and groups of parents to set up new schools in the state sector.[13]

The competition policy agenda

Social policy is traditionally viewed to be the most likely policy arena (with the possible exception of economic policy) to find differences between the two parties. However, Cameron intends to extend the reach of the post-welfare contracting state through the extension of active labour market programmes or what the Conservatives term 'Work for Welfare'. This will include long-term community projects to help integrate the unemployed back into the labour market and those not willing to take part would face tough sanctions.[14] Other areas of social policy innovation crystallized around Cameron's notion of social responsibility – such as increased taxation on beer and wine to battle binge drinking; additional working tax credits for married couples to help rebuild Britain's 'broken society'; the reclassification of cannabis as a dangerous drug; and, the suggested expansion of abstinence-based drug rehabilitation centres – do not represent a departure from the competition state model.[15] Rather, they help to reinforce conceptions of individual responsibility which underpin the market state.

On economic policy, Cameron's competition state project extends the logic of the pre-crisis New Labour competition state project but represents a damning critique of Brown's post-crisis management. This pragmatic policy juxtaposition is illustrated by Cameron's initial focus, on becoming party leader in December 2005, on the need to fix Britain's 'broken society'. At this time there was no reference to the recently discovered 'broken economy'. Cameron sought to find some blue water in policy terms by defining his shadow cabinet's mission as social responsibility, quickly endorsing Iain Duncan Smith's report on Social Justice, and kite-flying deliberately vague egalitarian rhetoric such as 'sharing the proceeds of growth'. On economic fundamentals the Conservatives remained wedded to the competition state project. John Redwood's competitiveness agenda, for example, recommended by his review group is largely an extension of the logic of the pre-crisis New Labour competition state project with recommendations for: scrapping inheritance tax; cutting corporation tax to 25p; abolishing capital gains tax on assets held for more than ten years; reducing red tape for business by 3.7 per cent annually for five years and repealing working time regulations. Cameron and Osborne's views on taxation have remained deliberately vague and often contradictory. They have declared their intention to 'shrink the size of the state' and 'share the proceeds of growth between public spending and tax cuts so that public spending is reduced as a share of national income'.[16] The Tories later sought to quell fears that they would cut public services by announcing that they would match Labour's public spending plans for the next three years and would not make any unfunded promises of tax cuts. However, in order to meet their commitments to social responsibility they have also declared their intention to ensure tax fairness for the poor, tax breaks for married couples and to raise green taxes but reduce the tax burden elsewhere.

The bipartisan approach to economic policy exhibited between 2005 to mid-2008 was destroyed in the aftermath of Cameron's support for the Brown government's recapitalization of the Royal Bank of Scotland, Lloyds and HBOS. The language of the 'broken economy' thereafter dominated the Conservative critique of Brown's economic policy and doctrine which Cameron claimed to be a 'complete and utter failure':

> Gordon Brown has left Britain's economy ill-prepared for a downturn: he borrowed in a boom and left us with one of the biggest budget deficits in the advanced world; he stripped the Bank of England of its powers to supervise the City; he actively encouraged the risk-taking culture in our banks; and he claimed to have abolished boom and bust.[17]

The prescriptions which follow this critique, however, centre on rebuilding faith in the competition state model rather than removing its key pillars. In the short term this would involve: freezing council tax for two years 'by reducing wasteful spending on advertising and consultancy in central government'; abolishing Stamp Duty for nine out of ten first-time buyers; raising the Inheritance Tax threshold to £1 million; providing a £2.6 billion package of tax breaks 'to get people into work'; cutting the main rate of corporation tax to 25p and the small companies' rate to 20p; introducing a £50 billion National Loan Guarantee Scheme to underwrite bank lending to businesses to get credit flowing again; giving small and medium-sized businesses a six-month VAT holiday; cutting National Insurance by 1 per cent for six months for firms with fewer than five employees; abolishing income tax on savings for everyone on the basic rate of tax and raising the tax allowance for pensioners by £2,000 to £11,490.[18]

However, for Cameron and Osborne, to 'repair the broken economy' in the long run would require:

> ... economic responsibility. That means: a responsible fiscal policy, bolstered by independent oversight. A responsible financial policy, bolstered by a renewed role for the Bank of England. A responsible attitude to economic development that fosters more balanced economic growth.[19]

This can be considered rather a timid response given their claim that Brown had presided over the biggest budget deficit in the advanced world! They have also availed themselves of the opportunity to lament that due to Brown's economic mismanagement 'we can't offer big upfront net tax cuts like some other countries'. However, in his first policy pledge of 2009, Cameron promised tax cuts for savers. As Nick Cohen notes, 'Conservative supporters applauded his desire to compensate the prudent who were suffering a cut in their interest payments as the government tried to clean up the mess left by its incompetent regulation of rapacious bankers'.[20]

It would be wrong, therefore, to characterize Cameron as an uncritical heir apparent to the New Labour competition state project. Discontinuities can also be identified in health policy with Cameron's focus on the need to improve health outcomes and promote clinical innovation rather New Labour's obsession with improving management processes.[21] Cameron is also unapologetically pro-marriage – 'the family matters to me more than anything else ... it's just common sense ... that kids have a better chance when mum and dad are both there to bring them up' (cited in Jones, 2008) – and appears a committed environmentalist. He is on the record declaring that '... now is not the time to lose our nerve over the green agenda ... The choice really isn't between the economy and the environment. The choice is between progress and the past.'[22] Indeed, it is on this issue that Cameron's credentials as both a genuine modernizer and as an agent of international policy transfer will be tested. For Cameron has pledged to follow the Californian model and implement an Emissions Performance Standard and emulate the German government in introducing a new system of 'feed-in tariffs', by which citizens are paid for the energy they produce.[23]

In conclusion – is David Cameron 'Tory Blair'?

Although Cameron is a critical heir apparent to the New Labour competition state project – more of a difficult sibling than an apostle – in most respects a Cameron government would mean a change in governing style rather than policy substance. For this is essentially a neo-liberal project; born from the Thatcher period and demonstrating the historical tendency for opposition parties to gravitate towards the ruling hegemonic project. In consequence, continuities can be identified in broad areas of public policy from the constitutional reformation and the shift from government to governance to the extension of the post-welfare contracting state. This is, of course, unsurprising given the success of New Labour in stealing the electoral centre ground from the Conservatives by taking the hard edges of Thatcherism through social policy innovation but retaining much of its economic policy. Moreover, it could be argued that the most dramatic period of policy convergence between Britain's two main political parties occurred between 1989 and 1997 with the development of the New Labour project in opposition (Evans, 2004).

The British state has therefore increasingly adopted the features of a competition state and traditional landmarks between left and right have only become conspicuous in times of profound economic crisis and even then are likely to be short-lived. In the ensuing two years both government and opposition will need to focus more on conflict management and statecraft in times of crisis – understanding the competition state as a contested discourse and identifying new instruments for managing citizen and stakeholder expectations (e.g. through deep democratization and processes of shared governance). However, the medium-term future governance of the competition state is likely to be characterized by a return to stable management and economic prudence because of the global economy; the return to neo-liberal anti-inflationary monetarism combined with greater financial regulation; a post-crisis management change in the emphasis of government intervention so that it deals with education, training and infrastructure and not things like industrial intervention or tax and spend; continued reform of the welfare state through extending the scope of the post-welfare contracting state; and, reinventing government through decentralization.

Whether these forces of convergence will lead to a stable, pluralistic world based on liberal capitalism and the vestiges of liberal democracy or to greater divergence and inequality remains to be seen. But whatever direction the future takes, the competition state has become both the engine room and the steering mechanism of a political globalization process, which will further drive and shape processes of economic, social and cultural globalization.

Notes

1. The full text is available at: http://news.bbc.co.uk/1/hi/uk_politics/7026435. stm (accessed 7 January 2009).
2. An extreme version of the concept of the competition state has recently been popularized by Philip Bobbit in his book, *The Shield of Achilles* (2006) where he talks about globalization leading to the replacement of the nation state by a market state characterized by a dependency on 'the international capital markets and, to a lesser degree on the modern multinational business network to create stability in the world economy, in preference to management by national or transnational political bodies'.
3. Reported in *The Times*, 8 January 1998.
4. Hypotheses 2 to 10 have been developed from the work of Dan Horsfall (2009, forthcoming). Although it must be noted that these hypotheses were also developed from my own work in Cerny and Evans (2004).
5. Horsfall's excellent study adopts a methodology based on the Z-scores of different government actions in certain policy fields. The Z-score based approach (ZBA), like Esping-Andersen's (1990) famous decommodification

index, was devised to place welfare states into different ideal types, based upon deviations from the mean. By using Z-scores, the ZBA is able to standardize the data, transforming it into a form whereby the mean becomes zero and the standard deviation becomes '1'. Z-scores are used to compile the international index of childhood well-being across nations (see UNICEF, 2007), and the compilation of university league tables (see Chauhan, 2005).

6. See the Cabinet Office's overview of the Professional Skills for Government programme at: http://psg.civilservice.gov.uk/ (accessed 7 December 2008).

7. See: Dolowitz et al. (2000), Jones and Newburn (2001), King and Wickham-Jones (1999), Lightfoot (1999), Marmor (1997), Theodore and Peck (1999).

8. See the policy section of the Conservative Party's website available at: http://www.conservatives.com/Policy.aspx (accessed 12 January 2009).

9. The full text is available at: http://news.bbc.co.uk/1/hi/uk_politics/7026435.stm (accessed 7 January 2009).

10. See Conservative Party policy on 'Democracy' available at: http://www.conservatives.com/Policy/Where_we_stand/Democracy.aspx (accessed 11 January 2009).

11. Ibid.

12. See Conservative Party policy on 'Local Government' available at: http://www.conservatives.com/Policy/Where_we_stand/Local_Government.aspx (accessed 12 January 2009).

13. See Conservative Party policy on 'Schools' available at: http://www.conservatives.com/Policy/Where_we_stand/Schools.aspx (accessed 11 January 2009).

14. See Conservative Party policy on 'Welfare and Pensions' available at: http://www.conservatives.com/Policy/Where_we_stand/Welfare_and_Pensions.aspx (accessed 11 January 2009).

15. See Conservative Party policy on 'The Family' available at: http://www.conservatives.com/Policy/Where_we_stand/Family.aspx (accessed 12 January 2009) and the findings of Social Justice review group chaired by Iain Duncan Smith (Social Justice Policy Group, 2006, 2007).

16. It is noteworthy that health spokesperson Andrew Lansley was chastised for his pledge to increase health expenditure by 2 per cent.

17. For the Conservative Party's response to the 2008 financial crisis, see 'Reconstruction – Our Plan for a Strong Economy', available at: http://www.conservatives.com/Policy/Where_we_stand/Economy.aspx (accessed 13 January 2009).

18. Ibid.

19. Ibid.

20. Nick Cohen, 'Loath as I am to give Joan a kicking ...', *Guardian*, 11 January 2009.

21. See Conservative Party policy on 'Health' available at: http://www.conservatives.com/Policy/Where_we_stand/Health.aspx (accessed 13 January 2009).

22. David Cameron on 'Environmental Policy' available at: http://www.conservatives.com/tile.do?def=news.story.page&obj_id=145279 (accessed 13 January 2009). See also: http://www.conservatives.com/Policy/Where_we_stand/Environment.aspx (accessed 13 January 2009).

23. Ibid.

9
Voting Blue, Going Green? David Cameron and the Environment

James Connelly

The slogan 'Vote Blue, Go Green' is now very familiar to the British public. But to what extent is it more than a neat slogan: to what extent does the Conservative Party go beyond sloganizing and embrace a real commitment to environmental concerns? This chapter evaluates David Cameron's environmental policy since he became leader of the Conservative Party. In so doing it will both compare and contrast this with previous Conservative leaders' attitudes towards the environment and ask whether there has been a significant shift in policy or (despite appearances) an underlying continuity.

It was a distinguishing feature of Cameron's assumption of the leadership of the Conservative Party that he immediately made the environment high profile. It became part of his public image, a matter of personal identity and identification. This was certainly a first for a Conservative leader. Not since Mrs Thatcher in 1989 has the environment loomed so large in Conservative Party thinking: certainly under William Hague, Iain Duncan Smith, and Michael Howard it never achieved anything like the same prominence. Earlier, under Thatcher and Major, there were definite advances in Britain's attitude to environmental concerns. However, although Mrs Thatcher 'discovered' the environment in 1989, this seemed less a genuine conversion to green values than a tactically driven response to the unprecedented 15 per cent share of the votes attained by the Green Party in that year's elections to the European Union Parliament. Prior to that her comments on environmentalism, its advocates, and their proposed lifestyle choices were typically less than sympathetic. Indeed, they were frequently anti-green in rhetoric and policy. Despite this, it should be noted that it was Heath's government which established the Department of the Environment, and that the Thatcher regime at the turn of the 1990s, under Chris Patten as Secretary of State, exhibited some real signs of interest in the environment. In the wake of the 'greening of Thatcher', and a decade after taking office, the administration produced its first white paper on the environment, *This Common Inheritance* (DOE, 1990). However, although it was steered through by a strong and sympathetic minister, Chris Patten, it did little more than summarize ad hoc policies already being undertaken and included no action plan for change. Radical ideas in the white paper, such as proposals for the use of economic instruments and green taxation were relegated to an annex, and his specific proposal for a carbon tax was resolutely opposed by the energy minister, the Treasury and the transport ministry. Recession was also setting in and Thatcher's contingent support for environmental issues became increasingly apparent. As we shall see, the ability to retain a strong commitment to the environment at a time of economic recession is a matter for renewed discussion in the present day.

Although in many ways an impressive document, the content of the Environmental Protection Act (1990) was largely centred on national implementation of EU directives on the environment. So much of the credit for substantive policy has to go to the EU, not to the government; indeed, it was during the Thatcher and Major years that Britain attracted the label of 'the dirty man of Europe', a label which it is now at last beginning to peel away. The role of the EU does illustrate an important point, which is the extent to which *any* government is required to implement environmental legislation simply by virtue of Britain's membership.

Between the publication of *This Common Inheritance* in 1990 and the Rio Earth Summit in 1992, Thatcher was replaced by Major. He was enthusiastic about the Rio process and he made a commitment to publish a national plan to implement Agenda 21. He was also active in persuading other G7 and EU countries to follow his example, thereby enabling the United Nations' Commission on Sustainable Development to begin its work. In 1994, the government made a formal response to the UNCED agreements and published white papers on sustainable development, climate change, biodiversity and sustainable forestry.

Whether self-driven, or externally imposed, therefore, there were certainly green straws in the Conservative wind from the early 1990s onwards, so to that extent the Conservative Party's current interest is not without precedent. However, none of his predecessors has so openly and completely allowed themselves to be identified with environmental concerns in the way that Cameron has. Mrs Thatcher discovered the environment in a secondary fashion and left policy largely to her ministers, one of whom, Patten, was enthusiastic, and others of whom (for example, Nicholas Ridley, who was credited with popularizing the acronym NIMBY – not in my backyard – as a way of denigrating those who protested against developments) were not. John Major was not inactive, but he was largely driven by external events and his identification with the issue was pale by comparison with Cameron's. To that extent there is certainly something unprecedented going on under the leadership of David Cameron. Whether it is driven by genuine concern or political tactics, the effects have been marked enough to spark the following sorts of remark:

> Under the slogan of 'Vote Blue, Go Green', David Cameron as leader has placed environmental concerns, in particular the issue of climate change, at the forefront of current Conservative Party policy. This focus has not only been emphasised by Blair's successor Gordon Brown, but has also been picked up by the opposition Conservatives, and their leader David Cameron, leading to arguments over which party is indeed more green – an event American environmental activists can only sit back and watch in amazement. (Schlosberg and Rinfret, 2008: 257)

To coin a phrase, Mr Cameron got his green credentials in early; indeed, it was noted that:

> On the very day that Mr Blair publicly doubted the value of a new climate change treaty, Mr Cameron put forward ... the most radical measures to tackle global warming ever proposed by a leading British politician. Then he was still a leadership candidate. When he won, he focused on the issue both in his acceptance speech and in his first Prime Minister's Questions, and, within days, recruited the radical environmentalist Zac Goldsmith to help lead a review of Conservative policies. At the same time he appointed Peter Ainsworth, probably the most respected green politician in parliament, as his Environment spokesperson. (*Independent on Sunday*, 2006)

So far so good, and despite the now notorious scenario of Mr Cameron cycling to parliament with his official boxes being chauffeured right behind, he has succeeded in making a good case to be taken seriously as an environmentally committed leader. But questions remain and will tease the minds of the sceptical or cynical until, when and if the Conservative Party under Cameron's leadership has its green credentials put to the test following an election victory. At this stage, it might be said, their environmental policies could be (in the immortal words of Mary Poppins) 'pie-crust promises – easily made and easily broken'; as Polly Toynbee observes:

> Cameron's 'revolution' is also pain-free ... it is strong on fantasy technology that doesn't yet exist: carbon capture will solve the dirty coal problem, there will be street plugs for electric cars everywhere. Every home will be entitled to be fitted with up to £6,500 of wall and roof insulation, paid for with loans from energy companies. ... But how green is Cameron really? Only this week he opposed the compulsory switchover to new light bulbs. (Toynbee, 2008)

It should be observed that the Conservative stance on the environment, although it could be dismissed as rhetorical, has had measurable effects. For example, through pressure on the government, in calling for a bill to set a target for cutting Britain's carbon emissions by 2050, they caused them to act in introducing a climate change bill. The Climate Change Act, which received the Royal Assent at the end of November 2008, requires the UK to cut its greenhouse gas emissions by 80 per cent (based on 1990 levels) by 2050. To achieve this, a series of five year interim 'targets' will also be set. These will take into account the UK's share of international aviation and shipping emissions. This implies that any future government, irrespective of colour or environmental commitment, will have to address the meeting of some difficult targets whether or not the economy is in recession. The Energy Bill, also passed in November 2008, made provision for the introduction of a feed-in tariff for renewable electricity and renewable heat incentives. This was inserted into the bill as a result of an amendment tabled by the Conservative and Liberal Democrat parties. It can readily be seen, therefore, that Cameron certainly changed perceptions of the main political parties on the environment. He led, promoted and publicized the green agenda, and by outflanking the government on the environment thereby encouraging a more radical content to the Climate Change and Energy bills in effect forced the government to go further than it had initially been inclined to.

So, is this strong interest in the environment authentic and genuine? Will it fade either in the exigencies of power or under the onslaught of economic recession? David Cameron forcefully claimed in a speech in June 2008 that his green shoots would not wither in the frost of economic hard times: but given the depths of the recession that the United Kingdom and the western world are currently undergoing, how convincing is this claim? As noted above, in comparable circumstances in the mid-1990s the environment moved rapidly down the policy agenda. Further, shortly before making this speech it was noted by observers that Mr Cameron failed to mention the words 'environment' or 'climate change' in a 1,200-word statement about his priorities for government (Grice, 2008).

The point is this. The Conservative Party under Cameron has been highly successful in appealing to the green movement. Further, many environmental pressure groups, think tanks and activists are favourably impressed not only by Mr Cameron himself, but also by his choice of Shadow Environment Secretary. Mr Ainsworth is regarded generally as being genuinely engaged with green issues: his green credentials are impeccable and he lends a lot of credibility, commitment and policy weight to Cameron's rhetoric which, in his absence might seem more vulnerable to the charge of political opportunism. Indeed, Mr Ainsworth was at the heart of the Conservatives' outflanking of the Labour government in the introduction of the Climate Change Act (2008). As we shall see, there is also a depth not only in personnel but in policy advice. The Quality of Life group (led by John Gummer and Zac Goldsmith) has produced some important and radical policy documents which include proposals for parking charges at out-of-town supermarket and shopping malls; a moratorium on airport expansion and increased taxes on short-haul domestic flights. However, Mr Cameron was careful to put some distance between himself and the report. In his words, the group's report was 'to' and not 'for' the party (Grice, 2008). However, although some of this careful response and distancing is only to be expected by a leader who has to act carefully in the run in to the next general election, other doubts surface from time to time. One doubt concerns the commitment of the other potential ministers to environmental concerns: there are many who consider that the Shadow Chancellor, George Osborne, or the recently renewed Kenneth Clarke, Shadow Business Secretary, and many others, will do all they can to lower expectations on the environment and prioritize conventional notions of economic growth and welfare. A related doubt is whether recession will lead to a resurgence of commitment to economic growth irrespective of environmental cost. Related to this is the issue of whether the environmental commitment is genuine, whether it can be resolved in the relatively painless way (through the magical medium of ecological modernization) that the Conservatives seem to suppose. And finally there is the ever-present thought in the mind of many environmentalists that the Conservative Party is doing only what it deems necessary to avoid attacks by green groups.

Conservatism, the Conservative Party and the environment

Let us now consider the current Conservative approach to the environment a little more closely. In one of Cameron's early speeches as leader he expressed the view that the Conservatives and the environment had a natural affinity:

> To me, the most surprising thing is that ... we on the centre right ever allowed the environment to appear to be something that was not for us. This mistake is all the more surprising given the Conservative Party's proud green heritage. It was Disraeli's Conservative government which, in 1875, introduced the great Public Health Act, a measure heralding the first determined attempt to clean up the terrible environmental impacts of the Industrial Revolution. It was a Conservative government in the 1950s that passed the Clean Air Act, putting an end to the choking, killer smogs in London and other cities. It was Edward Heath who established the Department of the Environment; Chris Patten who was responsible for Britain's first White Paper on Sustainable Development, and Michael Howard who persuaded the US government, under George Bush Snr, to sign the Climate Change Convention – the forerunner of the Kyoto agreement. Conservative governments introduced the modern framework for countryside and wildlife protection; the ban on CFCs, tax incentives for unleaded petrol, the great clean-up of our rivers and lakes, the landfill tax, and the Home Energy and Conservation Act. And of course it was Margaret Thatcher who, in 1989, became the first world leader to raise the need to tackle global warming. (Cameron, 2006c)

Cameron continues by suggesting that it is false to regard the environment and economic growth as necessarily at odds. What we need now, he states, is green growth, which means 'harnessing existing and developing technologies in energy and transport', 'putting a price on carbon emissions and ensuring that the polluter pays'; and 'enabling the market to do what it has always done: find the most efficient and cost-effective way of doing business' (Cameron, 2006c).

This statement, persuasive as it sounds, raises many issues both political and theoretical. It is undoubtedly true that in theory the environmental initiative can be claimed by the Conservative Party under the heading of conservation. It is often claimed (for example by Conservative ideologues such as Roger Scruton) that the Conservative Party, conservatism and environment all fit naturally together. However, persuasive as this might be as a background commitment to conservation, it is not at all clear that the Conservative Party can be so comfortable with the policy implications of the environmental policies, especially those on climate change. This is because they point towards government intervention, control, regulation, green taxation, and tradable permits. The Conservative answer is (as we saw above) ecological modernization. That is, the claim that to a considerable extent, hard choices do not have to be faced because a win-win situation is available to the canny politician. We might characterize ecological modernization as a way of thinking which recognizes the structural character of environmental problems, but assumes that existing political, economic, and social institutions can be modified so as to internalize care for the environment (Hajer, 1995: 25). It is claimed to be a way of meeting the demands of sustainability through the creation of markets in environmental goods and services. Proponents of ecological modernization argue that these changes have the potential to make significant improvements in the environmental performance of industrial economies; ecological modernization is seen as a means whereby capitalism can accommodate the environmental challenge: 'rather than environmental protection being a threat to capitalism, it is seen as a spur to a new phase of capitalist development' (Gouldson and Murphy, 1998: 75). Ecological modernization thus offers governments an alternative policy approach which allows them to reconcile previously antagonistic environmental and business interests. Its advocates maintain that some advanced capitalist nations are already doing this and that we are seeing a 'decoupling' of economic growth from ecological damage. Another phrase often used in close proximity is that of 'sustainability' or 'sustainable development'. The two are related, but not identical: 'while the literature often confuses ecological modernization with sustainable development, ecological modernization is a more limiting concept. It does not address the underlying contradiction in capitalism: a logic of ever-increasing consumption in a world characterized by material resource limitations (Baker, 2007: 313). Thus, before we even consider whether it is possible to combine environmental goods with economic goods under the banner of sustainability – a point to which we shall return – it is immediately apparent why ecological modernization is attractive to modern politicians of left or right who have accepted the fundamental principles of market capitalism. It promises to do everything without disturbing anything; we can have our environmental cake and eat it too. But even here and already, we notice a certain squeamishness on the part of the Conservatives to unleash the full potential of ecological modernization. For example, although they seemed to commit themselves to a more extensive use of green taxation, it seems likely that they will play a lesser role in seeking to alter people's behaviour than originally envisaged. The reasoning seems to be that it is hard to talk about raising taxes during a downturn in the economy and that, in the words of a shadow cabinet minister, 'People think green taxes are stealth taxes because Gordon Brown has given them a bad name' (cited in Grice, 2008). This demonstrates how easily straight oppositional party politics reasserts itself: the party backs away from a policy not because it is a bad policy but because the government has given it a bad name.

Mrs Thatcher

Let us return for the moment to consider Mr Cameron's antecedents, both intellectually and as leader. Despite Mrs Thatcher's famous speech to the United Nations on climate change in 1989, a speech to which Cameron often refers, her more constant political approach and practice was noted neither for green rhetoric nor substance. She once remarked that anyone still using the bus by the age of 30 was a failure; and, although she was tempted to turn a little green in 1989, her commitment was certainly more pragmatic than principled. Cameron, by contrast, appears to be genuinely principled. We noted earlier the argument to the effect that conservatism is inherently allied with environmentalism. Many of the concerns of environmentalists appear to have their roots in central conceptions within traditional conservatism. Congruence can be found with ideas of tradition, continuity, stability, organic change, prudence, rejection of totalitarianism and appeals to community. Traditional conservative and ecological theorists often share an anti-capitalist stance and romantic visions of non-human nature. In a defence of the deep affinity between ecological theory and conservative philosophy, John Gray adopts a common criticism of neo-liberal market philosophy, stressing the similarities of the two streams of thought (Gray, 1993). Both share a multi-generation perspective, give primacy to the common life, see danger in novelty and give a central place to the virtue of prudence. There is considerable scepticism about the possibility, inevitability or desirability of 'progress' and an emphasis on continuity and change as occurring within a developing tradition rather than in the light of a rational blueprint for society. The ideals of harmony and stability are central conceptions to both traditional conservatism and green political thought. As Michael Freeden remarks, 'conservative arguments cannot be completely disentangled or excluded from all green positions' (Freeden, 1995: 15).

This line of thought clearly has some merits, but ultimately it rests on an ambiguity between conservatism *qua* disposition and conservatism *qua* Conservative Party doctrine or policy. To really work, it would have to maintain that the Conservative Party is genuinely and consistently conservative with respect to both environmental ends and means and that there is no conflict between the two. But this might simply not be the case. For example, the Thatcher governments were renowned for being conservative on social policy and the family whilst being radical in economic policy, and it is precisely their economic policy which runs counter to the sort of conservatism required to sustain environmentalism. Of course some argue that free market approaches to the environment are appropriate, and this might be so. But if it is so, it is not clear that policy towards the environment derives principally from the urge to conserve; rather, it appears to derive from another source of concern, that is economic well-being. The link between conservation and Conservative, in other words, is not a necessary one – just as the link between the historical tradition of the Conservative Party, its name, and its current policies is contingent rather than necessary. So recourse to the claim that the Conservative Party is committed to environmentalism simply because of its name and history is specious, but misleading. This is not of course to deny that certain strands of conservatism, and certain conservatives, have this commitment. But other strands in both party and conservative thinking certainly have other and competing commitments.

Advisers, think tanks and policies

From where is the Conservatives' current environmental thinking derived? Who are the thinkers and what are the influences on their environmental policy? We have already mentioned the environmental activist Zac Goldsmith (now prospective parliamentary candidate for Richmond Park) and the Shadow Environment Secretary Peter Ainsworth; to these names we might add that of John Gummer, who has been quietly active for many years in expressing and acting on green concerns. Gummer, a former Secretary of State for the Environment, is Chair of the Quality of Life Policy Group, which was set up by David Cameron in December 2005, shortly after becoming leader; the Vice-Chair is Zac Goldsmith. Its remit was to recommend policies to the shadow cabinet and which produced the report *Blueprint for a Green Economy* in September 2007. In their report they assert roundly that:

> Business as usual is not a sustainable option. Our future security and prosperity depend on tapping human ingenuity to rethink our use of energy and natural resources in a world that will have to accommodate 9.2 billion people by 2050. Capitalism is evolving around the world, and we believe that the critical next stage is to ensure that it 'tells the ecological truth'. It is in the interest of both rich and poor that we create a model of growth that can be sustained. (Quality of Life Policy Group, 2007: 3)

Among their many recommendations were those for higher taxes on short-haul flights and fuel-inefficient cars; a power station waste heat levy; a moratorium on airport expansions; curbs on energy-wasting household goods; feed-in tariffs for small-scale low carbon technologies; restrictions on energy-wasting stand-by lights; and a cap on energy use by domestic appliances. Although Cameron sought to distance himself a little from the group's proposals, it could be argued that he has accepted most of them and was simply resisting being shackled to their every utterance. Hence his statement that their work was advisory. The most recent policy pronouncements, including those on smart meters and domestic contributions to the national grid, are directly in line with the recommendations of the report.

In December 2007, the policy paper *Power to the People* was published (Conservative Party, 2007), and its major themes have recently been endorsed by the policy paper *The Low Carbon Economy: Security, Stability and Green Growth* published in January 2009 (Conservative Party, 2009c). The latter was published at the precise moment that the government announced its plans to support the building of a third runway and a sixth terminal at Heathrow airport, thereby neatly enabling the Conservative Party to recapture the environmental high ground by re-asserting its opposition to the expansion of Heathrow, but also to continue its more general outflanking of the government on environmental issues. But what does the policy paper say?

> First, it will strengthen our economy. Decarbonising Britain will help create hundreds of thousands of jobs, raise skills and improve Britain's competitiveness. These jobs and skills will give new hope to people

being hit by the recession. A decarbonised Britain will be a world leader in green technology, engineering, innovation and growth. (Conservative Party, 2009c: 3)

It includes proposals to: transform electricity networks with 'smart grid' and 'smart meter' technology; create a 'decentralised energy revolution' by introducing a system of 'feed in tariffs' for electricity generation to multiply electricity production from micro-generation; expand the amount of offshore wind and marine power by giving the National Grid the incentive to construct a new network of under-sea cables; and introduce incentives for electricity network operators to establish a new national recharging network, leading to the development of electric and plug-in hybrid vehicles (Conservative Party, 2009c: 4–5).

In January 2009, Peter Ainsworth introduced the Green Energy Bill into the House of Commons: this is a private member's bill, and thus illustrates his own personal commitment to the cause. The purpose of this bill is to take further what the government has already enacted in the 2008 Climate Change and Energy acts. It is in perfect accord with *Power to the People*, and seeks 'to trigger government action that will pay people for the energy they produce'. It also seeks to remove bureaucratic blockages in the planning system 'to make it easier for people to install technologies in their homes, businesses and farms that create or save energy' (Ainsworth, 2009). All of these proposals indicate the Conservatives' determination to keep pushing the government on climate change and energy. However, we cannot let the matter rest there; rather, we need to consider the extent to which this policy outflanking, no matter how genuine, is stable, sustainable and sufficient.

Challenges and difficulties

I have argued that, overall, there is a genuine and clear sense in which the Conservative Party under David Cameron has shown a genuine commitment to the environment, a commitment which has enabled them to outflank the government, not only rhetorically, but also on the basis of genuine and thorough policy thinking. It is simply politics that they could not, even if they wished, do everything that the policy groups have mooted or suggested, and to that extent Cameron's partial distancing of himself from their recommendations was wise rather than cynical. Indeed, Zac Goldsmith has been quoted as saying that 'I'd be happy if only half of it was accepted': policy reviews of this sort always exceed the ability of government to fulfil them. However, there are other considerations which need to be addressed here. We saw earlier that although the Conservative Party put its environmental policy-making in the hands of committed environmentalists, such as Gummer, Ainsworth and Goldsmith, there are others within and without the party who place these matters somewhat lower in their agenda, and these voices might come to dominate in the near future, leading up to and after the election of the next Conservative government.

The first point is that the issue of the environment will tease and provoke the key fault lines in Conservative policy and doctrine. There is a willingness to harness the power of markets and to create commercial frameworks that give businesses the confidence to invest in innovation; there is some willingness to embrace the idea of green and carbon taxes, but also some scepticism. The general view is that green taxes should only be employed if they change behaviour, and only if they are replacement taxes, not new taxes.

A central question here is simply whether the market is regarded as a problem or a solution; and, if it is seen to be insufficient, whether non-market solutions will be chosen. Ecological modernization, as an approach, assumes (broadly) that free market capitalism can achieve environmental ends using market means; the hard question is whether, if this is not enough, a Conservative government would prioritize environmental ends and impose greater regulation and control of business in the interests of the environment? This is a real test for the radicalism of the Conservative Party's new-found commitment to the environment. Is its commitment to business and the market greater than its commitment to the environment? There are many who would say that it is, and many (including business and commerce) who will insist that it should be. This problem can be seen as primarily political. There is however the issue of whether ecological modernization and the related discourse of sustainability, with its talk of sustainable green growth, can genuinely hold together as a coherent whole. Is there any logical or empirical reason to suppose that environmental problems (however defined) can be solved in a win-win situation in which serious hard choices do not have to be made, in which economic growth continues (although in an environmentally redirected way) and the market is supreme?

Although Cameron has developed a strong track record of environmental commitment, and employed advisers who have sought to address the problems seriously, there are other dimensions to his political thinking which might nonetheless constrain the radicalism of any solutions he is prepared to accept. For example, Policy Exchange is an important and influential Conservative think tank which is held to be the closest of all to the Conservative Party and its leader. George Osborne and Oliver Letwin provide their web page and publications with admiring quotations and statements of support. Policy Exchange generally takes a strongly business and market orientated approach to things (Beckett, 2008; Policy Exchange, www.policyexchange.org.uk). That is no great surprise in a conservative think tank: but the extent of its commitment to the power of the market might be. It has suggested that business should run parts of the welfare state; that planning laws should be radically relaxed in favour of developers. It has suggested 'a doubling in size of the current motorway network' and the lowering of fuel and road taxes: policies which fly in the face of Cameron's (but not necessarily every Conservative supporter's) environmental thinking.

The key point, however, is not precisely which policies Policy Exchange advocates, so much as in the fact that, for it, the solution lies, as a matter of principle, in the application of the free market. Transposed to the environment this implies both an extension and a limit: use of the market where there is one, creation of a market (and associated property rights) where there isn't; and a limitation of environmental policy within the confines of what the market can do – if the market cannot do it, then it has to remain undone. In so far as the Cameron-led Conservative Party adopts the same view there are bound to be severe constraints on any environmental policy that it will be able to formulate and implement on gaining power.

Independently of this is the merely political difficulty. Cameron wants to realize the values and aspirations of the British people: but to what extent will he have to accept those values and aspirations as they stand, and to what extent will he be able to mould them? To put it crudely, will Basildon man (or Clarkson man, for that matter) have their current values and aspirations attended to, in which case there will be a sharp conflict with the environmental policy proposals Cameron espouses; or will they need to be re-educated in their values and aspirations, and how will that be done?

Some of these tensions are already appearing. It is certainly the case that the Conservative Party declared early that they opposed the third runway at Heathrow and that when the government came out in favour of it they re-affirmed their opposition. But there are three critical comments to be made immediately. The first is that it is easier to oppose a third runway at Heathrow than to make cheap flights more expensive. Secondly, Theresa Villiers, the Shadow Transport Secretary, whilst stating the opposition's objection to the third runway nonetheless did not 'rule out airport expansion in the south-east' (Stratton, 2009). This casts doubt on the nature of the Conservative opposition to Heathrow expansion: it suggests that it is politically opportunistic because it appears to be based less on overall environmental considerations concerning climate change and carbon dioxide emissions, than on narrower concerns to do with local noise nuisance and the like. Thirdly, as part of her original statement on Heathrow, Villiers announced plans for the next phase of high speed rail, which she described as a 'momentous step forward for Britain's transport infrastructure'. The proposal is for a Conservative government to build a new high speed rail line between Leeds, Manchester, Birmingham and London. Villiers claimed that high speed rail would benefit businesses, heal longstanding divisions in our economy by shrinking the distance between north and south, relieve over-crowding on existing lines and help to protect future generations from climate change (Summers, 2008a).

These all sound reasonable enough aspirations: but on closer inspection they reveal some inconsistencies at the heart of both the Conservatives' thinking, and the thinking of many others, on transport matters. The problem is that, as with any other form of high speed transport, the fuel consumption curve rises sharply the greater the speed, and trains are no exception. A true high speed rail link is hugely expensive on fuel consumption and therefore also on associated emissions of greenhouse gases. The claim is sometimes made that the carbon dioxide emission figures for the Eurostar demonstrate that high speed rail links can be environmentally friendly, but this is to conspicuously overlook the reason why the cross-channel link has relatively low emissions. The answer, in a word, is nuclear power. Half of the power for the Eurostar comes from French nuclear electricity production, thereby at a stroke making the figures look much better than they would if they were solely reliant on UK sources of power for the entire train journey from London to Paris. This could, of course, be construed as an argument for nuclear power; but my point here is the simpler one that high speed rail links are no climate change panacea, they have huge energy and emission costs of their own, and this fact should not be obscured by failing to compare like with like.

Conclusion: Cameron's green world

The challenge for any mainstream politician who makes the claim that their party is going to be green or environmentally concerned is to not only decide in what manner this is to take place, but to persuade the party and its backers that it should take place and will not be damaging to their interests or perceived interests. The easiest way to do this is through the medium of ecological modernization, that is, by persuading them that the issue is a win-win situation rather than a zero sum game. However, there are obvious problems with this approach. Not the least is that ecological modernization might not itself be a solution at all and even if it is it might still require too much of a leap of faith to make it palatable to the party faithful and its backers.

One big and obvious question is whether the commitment to environmentalism can survive the credit crunch and economic recession. Although ecological modernization is presented as a win-win in which both the environment and the economy benefit, it is easier to say this than to implement it in economically hard times. Should we, then, be reassured that Cameron in June 2008 declared enthusiastically and resolutely that the party's new-found environmentalism would not be dropped in hard times?

> Today, I want to tackle an argument that seems to be as cyclical as the economy. The argument that when times are good, we can indulge ourselves with a bit of environmentalism – but when the economic going gets tough, the green agenda has to be dropped. ... According to this argument, protecting the environment is a luxury rather than a necessity – and it's a luxury we just can't afford in an economic downturn. I want this generation to be the one that bucks that trend: to be the generation that finds a way to combine economic, social and environmental progress. ... The truth is: it's not that we can't afford to go green – it's that we can't afford not to go green. (Cameron, 2008h)

Be that as it may, it is certain that Conservative policies, if adhered to, will reveal some of the splits in Conservative thinking and action and ideology and doctrine. An example, from the world of Basildon man, can be found in Macer Hall's comment on Zac Goldsmith's environmental policy-making, that:

> Goldsmith seeks to remove the ethical dimension – the exercise of free choice – from daily household decisions. Tories of his ilk seem to have stolen from socialism the idea that the tax system should be used to change human behaviour rather than being a necessary evil for funding essentials such as defence and policing. (Hall, 2007)

And towards the end of 2008 it was reported that a senior Conservative frontbencher had said that higher green taxation is very unlikely to feature in the next manifesto (ConservativeHome, 2008). This is typical of a more general belief that, with the intensification of worries about recession and the economic downturn, Cameron might already have seriously begun to downplay his concern with the environment. Following the financial crisis of the summer and autumn of 2008, Mark Lynas commented that 'Certainly, David Cameron – having established his reputation with the "Vote Blue, Go Green" pledge – seemed scarcely to mention climate change any more' (Lynas, 2008). There might of course be other forces keeping the environmental pressure up: we have already noticed the work of Peter Ainsworth, who has not only recently promoted a new Energy Bill, but also has been insisting on the importance of 'holding fast' to the green agenda in tough economic times. He was reported to have said that, 'With our dependency on foreign oil, with food prices spiralling and jobs at risk, there is an urgent need to forge a greener economy that promises less dependency, more security, less risk, more jobs.' Further, he suggested that we did not have to choose between the economy and the environment, because going green will make us safer and better off, and he concluded by remarking that 'Going green means being safer by being more self sufficient; it means building a more robust and resilient Britain in a troubled world' (*Independent*, 2008).

On the reasonable assumption that Cameron, Ainsworth and Villiers are sincere in most of their pronouncements on the environment (and allowing for some ambiguity, e.g. on airport expansion), we can reasonably infer that the next Conservative government will address the problem of the environment in a manner unprecedented in any of its predecessors. The nature of the commitment is likely to be radical in certain ways: there is no reason to doubt Cameron's genuine commitment to extending the thinking of the Conservative Party beyond measuring well-being in simple economic terms and to include other forms of indicator of well-being. Equally, there is no reason to doubt that the party is committed to exploring new forms of technology to solve environmental problems and to harness the power of the market in doing so. The corollary is that the Conservatives' theory and practice is likely to be limited by their reliance on these very policy approaches. While they recognize that well-being might not always be reducible to measures such as average GDP per capita, they do not recognize the potential incompatibility between reliance on the means of market based approaches (which require pricing and monetary valuation to work, where they do work) and their stated goal, in which they seek to measure well-being in a rather different manner. Assuming that this manner of thinking prevails, we can expect at least a genuine environmental commitment in the next Conservative government, centred largely on a weak interpretation of sustainable development and the notions of ecological modernization. Beyond that it would be inappropriate to expect deeper green radicalism. The choice of means is both a constraint on, and an indication of, the limits within which the Conservative Party's commitment will operate.

10
Conservative Defence and Security Policy under David Cameron

David Lonsdale

It is axiomatic to note that a future Conservative government led by David Cameron would face a security environment significantly different from the one when the party left office in 1997. Nonetheless, this is still an important point to make, because in defence and security policy events are often more influential than party traditions and ideology. This reflects the nature of security and strategy, which demands an approach grounded in the Realist intellectual tradition. Ideologically driven security policy often suffers in the face of pragmatism.[1] Thus, when comparing the Conservative position on defence under Cameron to past Conservative leaderships, it is important to note that identified discontinuities may reflect the changing security environment more than they reflect a distinct Cameron approach. From this position, one might anticipate that significant discontinuities will be identified in the Cameron era. Whilst this certainly appears to be the case on certain issues (for example, a greater emphasis on the broader security agenda is one hallmark of the modern Conservative approach), there are certain themes and priorities evident in Cameron's approach that have long occupied a central position in Conservative thinking on defence and security.

At present the Conservative Party has no official defence and security policy. Thus, this chapter must rely upon speeches, articles, parliamentary evidence and in particular two published documents associated with the party. The two documents in question are *A Defence Policy for the UK: Matching Commitments and Resources* and *An Unquiet World*. The former, authored by Bernard Jenkin MP, is published by Conservative

Way Forward, a Conservative think tank that has the Shadow Defence Secretary Liam Fox as a vice-president. The latter is a report submitted to the shadow cabinet and produced by the National and International Security Policy Group, under the chairmanship of Pauline Neville-Jones, Shadow Security Minister and National Security Adviser to the Leader of the Opposition. Of course, neither of these documents represents official party policy. However, they do provide an insight into the intellectual influences upon the party leadership. Importantly, the content of both reports gives the impression that the Conservative movement has undertaken a reasonable degree of intellectual activity in an attempt to understand the changing security environment. For this they should be applauded.

In order to decipher the Conservatives' position on defence under David Cameron, and to establish the continuities and discontinuities with previous party leaderships, this chapter will address a number of issues. In the first instance, it will provide a brief overview of the changes to the security environment since the early 1980s. This will provide the context within which the different party leaderships have had to develop their policies and positions. Having established this background to policy formation, the essay will then identify the challenges faced by those constructing defence policies. The chapter will then be divided into two sections. The first will explore the main continuities in Conservative defence policy that Cameron honours. In particular, the significance of the transatlantic relationship and the attendant North Atlantic Treaty Organization (NATO) membership will be assessed. Another continuity examined is the retention of Britain's nuclear weapons. From here, the chapter will identify areas in which Cameron appears to have deviated somewhat from past practice. This will include an analysis of defence spending, the broader security agenda and structural reforms. Finally, the chapter will conclude with an assessment of the quality of Conservative defence policy, such as it is.

The changing security environment

It is rather obvious, but still valid, to note that the international security environment has undergone dramatic change since Thatcher came to power in 1979. During the 1980s British security policy was understandably focused on the threat posed by the Soviet Union in continental Europe. In response, British defence policy had three main priorities/characteristics: nuclear weapons, a continental commitment, and the NATO alliance. In contrast to the Labour Party at the time, the Thatcher governments remained steadfastly committed to maintaining Britain's nuclear deterrent forces. In addition, Britain deployed the British Army on the Rhine (BAOR) to play a part in the defence of Western Europe from the Soviet army. Finally, NATO was regarded as the most reliable instrument to ensure European security, primarily because it tied the United States into the defence of Western Europe. These priorities were reflected in the 1981 Nott Defence Review, which sought to reduce Britain's maritime capabilities in favour of a greater emphasis on the European central front and defence of the homeland. Although the review was guided by an assessment of strategic priorities, it was financial pressures that forced the government's hand on having to focus its defence efforts in one direction. A projected £400 million overspend on defence for 1980/81 demanded a rationalization of defence policy (Dorman, 2001; Freedman, 1999). Events beyond the main Soviet threat, such as the Falklands War, modified this approach to defence somewhat, but did not radically alter the main strategic focus. The conflict in the South Atlantic somewhat rescued the Navy's position in the Ministry of Defence, and certainly reduced the cuts in maritime capabilities, but did not lead to a significant re-ordering of defence policy priorities.

The end of the Thatcher years coincided with the end of the Cold War. The new Major government had to contend with a security environment in a state of flux. As the international system re-ordered itself various conflicts erupted, many of which involved Britain. At the same time, an economic downturn and demands for a 'peace dividend' in the aftermath of the Cold War indicated that a reduction in defence spending was required. Again, these pressures were reflected in the reviews 'Options for Change' (1990) and 'Front Line First' (1994). As the Conservative Party settled in to a long period of opposition, the security environment witnessed a series of significant events, many of which Britain became embroiled in. Whilst criticizing the manning levels and overstretch in the armed forces, the Conservative Party under William Hague supported British involvement in Kosovo; supported the Blair government during Operation Desert Fox in Iraq; and gave qualified support for the deployment of British forces to Sierra Leone. The greatest shift in the security environment since the end of the Cold War came with the terrorist attacks of 9/11. Once again, Britain has found itself heavily engaged in this new security reality. Reminiscent of the Hague years, the Conservative Party under Iain Duncan Smith and Michael Howard has steadfastly supported the deployment of British forces to major campaigns in Afghanistan and Iraq. In fact, at times the Conservatives have suggested additional commitments in such places as Darfur and Zimbabwe (Tempest, 2004). During this period, the

Conservatives continued to raise concerns about under-funding, but would only commit themselves to increases in spending that could be funded by savings in the defence budget (Hoggart, 2004).

Beyond these more traditional security concerns, the current international system has witnessed a growing prominence for the broader security agenda. In particular, there has been a growing emphasis on issues of environmental and energy security. Thus, it is clear that since the election of Thatcher in 1979 the security environment has changed significantly, presenting a series of new challenges every so often. It is thus interesting to examine, in the face of such dramatic changes, why certain continuities remain in Conservative defence policy, and how the new priorities have been integrated.

Defence planning

Any assessment of defence policy creation must be made on the understanding that defence planning poses a set of inherently difficult challenges. Indeed, Colin S. Gray contends that developments such as air power, nuclear weapons and cyberspace in the twentieth century have further complicated the role of the defence planner (Gray, 1999: 4). There are at least four dominant challenges, which taken together limit one's chance of 'getting it right' and restrict the options available. Firstly, and most obviously, defence planning has to deal with an uncertain future. However, the level of uncertainty is not absolute. Trends and their associated policy requirements can be identified to some degree in the security environment. Although the intelligence services spend most of their time on 'current intelligence', they still commit a reasonable amount of effort to long-term analysis, so-called 'research intelligence' (Johnson, 2008). Therefore at some level those responsible for defence policy can estimate what capabilities may be required, in what numbers, and how they should be balanced. Nonetheless, events such as the Falklands War and 9/11 provide sufficient evidence that surprises can occur for which one is ill-prepared.[2] Consequently, the defence planner must prepare for what is most likely to occur, whilst at the same time building some degree of flexibility into the system, and thereby being able to shift stance if required.

The challenge of dealing with uncertainty is further complicated by the fact that there are likely to be existing commitments that demand a significant proportion of current defence capabilities and budget. Current operational requirements obviously have a compelling case for prioritization. These existing commitments may be due to ongoing operations, alliance membership, or indeed the result of the state's international position. For the United Kingdom, its permanent seat on the United Nations Security Council and its NATO membership place demands, or have the potential to, on its armed forces. This clearly restricts the ability of the defence planner to innovate in an especially radical fashion. Thus, United Kingdom defence planners cannot start from scratch when undertaking a defence review. A number of existing commitments and responsibilities are always on the table and limit room for manoeuvre. Beyond existing commitments, a defence planner is also restricted by the limits of the defence budget. Of course the defence budget can always be increased. Nonetheless, realistically this can only be done within a certain margin. Finally, procurement cycles exert a significant influence on what capabilities are available to support defence policy. One of the most obvious examples of this is the lengthy procurement cycle for Eurofighter. Originally intended as a Cold War air superiority fighter to challenge Soviet aircraft, current and future British defence planners are now essentially stuck with fulfilling the order for 232 Eurofighters (Jenkin, 2007: 50). Although Eurofighter is undoubtedly a very capable aircraft, it is not necessarily the capability one would choose in the current security environment. Taken together, the four challenges above establish some boundaries and restrictions on the direction British defence policy can take.

The above challenges in defence planning have exerted significant influence on British defence policy. Since the Second World War there has been a dominant theme in British defence policy: the difficulty of balancing resources and commitments. Although this is the norm for most states, Britain's experience has been particularly acute due to a combination of factors. In particular, Britain has maintained a global role during a period of relative economic decline and defence inflation. On the latter it is reported that from 1980/81 to 2000/01 real defence spending for each member of the armed forces increased by 26 per cent (Hartley, 2001). Michael Alexander and Timothy Garden summarize the defence inflation problem thus: 'Personnel costs rise at a rate slightly above inflation; equipment costs rise much faster than retail price inflation; and running costs rise in line with inflation' (Alexander and Garden, 2001: 517). Margaret Thatcher was acutely aware of the problem: '[T]he real cost of ever more sophisticated weapons was remorselessly increasing the pressure' (Thatcher, 1993: 249). Almost every defence policy review has attempted to provide an answer to the perennial imbalance of resources and commitments. Various approaches have been tried. These include reductions in commitments, such as the withdrawal from east of Suez;

specialization in defence roles, such as under the Nott Review, which saw a significant reduction in naval forces; the search for efficiencies, such as the Private Finance Initiatives during the Thatcher and Major years; and finally increases in defence spending, such as the 3 per cent increase under Thatcher and current increases under the Labour government (HM Treasury, 2007b).

Rarely have the various attempts to redress the balance between resources and commitments succeeded. In fact, the situation has often deteriorated. Whilst levels of commitment have remained static or even increased, the percentage of GDP devoted to defence has reduced quite significantly since 1986. From a high of 5.3 per cent in 1986, the current level is approximately 2.3 per cent. It has been reported that this now takes Britain's spending on defence as a proportion of its wealth down to the level of the 1930s, prior to the period of rearmament before the Second World War (Hope and Jones, 2008; UKNDA, 2008a). This low level of GDP dedicated to defence comes at a time when Britain's armed forces have been deployed on five unforeseen occasions: Bosnia, Sierra Leone, Kosovo, Iraq and Afghanistan (UKNDA, 2008b). Liam Fox, the Shadow Defence Secretary, bluntly concludes: 'the critical situation our Armed Forces face is the inevitable result of Labour's failure to match commitments with resources' (cited in Martin, 2008). And yet, it is not clear if the situation would improve under a Conservative government, since 'He [Fox] is not yet pledged to spend a penny more on our forces' (Martin, 2008). Thus, one of the primary measurements of Conservative defence policy under David Cameron must be concerned with how they intend to deal with the resources/commitment challenge.

Continuities

Any cursory assessment of the Conservatives' view on British defence policy priorities will quickly identify that one of the most prominent themes is the transatlantic relationship. Indeed, the current leadership is quick to point out that this has been a longstanding position of the party. David Cameron himself stated this with great clarity: 'Atlanticism is in my DNA and in the DNA of the Conservative Party' (Cameron, 2008i). Such an Atlantic focus has a significant impact upon a number of defence and security policy areas. In particular, it largely determines the institutional bias in security affairs. For the Conservatives this produces a clear leaning towards NATO and a much less important role for the European Union. The Conservatives regard NATO as the primary instrument to retain American engagement in European security. When discussing his four key principles for NATO, it is interesting to note that David Cameron includes the United States at the centre of each of them. These principles include not only retaining American involvement in European security, but also the importance of helping to influence American policy choices (Cameron, 2008i). This sense of keeping America partially in check is also evident in *An Unquiet World* (Neville-Jones, 2007: 179–81). More specifically, there is the sense of a need to influence America towards a more multinational approach to international security. This is clearly a response to the perceived unilateralism of the United States post-9/11. In this respect there appears to be a sense within the Conservatives that the United States is still vital to British security, but there also exists the notion that the Blair governments may have exercised insufficient influence over the hawkish Bush Administration. In this respect Cameron appears to be following the party position on this issue he inherited from Michael Howard. The then Shadow Foreign Secretary, Michael Ancram expressed a desire for an 'honest relationship with America based on shared values and beliefs and mutual respect' (Tempest, 2004).

Despite some slight misgivings about how the transatlantic relationship worked in recent years, the Conservatives exhibit a clear understanding of the privileged position enjoyed by Britain in its relationship with the US. This includes such vital areas of intelligence sharing, officer exchange, and military technology (including nuclear weapons). The Conservatives under Cameron would clearly loath to risk such a valuable bilateral relationship with the world's premier power. Interestingly, much of Tony Blair's foreign policy was influenced by a similar fixation on the transatlantic relationship. Indeed, it was the desire to promote that relationship which heavily influenced his decision to invade Iraq (Lonsdale, 2008).

In order to keep the US engaged with European security, Cameron realizes that NATO must be reformed in a number of ways. In particular, decision-making in the alliance must be streamlined, and there must be greater commitment from many of the European members to pull their weight in operations (Cameron, 2008i). The urgency of these reforms is evident in Afghanistan. In the early stages of the campaign the United States largely sidelined NATO. This was a response to the alliance difficulties encountered during the Kosovo campaign.[3] Now that NATO has been allowed a greater role in the war against the Taliban and Al Qaeda, it has become painfully evident that many of the European members have neither the will nor capability to engage in actual fighting. Cameron correctly has also called for the 1999 NATO Strategic Concept to be updated (Cameron, 2008i).

American engagement in European security is not only threatened by problems in NATO. It is also potentially undermined by the increasing development of a European Security and Defence Policy (ESDP). Traditionally, this is something previous Conservative leaderships have rigorously fought against. For example, the 2001 election manifesto warned: 'our primary alliance, NATO, is being weakened by a concerted drive to create an independent military structure in the EU ... A Conservative Government would pursue a very different policy' (Conservativemanifesto.com). Although remaining true to the essence of this statement, under Cameron the party appears to project a more balanced approach. One might even go as far as to suggest that there is some confusion within the party on this issue. On the one hand, Geoffrey Van Orden, UK Conservative Party defence spokesman in the European Parliament, has described the ESDP variously as 'a diversion, weakening wholehearted commitment to the North Atlantic Alliance', 'duplicative and divisive', and that it had produced 'no new military capabilities' and 'compete[d] with NATO'. He further noted that the development of EU Battlegroups was duplicative and wasteful and did not deliver any additional capability (House of Commons Defence Committee, 2008: 76–7). These negative views are echoed in *A Defence Policy for the UK*, which regards the creation of EU military staffs and the European Defence Association as an example of unnecessary duplication of NATO actions (Jenkin, 2007: 35). However, David Cameron is not entirely rejectionist of an EU role in security affairs. Indeed, he appears to regard NATO and the EU as complementary partners in security terms. Nonetheless, he made it clear in a recent article on the subject that he believes NATO should lead the way on military security matters, with the EU undertaking policing/ training operations when required, or providing security forces when the US has little interest in an issue (Cameron, 2008i). One can conclude that the current Conservative Party has a more nuanced perspective on the relationship between NATO and the ESDP. However, within that relationship the different roles should be explicit, duplication should be avoided, and NATO should have priority, especially on traditional matters of military security.

Overall, it is clear that the Conservatives regard NATO not only as the primary means of retaining American engagement in Europe, but also as the primary security institution on the continent. As Cameron himself has noted, 'the enlargement of NATO has helped to entrench European stability' (Cameron, 2008i). David Cameron's faith in NATO extends to supporting the accession of both Georgia and Ukraine into the alliance. This is despite Russian pronouncements concerning NATO expansion, which they perceive as bringing down a new iron curtain across Europe. Cameron has thus far taken a strong position against Russia, especially in the light of Russian actions in Georgia. The Conservative leader has gone as far as to suggest that Russia be suspended from the G8 and restrictions be imposed on the visa regime for Russian citizens (Cameron, 2008j). Aside from showing a significant level of faith in the aging alliance, this also reveals that Cameron is prepared to take a robust stance on certain security issues. His stance on Russia comes at a time when it can be strongly argued that the Cold War has re-emerged as Russia becomes increasingly belligerent. This is not only evident in its intervention in Georgia, but also in its increasingly aggressive response to the deployment of the US Ballistic Missile Defence System (BBC, 2008b).

Another area of continuity in Conservative defence policy is that relating to nuclear weapons. The recent debates surrounding the replacement for Trident indicate that the Conservatives under David Cameron have a fairly orthodox party view on Britain's nuclear forces (Hansard, 2007). During the 1980s the Thatcher government was on safe ground in relation to Britain's nuclear deterrent force. For much of that period the Labour Party was hamstrung on the issue, either because it supported unilateralism or took an unconvincing pro-deterrence stance. In contrast Thatcher's government not only replaced the Polaris SLBM system with Trident, but also supported the deployment of US nuclear weapons (most notably the Tomahawk Cruise Missile) on British soil. However, the Conservative track record on this issue is not one of unremitting support for nuclear weapons. Under the Major government Britain's nuclear forces were significantly reduced. Short-range land-based systems were abandoned, as were nuclear depth charges for maritime operations. In addition, the WE-177 free-fall bombs, and the aircraft designed to carry them, were severely cut (Freedman, 1999: 16). The latter was entirely retired from service in 1998. This has left Britain as the only declared nuclear power with just one means of delivery.

Lawrence Freedman has described the Thatcher approach to nuclear weapons as 'the course of least resistance' (Freedman, 1999: 6). In many respects this phrase can be used to describe Cameron's approach on the subject also. Supporting the replacement of Trident with another SSBN fleet and a Trident D-5 missile upgrade shows a distinct lack of strategic imagination at an important time in nuclear affairs. As with the Blair government, the Conservative Party under Cameron has chosen the least controversial option. This is not to say that the SLBM route is not a sensible strategic choice. In many important respects, SLBMs remain the most stable and useful delivery system for nuclear weapons. However, in a period of increasing proliferation of weapons of mass destruction (WMD), with its attendant range of possible futures, a wider range of nuclear options may have been prudent. With just Trident, and/or its similar replacement, Britain is left with a fairly large nuclear option, which may look decidedly unsuited to more limited WMD threats to either Britain or her forces overseas. The so-called 'sub-strategic' role for Trident, whereby the missile system can carry a lower yield warhead, has some significant drawbacks. In particular, an enemy on the receiving end of a sub-strategic Trident warhead could not be sure of the limited nature of the attack until the warhead actually detonated. Thus, the firing, or threat, of a sub-strategic Trident missile may escalate a situation far more than anticipated. In turn, fear of such a misunderstanding may persuade policy-makers not to fire or deploy in the first place. In addition, having only one means of delivery invites the possibility of a countermeasure that renders Britain's entire nuclear arsenal impotent. A far more appropriate and courageous policy for Cameron would be to diversify Britain's nuclear forces, and thereby build more flexibility into the system. As it is, it appears that the Conservatives have taken a similar stance to the Labour Party, and reluctantly accepted the need for a nuclear arsenal, but without much strategic imagination. The Conservative position on this is therefore consistent with previous Conservative policy, but lacks the imagination to be found in other areas of defence and security.

Discontinuities

An analysis of Conservative defence spending since 1979 raises some contradictory conclusions. Until 1986 the Thatcher government increased spending on defence in real terms by 3 per cent per annum (Thatcher, 1993: 125). This looks impressive, and at first glance implies that the Conservative Party might have an inclination towards increasing the defence budget. This perception is strengthened by the fact that the same government also increased the wages of military personnel by 32 per cent, and indeed increased the defence budget at a time when other areas of government spending were being reduced (Freedman, 1999: 6). However, it should be noted that the 3 per cent increase was a NATO commitment inherited by Thatcher. Once the commitment had finished in 1986, the government returned to level spending. Any notions of a Conservative commitment to increases in defence spending are dealt a severe blow by the Major years. During the first half of the 1990s we see a steady decline in real terms defence spending. This trend is matched by the percentage of GDP devoted to defence. From a high of 5.3 per cent in 1986, by 1997 it had fallen to below 3 per cent. One could also argue that a number of Conservative defence reviews have resulted in significant cuts in the British armed forces. Under the 1981 Nott Review the Navy was due to lose 17 ships from its frigate and destroyer (reduced to 42) fleet, in addition to the sale of the carrier HMS *Invincible* to Australia. As it was, the Falklands War intervened, and in the end naval losses were reduced by a half. The navy lost further capabilities during the Major years under the reviews 'Options for Change' and 'Front Line First'. The other services were also hit during this period. The army's numbers were reduced, including the loss of a number of historic regiments, and the RAF lost squadrons and air bases. Finally, as part of the search for savings under 'Front Line First', support services were cut. Most notably, this included the closure of two of the three dedicated military hospitals (Dorman, 2001). However, it should be noted that some significant savings were made through various efficiency drives and private finance initiatives (Uttley, 2001). As noted above, in more recent years although the Conservatives have become increasingly critical of Labour's under-funding of defence, they have not committed themselves to outright increases in defence spending. Rather, as under the leadership of Michael Howard, they merely promised to find more money through savings.

To which tradition does David Cameron belong? Will we witness cost-cutting exercises under a Cameron-led Conservative government, or will we see a return to the early Thatcher years? As previously noted, the Conservative Party has yet to announce an official defence policy, and understandably has yet to outline any spending plans on defence. In fact, with the promise of a strategic defence review upon coming to power, it is unlikely that any specific spending details would be forthcoming before a general election. Nonetheless, the party has been very active and vocal in the area of defence. Indeed, the party makes one very clear, if somewhat general, commitment on its website: 'A Conservative Government will *match resources with commitments*' (Conservative Party, 2008i, emphasis in original). More specifically, the party's website highlights 'a decade of neglect by Labour has left them [the armed services] overstretched, undermanned, and in possession of worn-out equipment' (Conservative Party, 2008i). Thus, with such an emphasis on under-funding in recent years, one might expect an incoming Conservative government to rectify these shortages to some degree.

Much of the Conservative stance on these issues is encapsulated in the attention they have given to the Military Covenant. Indeed, David Cameron established a commission on this very subject.[4] The covenant refers to a customary agreement, which stretches back at least to the

Elizabethan period, between society and its armed forces. In exchange for service, with the possibility of death or injury, the armed forces can expect to receive decent recompense and care (for both themselves and their families). Although this does apply to serving personnel, special attention is often given to the care of veterans, especially those injured in the line of their duties. There is clearly a perception amongst the armed services and society that the covenant has not been properly honoured by the government in recent years. High profile individuals, such as Lord Guthrie (former CDS) and General Dannatt (Chief of the General Staff) have publicly commented to that effect. In addition, the Royal British Legion has launched a campaign on this issue. Thus, on the issue of the Military Covenant the Conservatives are pursuing what certainly appears to be a genuine problem. However, it should also be taken into account that such an issue is an easy stick with which to beat the government. The armed services are generally held in high regard by the public, and are currently taking regular casualties during the war in Afghanistan. There are potential votes in this issue. Therefore, it is important to explore in some detail what the problems are that have been identified, and whether Conservative policies would alleviate them, and at what cost.

The Military Covenant debate has highlighted a number of areas of genuine concern for the armed services. These include overstretch, accommodation and healthcare. Another area that has received quite a degree of attention in the press, and from the Conservatives, is the quantity and quality of equipment available to the forces. The issue of overstretch is perhaps one of the most pressing problems facing the armed services. The operations in Iraq and Afghanistan have led to increasing breaches of the 'harmony guidelines'. These guidelines give an indication of how often forces should be deployed in relation to leave. The problem of overstretch has led to problems of retention within the forces, especially of NCOs. In addition, in order to resource extra operations the armed services have had to reduce training and readiness regimes. Finally, because of increased use on combat operations, equipment (such as helicopters) is being depleted more rapidly than was planned for (Rayment, 2008; Jenkin, 2007). This situation is exacerbated by the fact that defence spending has been the poor relation next to spending on health and education. Put simply, the military have been asked to do far more with the same capabilities. Also, because frontline forces have rightly received priority in the defence budget, infrastructure issues such as housing have been neglected. Finally, there has been growing concern about the standard of healthcare for veterans and the compensation scheme for those injured in the line of duty.

The area that is perhaps less clear-cut is that concerned with equipment. Whilst it is clear that inadequate equipment will hinder the operations of military forces, this is an area that requires careful analysis. Whether as a result of careful analysis or not, the Conservatives have made much of this issue. For example, equipment shortfalls are highlighted in the Military Covenant Commission report *Restoring the Covenant* (Military Covenant Commission, 2008). In addition, the last page of *A Defence Policy for the UK* is adorned with a number of poppies, each with a number of servicemen killed in certain areas of operations adjoined, and with the question: 'How many would be alive if they'd been properly equipped?' (Jenkin, 2007). In the face of such stark statements, one question that needs to be asked is: How does one define 'properly equipped'? There cannot be a casualty in the history of warfare that could not have been prevented had more and better equipment been available. This is not to suggest that one should not strive to ensure that one's forces are well equipped, relative to the enemy. However, to reduce military success or failure (including individual casualties) to the availability of good equipment is far too reductionist. The nature of war is such that even well-equipped forces sometimes suffer defeat or heavy casualties. By stressing this part of the military covenant debate, the Conservatives may contribute to the ill-informed opinion, increasingly prevalent in society, that war can somehow be carefully managed to a point at which casualties are reduced to an absolute minimum. Such a perspective may contribute to unrealistic expectations and rapid disillusionment regarding military operations. In turn, this may affect our will to stay the course in war, which at one level is a battle of wills amongst belligerents. Have the Conservatives really thought through the implications of their stance on military equipment, and how would they judge how much is enough?

What then of the measures that the Conservatives have proposed to rebalance the Military Covenant? In the first instance it is important to note that, to some degree, the government has responded to the growing criticism on this issue. In the 2007 Comprehensive Spending Review, the government announced a 1.5 per cent annual increase in defence spending. The Review notes that alongside previous reviews since 2000, this represents a ten-year increase in defence spending. More specifically, the government has placed contracts for improved protected vehicles for the army (designed to counter the threat from mines and IEDs in Afghanistan), further air transport capability for the RAF, and £550 million investment in accommodation for the services (HM Treasury, 2007b). At minimum, a Conservative government would have to honour these commitments since they strike at the heart of the issues central to the military covenant debate. However, an analysis of funding issues in *A Defence Policy for the UK* and *An Unquiet World* suggests that the Conservatives under Cameron may wish to go further than the current government. The former report clearly states defence spending should receive priority status, in contrast to the Labour years when it played second-fiddle to areas such as health and education. The report also claims that manning levels in the armed forces should be increased, at minimum, to SDR recommended levels, at an extra cost of £59 million. Manning levels are particularly important due to the emphasis placed by the Conservatives on current breaches of the 'harmony guidelines'. In addition, there is a sense in Conservative statements on the Royal Navy that government cuts in forces should be overturned (Fox, 2007a, 2007b). All told, *A Defence Policy for the UK* suggests that an extra £3 billion must be found per annum, above current government spending plans, over five years (Jenkin, 2007). Similarly, *An Unquiet World* estimates that there now exists a shortfall in the equipment budget of £15 billion. The report concludes: 'The unpalatable choice lies between change in the shape and operational posture of the Armed Forces ... or the acceptance of the need for a significant increase in defence spending' (Neville-Jones, 2007: 177). It is worth noting that all of these plans would have to be funded during a period of severe economic downturn.

There is growing evidence that defence has become an increasingly important issue for the electorate. An opinion poll by ComRes for the United Kingdom National Defence Association (UKNDA) found that 78 per cent of voters believe that Britain's armed forces are 'dangerously over-stretched', and 70 per cent think that the government is 'failing to give the armed forces the resources they need'. Finally, 57 per cent of respondents indicated that they will consider each party's policy on defence when deciding how to vote in the next election (UKNDA, 2008b). Thus, based on the growing prominence of defence as an election issue, partly as a result of Conservative initiatives, in addition to the many areas of under-funding highlighted by the Conservative Party, it is reasonable to conclude that a Cameron-led government would have to buck the trend of Conservative governments since 1986 and increase defence spending quite significantly. Indeed, if the plans outlined in *A Defence Policy for the UK* are to be achieved a considerable increase will be required. In this respect, the UKNDA is undoubtedly correct in its assessment on this issue: 'They [Conservatives] will not be able to make good on their promises about improving the state of the Armed Forces unless they allow a significant increase in Defence funding' (UKNDA, 2008c). And yet, the final point made in the Conservatives' launch document for their Commission on the Military Covenant reads thus: 'Any recommendations made by the Commission must be paid for within existing and planned defence budgets' (Military Covenant Commission, 2008b: 6). This suggests that perhaps a Cameron-led Conservative Party falls somewhere between the early Thatcher years and the Major years: neither cutting nor increasing the defence budget. Should that be the case, it is difficult to see how Cameron could fulfil the party promise to match resources with commitments. This looks even less likely with the recent announcement by David Cameron that his party would not match the Labour government's spending plans for 2010/11 (BBC, 2008c).

There is of course an alternative route to matching resources with commitments: reducing the latter. This seems unlikely as *A Defence Policy for the UK* is critical of the reduction of British forces in Iraq (Jenkin, 2007: 24). Additionally, Cameron has expressed a serious commitment to the Afghanistan campaign (Cameron, 2007c). This has been recently reinforced by the Shadow Foreign Secretary, William Hague, who described Afghanistan as the first foreign policy priority for an incoming Conservative government (BBC, 2008d). If Cameron follows the advice of his army commanders once in office, he may have to increase British forces deployed there. Once again, this adds even greater impetus for a significant increase in manning levels. An interesting point to note in relation to the military covenant is how consistent Conservative manifestos have been in relation to service pay and conditions, including references to the quality of accommodation. These issues were commonplace in manifesto pledges from 1979 to 1992 (Conservativemanifesto.com). Thus, Cameron's recent campaigning on this issue can be said to represent a return to a traditional Conservative approach. Perhaps the Major years, faced as they were by economic downturn and demand for a peace dividend, were an anomaly.

Aside from an increase in defence spending, the Conservatives under Cameron also appear to have a number of innovative ideas regarding defence and security. Prominent among them is the notion of regular defence reviews along the lines of the quadrennial defence reviews in the United States. Again, this represents something of a shift from the previous Conservative approach to reviews. The Nott Review, 'Options for Change' and 'Frontline First' have all been criticized for being exercises in savings rather than actual root and branch reviews of defence policy. Therefore, in this sense Cameron appears to promote a more rational, one might even say a more strategic, approach to defence matters than some previous Conservative leaderships.[5] This rational approach is taken further with some institutional reform proposals.

The Conservatives have proposed the creation of a National Security Council, a unified national security budget, and a cabinet-level security minister. These measures are designed to bring together domestic and foreign elements of national security. This is particularly important in a security environment dominated by the threat from Islamist terrorism, which has blurred the boundaries between internal and external threats. In addition, there is a proposal for a unified border police force. Finally, there has been discussion of a dedicated Homeland Defence force with a permanent Headquarters. Such a force would provide important support to civil authorities during future crises and emergencies (Neville-Jones, 2007).

An area in which the Conservatives under Cameron have moved into new areas is the broader security agenda. Indeed, Dame Neville-Jones describes the approach taken in *An Unquiet World* as being based upon 'a very broad definition of what constitutes security' (Neville-Jones, 2007). The new leadership takes environmental security very seriously, and this happily merges with other major security concerns such as energy supplies. Demand for gas in particular leaves the United Kingdom somewhat dependent upon potentially unreliable countries, such as an increasingly belligerent Russia. Thus, it is evident that a number of Conservative security policies come together in the broader security agenda. The need for alternative forms of energy supply help to promote environmental security objectives. At the same time, Britain could leave itself less vulnerable to energy supply being used as a tool of coercion by Russia. Finally, the Conservatives' promotion of NATO dovetails nicely into its fairly robust position on Russia.

The broader security agenda is well represented in *An Unquiet World*. As noted earlier, such documents show an admirable degree of intellectual engagement by the party with a wide range of security issues and approaches. The notion of 'soft power' is particularly well represented in *An Unquiet World*. Soft power refers to those assets, not necessarily material in nature, through which policy can be pursued, and which are bound up with notions of legitimacy and the promotion of a positive set of values. For example, overseas development aid, the promotion of human rights, the British university system and the BBC are variously regarded as potential soft power assets (Neville-Jones, 2007). Whilst a rational grand strategy should involve all of the instruments at the state's disposal, including the assets of soft power, it is to be hoped that the Conservative Party does not become over-enamoured by the broader security agenda. Whilst not discounting the challenges involved in the use of military force, it should always be remembered that physical security assets provide the most compelling response to certain threats. Persuasion through soft power is to be encouraged, but not relied upon.

Conclusion

The Conservative Party under David Cameron faces a very different security environment than that faced by previous Conservative governments. In combination with a long period in opposition, this has enabled the party to develop policies and ideas potentially very different in nature from those of the past. Indeed, since defence and security is an area of government very much led by events, one might expect a fairly radical approach by the current leadership. In some areas this has been the case. A broader approach to security has been developed by the party and its associated think tanks. This is in line with a more fluid security environment and an increasing prominence for less traditional forms of security. Similarly, the call for regular defence reviews is both a rational move and one that correctly challenges the Labour and Major governments' neglect of this area. Finally, the promotion of certain defence capabilities suggests an approach that is some distance from the Major years, where cuts were the norm. However, it is unclear if a Cameron-led government would provide the extra funding required to maintain the needed capabilities. The big test for an incoming Conservative government is whether they go beyond current government levels of spending. Given the current mismatch between resources and commitments, a significant increase in spending appears to be the only credible way to rebalance Britain's defence policy. A more radical option would be to significantly reduce Britain's commitments. However, there is no evidence to suggest that the Conservatives are thinking along these lines.

Despite the radically different security environment demanding some changes in policy, the Cameron position on defence exhibits some striking similarities with previous Conservative policies. Most notably, the commitment to the transatlantic relationship and NATO as the primary vehicle of European, and increasingly global, security has been at the heart of Conservative policy for decades. It is interesting to note that at the same time that Cameron is rightly calling for reform of the alliance, the Cold War is re-emerging as Russia becomes ever more belligerent towards the West. Another area where Cameron can claim to be in tune with traditional Conservative thinking is on nuclear weapons. Indeed, one can go as far as to suggest that, like Thatcher and Major, Cameron has taken the path of least resistance. Although not alone in taking the obvious and safe Trident replacement position, it is disappointing that little intellectual energy has been exerted on nuclear strategy. This is especially problematic considering how much has been devoted to issues of soft power and the military covenant.

So, overall David Cameron holds a position on defence policy that can be described as a modern Conservative approach, meaning that he has retained the essence of traditional Conservatism but has adapted it to the modern environment. How do we assess such an approach in the modern security environment? If the Conservatives were to fully develop their indicated approach to defence, including the necessary increase in spending, Britain could look forward to a more balanced and rational approach to defence and security. Importantly, Britain would retain its commitment to Afghanistan, and would hopefully have the forces and equipment required to expand operations there. Just as importantly, Britain would remain firmly wedded to the United States in security matters. This may become increasingly important as the new Cold War develops. What we cannot predict is how a Cameron government would respond to a rapidly changing security environment. The Blair governments responded well to new challenges in an operational sense, but failed to adapt their spending plans to keep pace. As Prime Minister, David Cameron's credentials on defence would be tested as all others prior to him: on how well he can match resources with commitments in the face of a changing security environment. At present he has yet to provide any substantive evidence of his financial commitment to defence and security.

Notes

1. A classic example of this can be found in the sixteenth-century conflict between Elizabeth I's England and Imperial Spain under Philip II. The latter followed an approach deeply motivated and guided by his Catholic faith. In contrast, Elizabeth more often than not followed a prudent policy path. Philip's ideological approach led him to overstretch his empire, and ultimately persuaded him to undertake the ill-prepared invasion of England in 1588. This subject is particularly well covered in G. Parker, *The Grand Strategy of Philip II* (New Haven: Yale University Press, 1998).
2. Whilst it is true that in both of these cases there was some intelligence regarding the attacks, they still caught the respective policy-makers by surprise. This is partly due to the often uncertain nature of the business of intelligence.
3. For an analysis of the Kosovo campaign, including discussion of the problems faced by the NATO alliance, see B.S. Lambeth, *NATO's Air War for Kosovo* (Santa Monica: RAND, 2001).
4. See http://www.militarycovenantcommission.com/

5. This comment is premised on the notion that a Conservative 'strategic' defence review would genuinely seek to promote a defence policy guided by policy objectives. Further, that such a review would also be made on the basis of a genuine dialogue between the political and military components of strategy. For a discussion on these issues see E. Cohen, *Supreme Command* (London: Simon and Schuster, 2002), C.S. Gray, *Modern Strategy* (Oxford: Oxford University Press, 1999) and the original exponent of these core ideas of strategy, C. von Clausewitz, *On War* (Princeton: Princeton University Press, 1989).

11
David Cameron and Foreign and International Policy

Victoria Honeyman

At the 2002 Conservative Party conference, Theresa May, then Party Chairwoman stated that some people 'call us ... the nasty party. I know that's unfair. You know that's unfair but it's the people out there we need to convince ...' (May, 2002). When David Cameron became Conservative Party Leader on 6 December 2005, it was his job to change this, something his immediate predecessors had not been particularly successful at. However, while some policies were abandoned, in some key areas, and while a different style has been adopted, in overall terms the substance of policy has changed very little. One of those areas is foreign and international policy.

This chapter will focus on the foreign and international policy of the Cameron-led Conservative Party, arguing that while there has been continuity in Conservative Party foreign policy, it has been continuity primarily with the Blair Labour government, while there has also been continuity on issues such as the Anglo-American relationship with the governments of Thatcher or Major. Inevitably after 11 years out of office and constantly changing global circumstances, continuity with earlier Conservative government in some policy areas would be unrealistic. For example, the role of the British in the European Common Foreign and Security Policy has developed since its inception, and therefore policy continuation is simply not possible. While innovative thinking in foreign policy is not generally particularly well-received, there has been very little innovative thinking within the Conservative Party on foreign affairs, although there has also been relatively little innovative thinking within the governing Labour Party either. However, as Dodds and Elden noted, 'Brown's forays into foreign policy provide little room for manoeuvre' (Dodds and Elden, 2008: 348).

This chapter will also explore the ideas underpinning the foreign and international policy priorities which Cameron and Hague have identified, including the Anglo-American relationship, the wars in Afghanistan and Iraq, the reform of international organizations and the role of the Commonwealth. International development issues will not be considered as Cameron and Hague have made relatively few sustained public comments on this issue, despite Cameron identifying the 'moral obligation [of the party and Britain] to make poverty history' as one of his eight key policy areas in his *Built to Last* statement of Conservative Party aims and values (Conservative Party, 2006: 5). The Conservative Party did establish the Globalization and Global Poverty Group, with Peter Lilley as chairman and Ed Vaizey as deputy chairman, but Cameron and Hague have not directly participated in the group or spoken about it at length. Indeed, the group's work cannot be accessed from the Conservative Party website.

The foreign policy history of the Conservative Party

During the twentieth century, the Conservative Party has dealt with numerous foreign policy issues due to its longevity in government. However, this has not always been a wholly positive experience for the party. While there have been examples of conflict and overseas wars which have aided the party to win the next general election (such as the 1982 Falklands War, which contributed to Thatcher's 1983 election victory, and the 1991 Gulf War which contributed to Major's surprise 1992 election victory), there are many examples where the opposite is true. Generally, these conflicts and wars only have a positive effect on the party's electoral prospects if the conflict has had a positive outcome for the UK, bathing the party in reflective glory. Anthony Eden's political career was destroyed by his decision to send British troops into Egypt during the Suez crisis in 1956, the party only winning the next general election under the leadership of Harold Macmillan. Most infamously, Neville Chamberlain's appeasement of Hitler during the late 1930s certainly didn't win the party many supporters, and led to his replacement as Prime Minister and then Party Leader by Winston Churchill.

However, it isn't simply wars which have caused the Conservative Party political harm. The 1993 Maastricht ratification process through the House of Commons was fraught with difficulty and caused Prime

Minister John Major huge problems, both within his party and with the electorate, who recognized the deep divisions within the party over Europe. The impact of contentious foreign policy decisions and actions on the Conservative Party's electoral prospects and the political careers of its leaders has been very mixed and it seems likely that this collective experience, coupled with the debacle of the invasion of Iraq under Blair's leadership has had an impact on Cameron and his foreign policy processes and objectives. Britain's membership of the EU remains a hugely contentious issue for the party and collective international action is an important plank of foreign policy planning. By focusing on the party general election manifestos of 1997, 2001 and 2005, areas of continuity can be identified between Cameron and former party leaders, and also areas of change.

The 1997 general election campaign was fought while the Conservative Party were in government, with John Major as their leader. The manifesto focused on numerous areas, with foreign policy only covering a very small part of the manifesto, a practice which is not unusual, due in large part to the spontaneity of many foreign policy decisions. However, there were several foreign policy initiatives which were worthy of mention in the manifesto, including the importance of NATO, the desire to reform the UN, and the role of Britain within the EU. Also mentioned was the role of the Commonwealth, specifically in relation to the distribution of aid in developing nations. The manifesto stated that 'We will continue to support the Commonwealth, our unique global network, to encourage the spread of democracy; as set out in the Harare Declaration' (Conservative Party, 1997). Additionally, the party committed to strengthening the armed services by continuing to 'ensure the Services have the modern weapons they need to guarantee their superiority against potential aggressors. We will make sure we can conduct military operations throughout the world, and develop our capability to deploy the three services together and rapidly, including the ability to transport heavy equipment into an operational zone' (Conservative Party, 1997).

Under the leadership of William Hague, the 2001 general election manifesto focused on one main foreign policy issue – the United Kingdom's role in the EU and the Single European Currency. This is not surprising considering that the main focus of the entire campaign was the aim of the party to ensure that the United Kingdom remained outside of the euro-zone. In addition to this policy, the party also wanted to strengthen the United Kingdom's military forces and strengthen NATO, specifically to avoid any competition between it and the EU's Common Foreign and Security Policy (CFSP) (Conservative Party, 2001).

In addition, the manifesto called for an increase in aid to developing nations, and also, to utilize the Commonwealth to tackle global problems and conflicts: 'The Commonwealth has huge potential – as a force for stability, for promoting the rule of law, democracy and the open economy, and potentially as a means of focusing UK aid. We will consult with our partners on implementing many of the recommendations of the Commonwealth Commission' (Conservative Party, 2001).

Several themes which appeared in the 2001 manifesto also featured in the 2005 manifesto, showing the continued commitment by the party to certain key policy aims. The first foreign policy which appeared in the manifesto was the commitment to strengthen British troops within NATO, a policy which had featured in the 2001 manifesto (Conservative Party, 2005: 25). As in the 2001 manifesto, the focus was on the United Kingdom's relationship with the EU, and the desire of the party to ensure that the EU was reformed to create a 'more flexible, liberal and decentralised' organization (ibid.: 26). Again, the issue of aid to developing nations was mentioned, although no figures were attached to the general intent, but interestingly the role of the Commonwealth was not mentioned (ibid.: 26). Unsurprisingly, the actions of Blair in the run-up to the invasion of Iraq were criticized with the manifesto promising that the party would tell the public why it was important to go to war if they ever had to make that decision, pointing out Blair's misrepresentation in the run-up to the invasion (ibid.: 26). The aims listed in the manifestos were rather general, as is the habit of manifesto commitments, but there is some considerable continuity in foreign policy aims and objectives between the Conservatives under the leadership of Hague, Howard and Cameron. This continuity demonstrates how Duncan Smith, who did not lead the Conservative Party during a general election campaign, did not substantially change policy in this area either.

Liberal conservatism

On 3 March 2007, Shadow Foreign Secretary William Hague argued that Blair's style of 'sofa style decision making' was leading to serious errors in decision-making in terms of foreign and international policy, suggesting that this was something he and David Cameron were determined to 'put right' (Hague, 2007a). This statement was rather indicative of Hague and Cameron's wider thinking on international policy. While not necessarily disagreeing with the decisions made by the Labour government in terms of international policy, Cameron and Hague have been keen to provide an alternative approach to the decision-making process and an alternative vision of the United Kingdom in global politics. The sub-text is that while the decision might not necessarily be wrong in one instance, the flawed decision-making process makes mistakes in the future inevitable.

The Conservative Party is attempting to develop a new approach to policy-making in foreign and international policy, which Cameron has dubbed 'liberal conservatism'. In September 2006, Cameron outlined the basic ideas of liberal conservatism, adopting his preferred stance of stating that 'where possible we should offer support to the Government so ministers can speak abroad with the authority of the whole country', highlighting how responsible the Conservative Party is (Cameron, 2006d). This is a sentiment which Cameron has repeated several times in relation to numerous policy areas, including the handling of the credit crunch (Summers, 2008b). However, Cameron argued in his September 2006 speech that the Blair government had made decisions with an absence of 'humility and patience', referring specifically, although not necessarily restricted to, the war in Iraq. Interestingly, Cameron was keen to point out that he was not a neo-con, a term which does not have particularly positive connotations in Britain and certainly doesn't have connotations of humility or patience (Cameron, 2006d). He has distanced himself from much of the more hard-line party rhetoric on the EU and has populated his shadow cabinet with younger Conservative MPs, separating himself and his party from the Conservative Party of old. However, as Hague himself has pointed out, 'all governments find that idealism in foreign policy has to be tempered with realism' (Hague, 2007b).

Cameron argued that liberal conservatism was based on five basic principles: 'First, that we should understand fully the threat we face. Second, that democracy cannot quickly be imposed from outside. Third, that our strategy needs to go far beyond military action. Fourth, that we need a new multilateralism to tackle the new global challenges we face. Fifth, that we must strive to act with moral authority' (Cameron, 2006d). These five basic principles are fairly similar in content, if rather briefer in style, to the six principles which Tony Blair outlined in his April 1999 speech on the doctrine of International Community (Blair, 1999). Blair's speech focused initially on Kosovo but he discussed the future of Kosovo in terms of the future of the global community. His six basic principles were, first, in global finance, a thorough, far-reaching overhaul and reform of the system of international financial regulation. Second, a new push on free trade in the WTO. Third, a reconsideration of the role, workings and decision-making process of the UN, and in particular the UN Security Council. Fourth, for NATO, a critical examination of the lessons to be learnt, and the changes that need to be made in organization and structure. Fifth, in respect of Kyoto and the environment, far closer working between the main industrial nations and the developing world as to how the Kyoto targets can be met and the practical measures necessary to slow down and stop global warming. Sixth, a serious examination of the issue of third world debt (Blair, 1999).

In addition, Blair identified five considerations to be made before the United Kingdom should intervene in the affairs of another state. These were 'first, are we sure of our case? Second, have we exhausted all diplomatic options? Third, on the basis of a practical assessment of the situation, are there military operations we can sensibly and prudently undertake? Fourth, are we prepared for the long term? And finally, do we have national interests involved?' (Blair, 1999). Despite Blair's rhetoric and good intentions in 1999, all of these considerations were ignored or overlooked in the run-up to the invasion of Iraq.

Blair's six principles were far more specific than Cameron's, but his failure to honour them is partially explained by the fundamental differences between being a leader of the opposition and Prime Minister. Prime ministers are expected to be specific, while it is often easier for opposition leaders to talk in far more general terms, something which Cameron often does. By focusing on generalities, it is easier for him to communicate his ideas to the public and remove ammunition from political opponents, who can attack more detailed plans with far more ease. Dodds and Elden are not quite so charitable, arguing that 'some of these are assertions where nobody would really assert the opposite – especially relevant for points 1, 3 and 5 – which are, at best banal. Many of Cameron's pronouncements fall into this category: What is novel is probably trite and what is not trite is not novel' (Dodds and Elden, 2008: 358).

In October 2007, when Cameron first announced his five basic principles, he was clearly conscious of criticism that they were simply a less-detailed copy of the Blair doctrine. Cameron argued that while Blair has focused on the doctrine of 'liberal interventionism' as Blair describes it, he was instead focusing on the doctrine of liberal conservatism (Cameron, 2007d). He argued that 'liberal interventionism – the idea that we should just get out there into the world and "sort it out" was the right impulse; was morally correct, but failed to strike the right balance between realism and idealism' (Cameron, 2007d). While Cameron has attempted to highlight the different approach which he adopted in comparison to Tony Blair's guiding principles, set out eight years before, Cameron also has been keen to note that he was willing to support foreign policy aims and objectives if they fitted in with his views. He highlighted his position as a responsible politician, and certainly one that can be trusted to run the country by noting that 'we are Her Majesty's loyal opposition – and I take the "loyal" part seriously' (Cameron, 2006d).

One area of continuity in Conservative Party thinking has been regarding the United Kingdom's relationship with her two main allies – the United States (i.e. the Anglo-American special relationship) and the EU. Hague has spoken about Britain's position at the crossroads of the US–EU relationship, pointing out that 'our country enjoys a unique position – the place where America, Europe and the Commonwealth meet' (Hague, 2006a). This is very reminiscent of Winston Churchill's discussion shortly after the end of the Second World War of the three interlocking circles which made up Britain's primary overseas interests, although the Europe he referred to was continental Europe rather than the EU (Sanders, 1990: 1). However, it seems clear that Conservative Party thinking about the United Kingdom's preferred international relationships has moved on very little in the last 60 years, despite the impact of globalization and the changing economic and political status of nations such as China, India, Japan and Germany. It would be unfair to claim that the Conservative Party has not responded to the changes of the global economy or changing global circumstances. For example, its views on UN Security Council membership reflect the growing importance of various nations and will be discussed further below.

Some of the Conservative Party's policy ideas on the development and reform of NATO and the UN have been adopted by the Brown government. Indeed, Gordon Brown has discussed them in various forums, including on a trip to India and at the UN itself. Brown, himself continuing Blair's calls for reform of these organizations made in 1999, identified the need for reform of the UN Security Council, particularly in terms of its membership (Blair, 1999). In a November 2007 speech, Brown named 'Japan, India, Brazil, Germany or any African country' as likely new members of the UN Security Council, eight months after the same nations had been identified by William Hague (Brown, 2007).

Cameron and the 'special relationship'

The relationship between the United Kingdom and the United States of America has had a crucial, central role at the heart of British foreign policy since the end of the Second World War. The 'special relationship' was initially forged between Franklin D. Roosevelt and Winston Churchill, perhaps the greatest Conservative Prime Minister of the twentieth century. While the relationship has been maintained by both Conservative and Labour prime ministers in the 60 years since the end of the Second World

War, it has changed depending upon the particular political priorities of the two states. The relationship has often been based on the shared objectives of the two states, and tends to be closest when these objectives are in unison, as can be seen in the joint invasion of Afghanistan and Iraq by British and American troops following the terrorist attacks of 11 September 2001.

The relationship has also reflected the political beliefs and personalities of the individuals in office. Conservative prime ministers have often shared better relationships with their American counterparts than Labour prime ministers, and one of the reasons for this seems to be based on the ideological bases of the two major United Kingdom political parties. Traditionally, the Labour Party supported, in name at least if not action, a socialist agenda, which was not greeted with enthusiasm in America, the leader of the capitalist world. The closest examples of the 'special relationship' have tended, until 1997, to involve Conservative prime ministers – Churchill and Roosevelt, Macmillan and Kennedy, Thatcher and Reagan. It is, therefore, unsurprising that the Conservatives have great faith and belief in the effectiveness of the Anglo-American 'special relationship' and the influence which it gives the United Kingdom on the world stage. Traditionally, the United Kingdom has been accused of 'punching above her weight' and the special relationship with the US has ensured that the United Kingdom has maintained a high profile on the international stage.

Since the Blair–Bush relationship and the invasions of Afghanistan and Iraq, the Anglo-American relationship has remained popular in principle, being supported by all three main parties, but open to criticism regarding the relative strengths of the two nations and the dynamics of the Bush–Blair relationship (Cohen, 2001: 31). Dodds and Elden argued that this 'narrowed Cameron's options and curtailed his freedom of manoeuvre' (Dodds and Elden, 2008: 360). However, David Cameron's Conservative Party has maintained its strong public support for the special relationship and has attempted to outline in various foreign policy speeches and statements how the special relationship has to be changed in the light of the Iraq war and Bush's tenure as President, while maintaining the key facets of the relationship and protecting the benefits which Britain gains from it. As early as September 2006, less than a year after becoming party leader, Cameron defended the United Kingdom's relationship with the US. He argued that 'anti-Americanism represents an intellectual and moral surrender. It is complacent cowardice born of resentment of success and a desire for the world's problems simply to go away' (Cameron, 2006d).

In addition, Cameron proceeded to explain the importance of this relationship to the modern day Conservative Party, rather than it simply being an overhang from a previous era. He highlighted the benefits of this relationship in the twenty-first century, arguing that 'we believe in the alliance for both emotional and rational reasons ... the fact is that Britain just cannot achieve the things we want to achieve in the world unless we work with the world's superpower' (Cameron, 2006d). In fact, Cameron went further and argued that it is a crucial part of being a member of the Conservative Party to support a strong Anglo-American relationship. He stated very clearly that 'when it comes to the special relationship with America, Conservatives feel it, understand it and believe in it. All Conservatives share this attitude' (Cameron, 2006d). Cameron has not offered this kind of instinctive support to other nations, highlighting the importance of the relationship, both to the United Kingdom and the Conservative Party.

However, due to the perceived unpopularity of the recent Anglo-American relationship, where Blair was regularly accused of being subservient to Bush, Cameron and his influential Shadow Foreign Secretary, former party leader William Hague, have been at great pains to discuss how a Conservative Prime Minister would handle the special relationship differently. As Dodds and Elden have stated, 'his [Cameron's] views on foreign policy have been forged much more in collaboration with Shadow Foreign Secretary William Hague' (Dodds and Elden, 2008: 348). As a former party leader, Hague is an influential figure and Cameron has positioned Hague at the centre of his decision-making on foreign policy, as demonstrated by speeches and statements by both Cameron and Hague. The key phrase, which both men have used is 'solid, but not slavish' (Cameron, 2006d; Hague, 2006a). This reflects the popular perception that the relationship between Blair and Bush was not an equal relationship, and that while the United Kingdom often shares similar values and objectives to the US, there should still be room for the United Kingdom to pursue its own aims, regardless of whether they dove-tail with those of the US (Cohen, 2001: 31).

Hague, speaking in February 2006 argued that the relationship should, as well as being 'solid but not slavish' also be 'firm but also fair' (Hague, 2006a). There have been no solid proposals to support these sound bites, but these are rather difficult to provide without the practical experience of government, and perhaps an unfair criticism of the Conservative Party. Hague's remark was made in the context of the Iraq war and the invasion of Afghanistan and he argued that 'in dealing with such dangerous issues, the US and the United Kingdom must remain close allies' (Hague, 2006a).

However, Cameron went further in his discussion of how Britain should and must maintain her independence of movement while retaining the friendship of the US. He argued that 'we [Britain] have never, until recently, been uncritical allies of America ... I fear that if we continue as at present we may combine the maximum of exposure with the minimum of real influence over decisions' (Cameron, 2006d).

David Cameron and William Hague have had to tread a careful line when discussing the Anglo-American relationship. To simply state that the relationship is good for Britain would not distinguish the Conservative Party from the Labour government and might feed the perception that the United Kingdom is, in the twenty-first century, being cast as the junior (and very subservient) member of the relationship, although there is a strong argument that that has always been the reality of the situation. Instead, Cameron and Hague have, very astutely, portrayed the United Kingdom as the junior partner in the relationship, but still capable of influencing the behaviour of the US and capable of pursuing her own agenda, rather than unthinkingly following the lead of the US. By recognizing the benefits of the Anglo-American relationship while adopting a different tone with Washington, Cameron and Hague appear to have adopted a policy which demands change while being realistic about the United Kingdom's global position.

Liberal conservatism on Iraq and Afghanistan

The invasion of Afghanistan and the war in Iraq which followed caused very considerable problems for the Labour Party, particularly Tony Blair, but it also presented considerable problems for the Conservative Party. Admittedly, Cameron was not leader of the party in the run-up to the invasions of Afghanistan and Iraq or when the initial Commons vote on the invasion of Iraq was conducted, but the Conservative Party did pledge its support for the invasion of Afghanistan. The lack of weapons of mass destruction in Iraq and the increasingly difficult situation in both nations, compounded by the death of British troops and the increasing criticism which George Bush and Blair have faced over their motivations and actions, has obliged David Cameron to restate his views on this issue repeatedly, and to be very clear about where his views coincide with the government's and, more importantly perhaps, where they don't.

The Conservative Party has never withdrawn its support for either the war in Afghanistan or Iraq. Indeed, Cameron has restated his support for both wars and his 'yes' vote in the Commons debate on the invasion of Iraq on 18 March 2003. While the initial reason why many in the country and in parliament (including many Conservative MPs) supported the invasion of Iraq was the intelligence on Iraq's weapons and claims regarding their speed and effectiveness, this evidence has been disputed and discredited. Despite this, Cameron and the wider Conservative Party have continued to support the wars, largely because British troops are active in both areas, and because questioning the motivations of a military incursion when British troops are still fighting overseas is considered disloyal and not the role of a responsible opposition, something David Cameron is keen to ensure his party is portrayed as. Speaking in February 2006, Hague noted that 'in Afghanistan we are not only fighting terrorists but working to build a country. In Iraq, we are helping build a democratic country that is unified, free and at peace with itself and its neighbours' (Hague, 2006a).

The Conservative Party has been, unsurprisingly, keen to identify the mistakes which were made in the run-up to both wars and identify policy initiatives to deal with these for the future. Dodds and Elden have argued that 'while more recently the Conservatives have broken the largely bipartisan approach of the two main British parties concerning Iraq, this has been around detail, hindsight and political positioning rather than any fundamental ideological division' (Dodds and Elden, 2008: 349). William Hague promised that when the Conservative Party regained office it would:

> restore proper Cabinet government to our foreign policy decision making. The sofa style decision making of Blair's Downing Street has led to weak and last minute decision making, without the full flow of information available to Cabinet colleagues, probably contributing to serious mistakes even in circumstances of war, and this is something that David Cameron and I are determined to put right. (Hague, 2007a)

Hague also noted that the Conservative Party was keen to establish a Privy Council inquiry into the 'origins and conduct of the Iraq war and its aftermath, and if the government does not announce such an inquiry in the coming months we will table a motion in the House of Commons requiring them to do so' (Hague, 2007a). While this inquiry did not take place, it does demonstrate that while showing support for British troops and not renouncing formal support for both the invasion of Afghanistan and the war in Iraq, both Cameron and Hague were keen to demonstrate their uneasiness with the process which took the United Kingdom to war and the actions of the government. Subsequently, the Conservative Party has not suggested an immediate withdrawal of troops from either Afghanistan or Iraq, although there have been suggestions about troop reductions leading to a phased handover of control. Hague argued that withdrawal from Iraq and Afghanistan quickly would be counterproductive, leading to the abandonment of the people, handing Afghanistan back to the Taliban (Hague, 2006a).

In terms of Afghanistan, where the causes of invasion are far less divisive, but the future of British troops is still problematic, Hague has argued in favour of NATO becoming a much bigger player. He stated that:

> we have to do our utmost to galvanise NATO into doing what is necessary to make a success of the deployment in Afghanistan, persuading other countries to summon the political will to make a major contribution to what is, after all, their defence, rather than always relying on British, Canadian and American forces to take on the greatest dangers. (Hague, 2007a)

However, Hague has drawn connections between the actions of terrorists in Afghanistan and Iraq and other problems in the Middle East, arguing that tackling global terror does not begin and end with Afghanistan and Iraq and better security at home. Instead he argued that:

> the next administration to take office in America or in Britain could face a nuclear armed Iran, continued violence in Afghanistan, a still unstable Iraq, a stalled peace process between Israel and Palestine and major instability in one of our major Arab allies. All of these conflicts have the potential to feed into or be hijacked by forms of terrorism. (Hague, 2007b)

Gordon Brown has also considered the various factors which are utilized by terrorists, both home and abroad to justify their actions (Brown, 2006). Unfortunately, like the Labour Party, the Conservative Party has not been able to put forward any plans on how to deal with these issues, many of which are extremely problematic and long-running. The main suggestion of Cameron and Hague seems to centre on the strengthening and deepening of international organizations, and a strong Anglo-American relationship.

Liberal conservatism on the UN, NATO and the European Union

Despite both having been created in the immediate aftermath of the Second World War, the UN and NATO have retained their position at the very heart of the global community in the twenty-first century. Many global disputes and difficulties are tackled through either NATO action or UN intervention, despite these organizations having a rather mixed record of success and speed of action. In the light of global conflicts, such as the situation in Darfur and the rule of Robert Mugabe in Zimbabwe, the membership and credibility of these organizations has been called into question. Speaking in 1999, Tony Blair argued that the membership of these organizations needed to be reconsidered in light of the changing global circumstances, notably the economic rise of India and recognition of the increasing strength and influence of South American nations, such as Brazil. Gordon Brown reiterated these suggestions in November 2007 (Brown, 2007). This is an issue which David Cameron and William Hague have both considered since Cameron became leader, as part of their restatement of liberal conservatism in foreign policy.

While NATO and the UN are often bundled together in discussion of international organizations by politicians, they are in actual fact very different entities with very different remits and memberships. Therefore, the reforms which politicians suggest for these organizations have to reflect these differences. Speaking in March 2007, William Hague stated that what was needed with regard to international organizations generally, and the UN specifically, was a 'freshening and deepening of our multi-lateral alliances'. This would mean in practice that the United Kingdom should become a 'powerful advocate of its [the UN's] reform, giving, for instance, Japan, India, Germany and Brazil permanent seats on the UN Security Council' (Hague, 2007a). In the same speech, Hague justified his suggestions for reform by indicating that the composition of the UN Security Council still reflected 'the outcome of the Second World War' (Hague, 2007a). By increasing the representation of the UN, it would almost certainly increase the credibility of the UN across the globe and give it a greater voice, and increased credence, when dealing with global issues.

In terms of NATO, the reform which the Conservative Party has suggested is rather different. The membership of NATO is largely confined by it being the *North Atlantic* Treaty Organization, meaning that many powerful nations cannot expect admission simply due to their geographical position. NATO is one of the cornerstones of British foreign policy and is one of the most powerful international organizations in existence. While both the Conservative and Labour parties have suggested that reform is necessary of this organization, neither has actually put forward concrete proposals on how to achieve change or what the ultimate aim of such reform would be. Hague argued that, for its deployment to be successful in Afghanistan, the United Kingdom must galvanize NATO (Hague, 2007a). Cameron has identified his desire to reform international organizations, without naming NATO specifically, but he has not put forward any concrete proposals for reform of this particular organization. It is therefore difficult to know how the Conservatives would like NATO to look or what reforms they feel would be necessary to make that happen.

Unsurprisingly, Cameron and Hague have tended to focus on another organization in need of reform – the European Union. The EU has been a difficult and divisive issue for the Conservative Party. Cameron and Hague have both spoken of their desire to enlarge the EU and it seems likely that there are two main reasons for this desire, although these are very rarely discussed. Firstly, the larger the EU is, the harder it would be for the organization to become supranational, maintaining the inter-governmental system which the Conservative Party prefers, rather than the increasing integration which countries such as France and Belgium desire.

Secondly, the enlargement of the EU can act as an incentive to countries keen to join and experience the financial benefits of membership. Cameron highlighted the incentive which EU membership had provided for Serbia. As he stated, 'there is no doubting that the prospect of membership, one day of NATO and of the European Union has – until recently – acted as a powerful driver for progress right across the Balkans, just as it did for the countries of Central and Eastern Europe' (Cameron, 2007e). However, in the same speech, Cameron highlighted current fissures over the actions of the EU towards Serbia. Cameron railed against the change of approach by the EU to Belgrade by allowing the EU accession process to move forward without the handover of indicted war criminal Ratko Miladic. He stated: 'The hope is that by giving Serbia something in exchange, it will adopt a more emollient attitude towards the independence of Kosovo. But this is the wrong sort of linkage. It undermines reformers across the region, and moderates within Serbia itself' (Cameron, 2007e). Cameron's solution was for continued strong relations between the UK and the US, including both the EU and NATO within a global partnership to create 'a stable and peaceful future, with the full backing of the international community' (Cameron, 2007e). He stressed the role of the EU in foreign policy in conjunction with NATO, and has repeatedly focused on the interconnectedness of the global community and how organizations such as NATO and the UN have to reflect this in their membership and approach.

Cameron and Hague have also suggested that while the EU should be allowed (and encouraged in some situations) to intervene militarily in certain conflicts, this must be conducted in concert with rather than instead of NATO involvement, a touchstone for many members of the Conservative Party, regardless of whether they be eurosceptic or europhile. Hague stated that 'today the European nations working through NATO have an unprecedented chance to prove their military credibility. Europe wants to do more, and should be able to do much more, but only under NATO auspices' (Hague, 2006a). Indeed, Hague went on to stress the consequences if the EU took on more independent military action or the US ignored the importance of NATO. He argued that 'NATO has a vital ongoing role to play which must not be diluted by the EU on the one hand, or rendered inadequate by the US, on the other' (Hague, 2006a). The strengthening of NATO, and the role of the EU within it in terms of military intervention, coupled with the reform of the UN Security Council is an ambitious programme for the Conservative Party to pursue, but not particularly different from the policy aims of the Labour Party.

Liberal conservatism and the Commonwealth

The importance of the Commonwealth to the UK has declined quite considerably and the organization is often overlooked in the twenty-first century. Gordon Brown has barely mentioned the Commonwealth since becoming Prime Minister, while giving speeches on many other aspects of international policy and organizations (Honeyman, 2009, forthcoming). Indeed, while politicians in both the Conservative and Labour parties tend to focus on the UN and NATO, the Commonwealth is barely ever mentioned. However, the Commonwealth still exists as a working organization and provides links for the UK with countries which are not members of either the UN Security Council or NATO. It additionally provides another forum for global discussion and can allow the UK to exert additional pressure on nations otherwise beyond her reach. A recent example of this is the situation in Zimbabwe with Robert Mugabe's land grab of white-owned farms and the disputed election results in 2008.

Outside of the Commonwealth, the UK has very few methods of applying pressure to nations within the global community without the support of certain countries generally reluctant to take part in global action, such as China and Russia. In addition, because of the history of Zimbabwe and the rule of the white minority under Ian Smith, which had begun in 1965 with Smith's unilateral declaration of independence from the United Kingdom, the Commonwealth is composed of other nations who understand the pressures of decolonization and can therefore apply pressure on Zimbabwe (with British support) when the UK cannot do this singularly due to calls of hypocrisy.

While the Conservative leadership has not concentrated its discussion of international organizations or foreign policy on the Commonwealth, William Hague made special reference to the Commonwealth in October 2006, highlighting how the organization is overlooked by the Labour Party. He noted that 'we need to be able to make much more of a body Labour ministers hardly ever mention: the Commonwealth' (Hague, 2006b). However, Hague did not expand on how the Conservative Party would utilize the Commonwealth effectively or pursue the United Kindom's foreign policy objectives through it. Interestingly, in the same speech, Hague alluded to Churchill's spheres of influence by arguing that 'our country enjoys a unique position – the place where America, Europe and the Commonwealth meet' (Hague, 2006b). The relative unimportance of the Commonwealth in the thinking of the Conservative leadership on foreign policy is demonstrated by the fact that other than these mentions of the Commonwealth, it does not appear predominantly in either Cameron's or Hague's speeches on foreign policy. This suggests that while the Commonwealth will remain one of the international organizations which the United Kingdom is a member of, its importance will not be increased under a Cameron government, and there have been no public announcements of plans for reform of the Commonwealth to streamline its processes or make the organization easier to mobilize.

Conclusion

Unlike other policy areas considered within this book, foreign and international policy tends to elicit more agreement between the two main political parties. The most contentious foreign policy issue currently – the presence of British troops in both Afghanistan and Iraq – is being dealt with in a fairly muted way due to the danger which British troops find themselves in, with criticism being levelled at the breaking of the military covenant and equipment shortages rather than the legitimacy of the war itself. This leaves the Conservative Party in a very difficult position. The party is keen to identify areas of divergence between itself and the Labour government, in addition to pointing out the errors and mistakes which it perceives the government has made. However, it also needs to make sure that, should it form the next government, it hasn't backed itself into a corner and criticized the very nations which are essential allies of the United Kingdom. This has meant that Cameron and Hague have adopted a strategy of pointing out mistakes which the Labour government have made and suggesting remedies to these for the future, while also being a responsible opposition and highlighting areas of continuity between themselves and the government.

Foreign and international policy is hugely affected by the actions of others and the development of other nations. Therefore, it is unsurprising that there has been considerable continuity between the Cameronite Conservative Party and the Brown government. While there are continuities between the Conservative Party under Thatcher and Major with the Cameron Conservative Party, these tend to be in areas which have a strong ideological basis. For example, the importance of the Anglo-American relationship and concern over a supranational EU are ideologically based and not dependent on individual events or crises. The need for the UN Security Council to be reformed in terms of its membership is a much newer issue and is largely driven by the economic and regional importance of certain nations, such as India and China, which was not so pressing when the Major government left office in May 1997.

While a certain amount of continuity between the Conservatives and the Labour government might be expected, in areas relating to the activities of British troops in Afghanistan and Iraq for example, there does seem to be a considerable amount of common ground between the two parties. In large part, this is due to the fact that many of the Labour government's actions in foreign policy have fitted in well with Cameron's 'liberal conservatism' and can be viewed as reasonable actions in this regard. However, it is rather surprising that the Conservative Party has not capitalized more on the mistakes made in the run-up to the invasion of Iraq. It seems likely that this is due to the support which the Conservative Party, with Michael Howard as leader, gave to the Labour government in the Commons debate on the invasion of Iraq in 2003. It has been very difficult for the Conservative Party to move away from this commitment, and has meant that the party has not been able to make as much political ammunition out of the situation as it might otherwise have. Cameron and Hague are pursuing an ambitious but realistic foreign and international policy approach, casting the Conservative Party as a responsible and realistic opposition which can be entrusted to lead the country. However, should the Conservative Party win the next election it seems likely that there will not be any seismic shifts at the Foreign and Commonwealth Office.

12
The Conservatives and the European Union: The Lull Before the Storm?

Philip Lynch

The issue of Britain's relationship with the European Union (EU) was a difficult and divisive one in the Conservative Party during David Cameron's formative years in politics. Cameron was a special adviser to Chancellor Norman Lamont at the Treasury on 'Black Wednesday' in 1992 when sterling was forced out of the European Exchange Rate Mechanism (ERM). The experience shaped Cameron's moderate eurosceptic outlook. He entered parliament at the 1997 general election as divisions on Europe contributed to the Conservatives' worst defeat of the modern era. During Cameron's period as leader, however, the Conservatives have had a settled European policy on which they are largely united, and the issue of Europe has not featured prominently in party discourse.

But Europe has the potential to once again prove a thorny issue for a future Conservative government. The Conservatives oppose the Lisbon Treaty and have stated that they 'will not let matters rest' should they come to power when the treaty is in force in the EU. How this, and the Conservative vision of Europe more broadly, might be realized is uncertain. Cameron's main initiative on Europe has been the pledge that Conservative MEPs will leave the European People's Party-European Democrat (EPP-ED) group in the European Parliament and form a new group. But this was put on ice until after the 2009 European elections when the leadership failed to recruit sufficient allies and met resistance from Tory MEPs. This frustrated eurosceptics in the party, many of whom want a significant reworking of Britain's relationship with the EU.

Conservative exceptionalism

Research on euroscepticism in political parties across the EU highlights the British Conservative Party as an exceptional case. As Leonard Ray puts it, 'in comparison to all European parties of similar ideology, experience in government, and size, the UK Conservative Party is strikingly Euroskeptical' (Ray, 2007: 171). Most eurosceptic parties are found on the political fringes and have little prospect of holding office. The Conservatives are the notable exception: should they win the next general election, a eurosceptic party will hold power in a large EU member state for the first time. Most centre-right parties in western Europe are located in the Christian Democrat party family and are pro-European in outlook. The Conservatives have moved from a relatively pro-European position of the 1970s and 1980s to their 'soft' eurosceptic position of the last decade. The shift occurred in the 1990s when the Maastricht Treaty's provisions for Economic and Monetary Union (EMU) and political union exposed the tensions inherent in Thatcherism between the support for the Single European Market that flowed from its economic neo-liberalism and the opposition to further integration that resulted from its attachment to national sovereignty. The move towards euroscepticism was driven by a potent combination of concerns about the impact of European integration on political economy, nationhood and executive autonomy, elements that lie at the heart of the Conservative Party's self-identity (Lynch, 1999; Baker et al., 2002). By the turn of the century, eurosceptics were in the ascendancy in the party.

The influential typology of party-based euroscepticism developed by Paul Taggart and Aleks Szczerbiak distinguishes between 'hard' and 'soft' euroscepticism (Taggart and Szczerbiak, 2008). Hard euroscepticism involves principled opposition to European integration as embodied in the EU. Soft euroscepticism occurs when there is not principled opposition to the European integration project of transferring powers to the supranational EU, but there is opposition to the EU's current or future trajectory based on the further transfer of competences. The UK Independence Party (UKIP) is the prime example of a hard eurosceptic party in Britain, calling as it does for the UK to leave the EU. The Conservatives are a 'soft' eurosceptic party, supporting EU membership policies such as the Single European Market, but opposing recent extensions to the EU powers including EMU and the Lisbon Treaty. However Conservative policies such as the renegotiation of treaty commitments and the repatriation of some competences, have the potential to go beyond the 'opposition to the EU's current or future planned trajectory' because they suggest significant changes to the basis of British membership. Some Conservative eurosceptics wish to go further still by, for example, reasserting the supremacy of parliament, but advocates of withdrawal are a small minority.

The Conservative critique and vision

At the time of writing – before publication of the manifesto for the 2009 European elections – the Conservative Party had not spelled out its European policy in a comprehensive fashion. Britain's relationship with the EU was not explored in detail by the policy review bodies, and Cameron had only made one keynote speech on European policy by the beginning of 2009. However, key elements of Conservative European policy can be pieced together by examining speeches by Shadow Foreign Secretary William Hague, statements by Conservative spokespersons in the House of Commons (particularly on the Lisbon Treaty), and other policy announcements. In doing so, it becomes apparent that there is a great level of consistency – more than in most other areas – between party policy on Europe prior to 2005 and since Cameron became leader. This is evident in both broad themes and policy detail, where many of the central planks of the 'in Europe, not run by Europe' position developed under Hague's leadership (1997–2001) remain in place. There is also continuity in the discourse on Europe used by Cameron and in the relatively low salience afforded to European matters in the Conservative narrative. Cameron's most significant initiative was the pledge to remove Conservative MEPs from the EPP-ED – one that he was unable to deliver before the 2009 European elections. There is a familiar pattern even here: Iain Duncan Smith also planned to leave the EPP-ED but could not fashion a new group during his short spell in office (2001–03).

The Lisbon Treaty

The Lisbon Treaty has been the most significant European issue of the Cameron period. Cameron became Conservative leader when the EU Constitutional Treaty (commonly known as the EU Constitution) was in cold storage following 'no' votes in referendums in France and the Netherlands in 2005. The Conservatives had declared the Constitution dead but the Blair government pressed for a less ambitious treaty to replace it. The main points of the Reform Treaty were agreed by Tony Blair in June 2007, with what then became the Lisbon Treaty signed by Gordon Brown that December.

Conservative opposition to the Lisbon Treaty drew heavily on the critique of the EU Constitutional Treaty developed under Michael Howard's leadership (2003–05). The central argument was that Lisbon was essentially the same as its discredited predecessor, which was said to mark a significant step towards statehood, so Labour's manifesto commitment to hold a referendum on the Constitution should apply to Lisbon. Since the Hague period, the Conservative position has been that any EU treaty surrendering further powers to Brussels should be approved in a referendum as well as by parliament. The 2004 European Parliament elections and 2005 UK general election thus saw the Tories commit to hold a referendum on the Constitutional Treaty and campaign for a 'no' vote. Blair's announcement ahead of the European elections that Labour would hold a referendum drew the sting from the Conservative position. But it would provide Cameron with his main line of attack when Blair and Brown refused to hold a referendum on Lisbon and claimed that it was merely an 'amending treaty' stripped of the constitutional elements of its predecessor. The Conservatives claimed that there was no substantive difference between the two and argued that the additional safeguards secured on the government's 'red lines' – on the EU foreign policy post, criminal justice, the Charter of Fundamental Rights, and unanimity – offered insufficient protection.

Conservative discourse on the Constitutional Treaty and Lisbon has been built around issues of democracy and trust. The traditional Tory concern with sovereignty and the nation state has figured more prominently in speeches from Conservative backbenchers than in those from the leadership. The government's refusal to hold a referendum despite its manifesto commitment is said to further erode trust in politics. Conservatives actively supported the cross-party 'I want a referendum' campaign.[1] Hague also claims that the EU will lack democratic legitimacy if the Lisbon Treaty is not put to national referendums (Hague, 2008). EU elites, he argues, ignored voters in France and the Netherlands by bringing the Constitution back in another guise. Whereas nine member states held or intended to hold referendums on the Constitution, only Ireland did on Lisbon and, when it delivered a negative verdict, the Irish government was pressed to call another. The EU suffers from a democratic deficit, understood as the transfer of decision-making from elected representatives in the nation state to supranational bodies that are not sufficiently accountable and lack the legitimacy of national institutions with which people identify. The transfer of competences has taken place by stealth and without popular consent. Hague points to EU employment regulations and the UK government's inability to deport criminals from other member states as issues where the EU's 'democratic disconnection' has contributed to the breakdown of accountability and trust in politics (Hague, 2007c). The Conservative solution is to strengthen national scrutiny of the EU, pursue intergovernmental cooperation and restore some competences to the nation state (see below).

Attention now turns to the Conservatives' detailed case against the Lisbon Treaty. They have long advocated intergovernmental cooperation in the 'area of freedom, security and justice', and in foreign, security and defence policy. The new post of High Representative of the Union for Foreign Affairs and Security Policy is criticized for being little different to the Constitution's 'Union Minister for Foreign Affairs', with the holder presiding over the Foreign Affairs Council and supported by the European External Action Service. The High Representative will act on behalf of the EU but will, however, only be able to implement policies agreed by unanimity. The UK secured a Declaration stating that foreign policy remains the responsibility of member states, but critics note that such declarations are not legally binding.

Lisbon gives the EU competence in judicial cooperation in criminal matters and police cooperation. Policy in these areas, such as the European Arrest Warrant, will follow the Community method of proposals from the Commission, qualified majority voting in the Council, co-decision and European Court of Justice (ECJ) jurisdiction. The UK maintains its right to opt-in to police and judicial matters without compulsion, but the Conservatives claim that when the government opts-in, it loses its right to veto future policy developments.[2] Transitional provisions in the treaty also raise the prospect of current EU measures relating to the UK being ruled inoperable if the UK declines to opt-in to their successors (European Scrutiny Committee, 2007–08: 14–19). The Lisbon Treaty extends legal personality to the European Union, meaning that the EU will be able to sign treaties in its own right on matters such as extradition. A Declaration states that legal personality does not authorize the EU to act 'beyond the competences conferred on it by member states'.

Lisbon gives the Charter of Fundamental Rights the same legal value as the treaties. A Protocol states that the Charter does not extend the ability of the ECJ or any British court or tribunal to rule that UK laws, regulations or administrative practices are inconsistent with the Charter. It also states that nothing in the Charter creates justiciable rights that apply to the UK above those that already exist in British law. The Protocol's effectiveness is disputed, critics claiming that the ECJ may still create EU-wide case law based on the provisions of the Charter on matters such as social security and collective bargaining when it is called upon to rule on cross-border cases.[3]

A new element in the Lisbon Treaty to attract Conservative criticism is the 'ratchet clause' allowing member states to agree that decisions currently taken only by unanimity can in future be decided by a majority vote (except on defence). This might allow EU treaties to be amended without an Intergovernmental Conference. Member states would, however, have to agree by unanimity that the 'ratchet clause' procedure be used and all national parliaments would have to give their approval. Finally, the Conservatives are concerned by an apparent weakening of the EU's commitment to competition signalled by the move from the Treaty preamble to a Protocol of the objective of 'free and undistorted competition', although protocols are legally binding.[4]

EU institutions and policies

The Conservatives have since the mid-1990s proposed significant changes to the main EU institutions which would shift the balance of power towards member states. The Commission should lose its monopoly right to initiate legislation, its prime function being to ensure the efficient working of the Single European Market. Conservatives are concerned by the way in which ECJ decisions have extended supranationalism. Under Hague they proposed that legislation interpreted by the ECJ in a way different from that originally intended should be subject to rapid amendment. For the Council of Ministers, the Conservatives support reform of the system of qualified majority voting (QMV) to reflect more accurately the size of large member states. But they want greater transparency and oppose the extension of QMV. The party opposes Lisbon's creation of a President of the European Council, its preference being a team presidency building on the current troika system.

The Conservatives propose the extension of the principle of subsidiarity, which they understand to mean the transfer of decision-making from the European to the national level. National parliaments should be able to block EU legislative proposals when a small number of them believe that the proposals do not comply with the principle of subsidiarity. This amounts to a 'red card' compared to the Lisbon Treaty's 'yellow card', under which EU proposals would be reviewed if one third of national parliaments believed they infringe subsidiarity, and an 'orange card' under which draft legislation proposed by the Commission would fall if deemed non-compliant by a majority of national parliaments and either 55 per cent of Council members or a majority in the European

Parliament.[5] The scrutiny of EU legislation at Westminster should also be improved (Hague, 2007c; May and Timothy, 2007).

On EU policies, the Conservatives continue to promote a deregulatory agenda, urging the completion of the Single European Market, the liberalization of protected sectors and tougher competition policy.[6] Measures taken to reduce regulation, enhance labour market flexibility and increase European competitiveness such as the Services Directive and the Lisbon agenda are viewed as too timid. Criticism of EU social and employment policy has also been a consistent theme of Conservative policy, with Cameron committed to a British opt-out from EU social and employment law. Another familiar theme is global free trade. The Conservatives oppose protectionism within the EU (e.g. 'national champions') and beyond, proposing a transatlantic free trade area. Cameron has added concerns about the costs of the Common Agricultural Policy (CAP) to farmers in the developing world and the environment to longstanding criticism of its inefficiency.

In his first major speech on the EU, Cameron said that it should focus on three issues – globalization, global warming and global poverty (Cameron, 2007f). The former means delivering the Lisbon Agenda and CAP reform. Member states should bolster their commitment to tackling climate change through the EU's Emissions Trading Scheme – but Cameron does not envisage an extension of EU competence on environmental matters. On global poverty, Cameron again suggests multilateral action and the Conservatives oppose provisions in the Lisbon Treaty linking development cooperation to the EU's common foreign and security policy objectives. They fear that this will see a further concentration of aid on the EU's near neighbours rather than on the poorest states.[7] Cameron's focus on global poverty as an EU priority is a departure from the position taken under Howard when international aid was identified as a competence to be repatriated to nation states.

Cameron inherited a definitive, settled position on EMU. John Major's 'wait and see' policy on British membership of the single currency had evolved under Hague into a commitment not to join for two parliaments and to campaign for a 'no' vote in a referendum. Only when Iain Duncan Smith defeated Kenneth Clarke in the ideologically-charged 2001 leadership contest did party policy become one of principled opposition to membership. This helped close down the issue, as did the negative verdict on the 'five economic tests' delivered by the Labour government in 2003. Speculation about British entry resurfaced in late 2008 as the value of sterling plummeted. Senior Conservatives reiterated that they would never support euro entry and rehearsed a case against entry that pointed to the loss of national control over key economic decisions and the structural differences between the British and euro-zone economies (Hague, 2009).

EU enlargement is another longstanding goal. The Conservatives support in principle the membership applications of Turkey and the Balkan states, subject to them meeting the appropriate criteria. Should the question of Turkish membership come to the fore under a Conservative government, Cameron will face dissent from MPs unconvinced of Turkey's suitability. Whereas the leadership focuses on the strategic and symbolic importance of admitting a secular Muslim state, critics claim that Turkey is not sufficiently European and warn of large scale migration.[8]

Flexibility

The Conservative vision is of a flexible Europe in which, aside from core Single European Market policies, member states are not required to follow other EU policies at the same speed – or at all if they have fundamental objections. Flexibility should not be limited to new EU policies, with the Conservatives seeking a limited renegotiation of existing commitments. At the 2005 general election they proposed the repatriation (i.e. the return of responsibility to Westminster) of social and employment policy, international aid and fisheries (Conservative Research Department, 2005: 577). Cameron has retained the commitment to repatriate social and employment policy, but rowed back from that on the Common Fisheries Policy, calling instead for its reform. The Conservatives cite the 2001 Laeken Declaration to support their case for flexibility. It stated that the EU must become 'more democratic, more transparent and more efficient' and that 'restoring tasks to the member states' might be considered.[9] They claim that this signals that the *acquis communautaire* (the body of existing EU law) is reversible, but this is a selective interpretation of a document that initiated moves towards the EU Constitution.

If a Conservative government enters office when the Lisbon Treaty has not yet been ratified by all member states, it would hold a referendum on the treaty and campaign for a 'no' vote. If Lisbon has entered into force, it would 'not let matters rest'.[10] This is a deliberately ambiguous phrase but it is safe to assume that the Tories would seek opt-outs on social and employment policy, and further assurances or opt-outs in other areas. Achieving this would not be easy as it would require treaty amendment and thus the support of all member states. The Conservatives might find sympathetic governments in the Czech Republic and the Netherlands, and persuade others that denying the UK would create greater problems. But some states would strongly resist British opt-outs, fearing that this would give the UK a competitive advantage and unravel the *acquis*. The leadership is understandably reluctant to speculate on what might happen if they failed to negotiate new opt-outs. A post-ratification referendum on Lisbon is a possibility, but one fraught with problems given the difficulty of separating the Lisbon provisions from earlier treaties. A referendum on Lisbon could become either too broad (i.e. on EU membership) or narrow (i.e. not covering parts of earlier treaties which the Conservatives oppose). Furthermore, a newly elected government could well argue that it had already secured a mandate to renegotiate. Another option could then be a manifesto pledge to renegotiate the terms of EU membership with a referendum to follow when the negotiations are concluded (Nelson, 2008).

A more intriguing possibility is that a Conservative government reasserts the supremacy of the Westminster parliament.[11] When Hague was leader, Conservative policy was to introduce legislation to establish reserve powers: the sovereignty of parliament would be ring-fenced in areas in which the EU does not have full competence, preventing EU law from overriding UK legislation. Future governments could participate in new EU initiatives but would require the express approval of parliament to do so. The issue of supremacy has resurfaced under Cameron. John Redwood's Economic Competitiveness Policy Group suggested that as a 'last resort' the European Communities Act 1972 should be amended to allow parliament to disapply EU regulations that are harmful to British business (Economic Competitiveness Policy Group, 2007: 62). As we will see, backbencher Bill Cash has proposed various measures to reassert the supremacy of parliament. A response by Hague to a question by Cash during the third reading of the bill ratifying the Lisbon Treaty is revealing on the current thinking of the leadership:

> Given the growth of the EU's powers, British sovereignty and the ultimate supremacy of parliament need a constitutional safeguard, but ... the legal implications of any such provision must be absolutely clear. More work would need to be done in the future on the context and formula by which it is achieved, but I have great sympathy with the constitutional safeguard of ultimate supremacy.[12]

A 'soft' eurosceptic party

The ratification of the Maastricht Treaty in 1992–93 brought a perfect storm in the Conservative Party, its measures on economic and political integration provoking an initially disparate group of MPs to launch the party's most damaging parliamentary rebellion of the post-war era (Baker et al., 1994). Since 1997, however, the Conservatives have been the most united of the main parties on European matters. Eurosceptics make up the vast majority of the parliamentary party, and support the soft eurosceptic position adopted by the leadership. The cluster analysis undertaken by Paul Webb shows the parliamentary party becoming solidly right-wing and eurosceptic, bar a small number of pro-European centrists (Webb, 2008). The classifications of Conservative MPs by Timothy Heppell and Michael Hill also show a decisive shift to euroscepticism. Heppell identifies 192 Conservative MPs (58 per cent) in the 1992–97 parliament as eurosceptic and 98 (30 per cent) as pro-European (Heppell, 2002). For the 1997–2001 parliament, Hill lists 140 of 164 MPs (85 per cent) as eurosceptic and just 13 (8 per cent) as pro-European; by 2001–05, 90 per cent of Conservative MPs were eurosceptic (Heppell and Hill, 2008; Hill, 2007). More eurosceptics entered the House of Commons at the 2005 general election. The eurosceptic presence now included veterans of the Maastricht rebellions (e.g. Cash and Richard Shepherd), former cabinet ministers (e.g. John Redwood and Peter Lilley) and a new generation of MPs (e.g. Greg Hands and Theresa Villiers).

Pro-Europeanism is, then, very much a minority position in the Conservative parliamentary party. Most of the senior pro-European Conservative figures of the Thatcher and Major governments have left politics, often through election defeat or retirement. Others have resigned the Conservative whip and defected to a rival party. The most recent to do so was Quentin Davies, the then chair of the Conservative Group for Europe, who defected to Labour in 2007 citing Cameron's decision to 'break a solemn agreement' on EPP-ED membership as a key factor in his departure.[13] The disproportionately high number of pro-European Conservative MEPs helped frustrate Cameron's plan to leave the EPP-ED.

Voting in House of Commons divisions on European matters provides further evidence of unity on the Conservative benches. Three-line whips requiring Conservative MPs to vote against the ratification of the Amsterdam Treaty, the Nice Treaty and the EU Constitutional Treaty were adhered to by all but a handful of pro-Europeans before 2005.[14] The European Communities (Amendment) Bill 2008, which ratified the Lisbon Treaty, again saw very high levels of unity. Only three MPs – Kenneth Clarke, David Curry and Ian Taylor – disobeyed the whip to support the bill at second reading. A fourth, John Gummer, rebelled on other votes on the treaty and opposed a referendum on Lisbon.[15]

Few pro-Europeans have held shadow cabinet positions since 1997. Curry, Taylor and Stephen Dorrell left their posts in the first year of Hague's leadership, while Quentin Davies served under Duncan Smith. More significant was Cameron's appointment of Kenneth Clarke as Shadow Secretary of State for Business, Enterprise and Regulatory Reform in January 2009.[16] Clarke's return brought a number of positives: his popularity with voters, down-to-earth manner and record as Chancellor (1993–97) helped counter claims that the Conservative frontbench was too posh and inexperienced. But it also brought risks. Some eurosceptics had not forgiven Clarke for what they perceived as an act of treachery when he shared a platform with Tony Blair and Gordon Brown at the launch of the pro-single currency Britain in Europe group in 1999. Clarke has been critical of party policy under Cameron: he supports eventual British membership of the single currency (albeit recognizing that this is unlikely to occur in his political lifetime), criticized the plan to remove Tory MEPs from the EPP-ED, voted for the Lisbon Treaty and opposed a referendum on it. Philip Cowley notes that prior to his appointment, Clarke was the most rebellious Conservative MP of the Cameron era, although 26 of his 33 dissenting votes were cast on the Lisbon Treaty (Cowley, 2009, forthcoming). On his return to the frontbench, Clarke accepted that the party had a 'settled view' on European matters and said that he would not 'oppose the direction' set by the leadership.[17] But political opponents anticipated dissent during the European elections and a second Irish referendum on Lisbon set for autumn 2009. Clarke's shadow ministerial brief also meant that he will be Conservative spokesperson on EU social and employment policy on which the party line is that the UK should have an opt-out.

Off-message comments from Clarke are likely to attract attention, but it is eurosceptics in the parliamentary party who may ultimately be of greater concern to Cameron. One hard eurosceptic, Bob Spink, joined UKIP in 2007 having resigned the Conservative whip after disputes with his constituency party. But public dissent has otherwise been rare from eurosceptic MPs who feel that Cameron has neither given sufficient priority to Europe nor adopted a tough enough position.

Two parliamentary amendments proposed by veteran eurosceptic Bill Cash provide pointers to the level of Conservative support for fundamental changes to Britain's relationship with the EU. In 2008 his new Clause 9 of the European Communities (Amendment) Bill stated that 'nothing in this Act shall affect or be construed by any court in the United Kingdom as affecting the supremacy of the United Kingdom Parliament'. Most Conservative MPs abstained on what was a free vote for all MPs, except for the members of the frontbench, but no fewer than 40 MPs (including Iain Duncan Smith) supported the amendment. The whips had not been as cautious in 2006 when Cash proposed an amendment to the Legislative and Regulatory Reform Bill which would override the European Communities Act 1972 by allowing parliament to repeal burdens on British business imposed by the EU and require British courts to comply with Westminster legislation where it is expressly inconsistent with EU law (Cash, 2007: 9). The whipped amendment was supported by 136 Conservative MPs.

Cash was the primary sponsor of the most significant eurosceptic Early Day Motion (EDM) of the Cameron period, EDM 2143 on the European Reform Treaty in the 2006–07 session. It insisted that the Prime Minister 'holds a referendum before or after ratification' on what became the Lisbon Treaty. Forty-six Conservative MPs signed the EDM. Private members' bills also give a flavour of eurosceptic sentiment. Owen Paterson's European Communities Act 1972 (Disapplication) Bill of 2005–06 sought to provide that EU law would only be legally binding when it did not conflict with subsequent, expressly inconsistent Acts of parliament. Paterson and another of the bill's sponsors, Theresa Villiers, later joined the frontbench. Cash introduced a bill to allow parliament to overturn EU legislation on employment rights in 2008–09. Finally, in 2007–08 Shadow Europe Minister Mark Francois voted for Christopher Chope's European Union (Audit of Benefits and Costs of UK Membership) Bill to establish a commission examining the costs of EU membership, and Peter Lilley's Members of Parliament (Pay and Responsibilities) Bill would link MPs' salaries to the transfer of competences to Brussels and their return to Westminster.

Membership of eurosceptic pressure groups was tolerated by Conservative Party managers in the 1990s as a way of managing divisions and removing dissent from the parliamentary arena. But, as Simon Usherwood points out, as a consequence eurosceptics were radicalized when afforded the opportunity to stray from the party line (Usherwood, 2002). The most interesting 'hard' eurosceptic group to emerge in the Cameron period is the Better Off Out campaign which calls for British withdrawal from the EU. It is a non-party group that includes UKIP and Labour eurosceptics, but was launched in 2006 by the Freedom Association. Those Conservative MPs listed as supporters are Douglas Carswell, Philip Davies, Philip Hollobone, Ann Winterton and Sir Nicholas Winterton.[18] Eurosceptics who voted for Cameron in the 2005 leadership election believed that they had received assurances that those favouring withdrawal could put their case in public. But Cameron made it clear that those doing so would not serve on his frontbench. Some eurosceptics complained subsequently that they had come under pressure not to associate with Better Off Out and argued that, with the return of Clarke, they should not be excluded from the frontbench because of their views on Europe.[19]

Predictions on the make-up of the post-election Conservative Party cannot be foolproof, but it is safe to say that there will be no influx of pro-Europeans, and that soft eurosceptics will outnumber hard eurosceptics. If the Conservatives win a majority, almost half of the parliamentary party will be first-time MPs. Eurosceptics entering parliament for the first time may be disinclined to rebel early in a Tory government but some among the 2005 intake (e.g. Philip Hollobone and Philip Davies) soon developed a habit of rebellion (Cowley, 2009, forthcoming).

Cameron is a pragmatic eurosceptic wary of re-opening divisions within his party. When appointing Clarke to his shadow cabinet, he reassured eurosceptics by giving Shadow Europe Minister Mark Francois a position in the shadow cabinet and bolstering Hague's role as his *de facto* deputy. His handling of the EPP-ED issue and courting of eurosceptic support during the 2005 Conservative leadership election also point to Cameron's desire to contain division and broker agreement on European matters.

Leadership elections

Europe has featured prominently in the three Conservative leadership elections held in opposition. Although the parliamentary party is predominantly eurosceptic, the most eurosceptic of the leadership candidates has only won on one occasion, when Iain Duncan Smith defeated Kenneth Clarke in 2001. This was not an auspicious outcome. In the MPs-only stage of the election, all of the MPs to vote for Duncan Smith (a former Maastricht rebel) were Thatcherite eurosceptics. Not only did Duncan Smith fail to reach out beyond his core constituency but his 54 votes on the third ballot represented the support of only a minority of eurosceptic MPs (Heppell, 2008: 151–2). The 61 per cent of the vote he secured in the ballot of party members was more impressive, but his lack of support among MPs meant that Duncan Smith was unable to establish his authority. Clarke's appeal reached beyond the party's divide on Europe in both the 2001 and 1997 contests. In the latter, eurosceptic votes on the first ballot of MPs were divided between Michael Howard, Peter Lilley and John Redwood. Clarke's attempt to clinch the leadership by brokering a deal with Redwood, who exited on the second ballot, that promised a free vote on EMU entry alienated many eurosceptics. William

Hague was the beneficiary, but only on the final ballot did he secure the backing of much of the eurosceptic right, and even then some voted for Clarke (Heppell and Hill, 2008).

Although it did not have as a high a profile, Europe was still significant in the election of David Cameron in 2005. Eurosceptic MPs associated with what became the Cornerstone Group indicated that they would support a candidate who made a firm commitment to leave the EPP-ED group.[20] This was a symbolically important issue for eurosceptics and one that could be delivered by the party leader in opposition. Cameron pledged to leave the EPP-ED, a decision borne from conviction rather than simple electoral calculation, as did Thatcherite eurosceptic Liam Fox. But the other eurosceptic candidate, and frontrunner, David Davis refused to do so because he feared that it would be too difficult to implement. Cameron's pledge enabled him to add support from the eurosceptic right, including David Heathcoat Amory who defected from the Fox camp after the first ballot. Cameron surged ahead of Davis on the second ballot and beat him comfortably in the vote of party members. Like Hague, he began with support primarily from the centre then added eurosceptic votes to create cross-party backing, but unlike his predecessor, Cameron was not the default choice of eurosceptics and had secured enough support from MPs and party members to establish his authority. Fulfilling his campaign pledge to pull Tory MEPs out of the EPP-ED would, however, prove problematic and prompt some eurosceptics to question his credentials.

The Conservatives in the European Parliament[21]

The distinctiveness of the Conservative position on Europe has left the party short of natural allies in the European Parliament (EP), where MEPs sit in transnational groups. In 1992 the Conservatives became allied members of the European People's Party (EPP), whose Basic Programme supports the social market economy and a federal Europe. But Tory MEPs were permitted to vote differently from the group line and the Conservatives have never joined the EPP transnational party. Domestic concern about the EPP link grew as the Conservatives became more eurosceptic. The Malaga Declaration of 1999 changed the group's name to the European People's Party-European Democrats (EPP-ED), the Conservatives becoming allied members in the European Democrat (ED) section with their right to vote separately strengthened. Duncan Smith demanded greater autonomy for the ED but, when this was not forthcoming, began discussions on the formation of a new group with parties from central and eastern Europe. Howard ended these and agreed a deal with the EPP-ED in 2004 that changed the group's constitution. A new Article 5(b) allows the ED to 'promote and develop their distinct views on constitutional and institutional issues in the new Europe'. MEPs applying to join the group could do so either on the basis of the EPP programme or the ED element. All prospective MEPs were required to commit in writing to the deal for the duration of the 2004–09 EP. All those elected in 2004 did so, some with misgivings. But day-to-day relations with the EPP were little changed.

Cameron's leadership election pledge to leave the EPP-ED was soon refined: the Conservatives would leave only when a viable new group could be formed. Finding suitable allies proved tricky. The European Parliament's rules required a group to have a minimum of 20 MEPs from at least one-fifth of the member states (i.e. five in 2005, then six from 2007). The Conservative leadership would only consider mainstream centre-right parties, but most were full members of the EPP and would not leave the group in mid-term, if at all. European Democrat section MEPs from Italy and Portugal also refused to quit. The most likely candidates were the Czech Civic Democrats (ODS), the Tories' closest allies in the ED, and the Polish Law and Justice party (PiS), which belonged to the Union of European Nations (UEN) group. Both had signalled their willingness to team up with the Conservatives during Duncan Smith's search for allies. Both were also on the verge of government, and it was domestic considerations that put paid to the ODS leaving the EPP-ED in the short term. Without the ODS, the chances of forming a viable group of some forty or fifty members receded. The minimum number required could still have been reached by enlisting the PiS plus smaller parties and independents from Sweden, the Baltic states and Ireland. Eurosceptics believed that other parties who had doubted the Tories' commitment to leave the EPP would then join. But this would have been a fragile alliance with limited ideological congruence, and one in peril of defection and collapse.

A lack of support for Cameron's plan among Conservative MEPs also contributed to its postponement. The 27-member delegation in the 2004–09 term is divided into three camps: one is pro-European and pro-EPP, another eurosceptic and anti-EPP, and a third group is pragmatic and loyalist.[22] The delegation has always contained a significantly higher proportion of pro-Europeans than the parliamentary party or wider membership. Key leadership positions in the delegation continue to be held by MEPs supportive of the EPP link. To avoid a split, Cameron had to convince the delegation leadership and pragmatic centre, but instead he antagonized both pro-EPP and anti-EPP MEPs. At least six MEPs would have refused to join a new group, and more would have refused to sit as non-attached members ('non-inscrits').

Postponing the formation of a new group became the least costly option for Cameron as others were closed off. Forming a new group before 2009 was unattractive once the ODS declined to leave in mid-term. Sitting as non-attached members – favoured by some eurosceptics as it would break the EPP link and give the delegation leader more speaking time in the EP – would mean a loss of influence and status.[23] Joining another existing group was not an option because the UEN included the post-fascist Italian Alleanza Nazionale and Fianna Fáil (who would not welcome the Tories). In July 2006 Cameron and ODS leader Mirek Toplanek duly announced that they would create a new group after the 2009 elections. They launched the Movement for European Reform (MER) to develop their agenda outside of the EP. This allowed Cameron to head off criticism of the delay and claim that the Conservatives are not isolated in Europe. But the MER failed to recruit other parties and has barely functioned since 2007.[24] Relations with centre-right governing parties in Germany and France had been damaged, but joint working groups were set up in 2008 as a thaw set in.

The pros and cons of forming a new group are finely balanced. If internal party considerations are more important to the Conservatives than objectives at the EU level, then leaving the EPP-ED would be the favoured option. Policy and office objectives in the EU are more likely be achieved through access to influential committee positions and rapporteurships, more of which go to the largest groups in the EP. Conservative MEPs have in recent years chaired important committees (e.g. environment, agriculture) and held rapporteurships on the EU budget and competition policy. Under the d'Hondt system used to distribute committee chairs, chairs of the most prestigious committees are not available to smaller groups, while rapporteurships are distributed through an auction system in which large groups are allocated the most points. Leaving the EPP-ED would reduce the chances of the Conservatives obtaining the most prestigious posts, but other important posts would be available to a new group. The Tories might, however, be obliged to award these to smaller parties in return for their membership of a new group. Eurosceptics counter that the European Democrat section lacks autonomy, that the EPP has prevented MEPs from joining the ED, and that a new group would control a £5 million budget which could be spent promoting their vision of Europe.

The behaviour of MEPs in roll-call votes in the European Parliament shows that the Conservatives are close ideologically to the German

Christian Democrats on key issues, with disagreements occurring most often on issues (e.g. institutional reform) where the EP has less power and which constitute less of its workload (Lynch and Whitaker, 2008). On such issues, the Conservatives can also vote differently from the EPP. Roll-call voting also reveals congruence between the Conservatives and the ODS and PiS, although they have less in common with other parties suggested as allies.

Cameron maintains that a new group will be formed and the ODS restated its commitment at its 2008 congress. But pro-European and eurosceptic Conservatives harbour doubts. A change to the EP's rules on political groups – a group will now require at least 30 MEPs drawn from seven member states – may complicate matters. However the UEN looks set to collapse, freeing some parties to join.[25] Were a new group to take root, the best-case scenario is that it then recruits those parties from central and eastern Europe unhappy with the hierarchical style of the EPP leadership, and breaks the EPP's monopoly of the centre-right. The post-election Conservative delegation will be more eurosceptic: of the ten MEPs not standing in 2009, seven favoured the EPP–ED link.[26] All candidates signed a declaration stating that they will respect Cameron's policy to form a new group, but this also contained a more ambiguous clause requiring candidates to 'become a member of whichever political group in the European Parliament is decided upon by the party leader'.[27] This leaves open the possibility of remaining in a strengthened European Democrat section of the EPP-ED, which is the preferred outcome of some senior Tory MEPs. This would anger eurosceptics, but with a general election only months away they would come under pressure not to rock the boat.

Conservative discourse and issue salience

Research by Geoffrey Evans shows that the Conservatives have been closer to public opinion on Europe than Labour since the mid-1990s (Evans, 2002; Evans and Butt, 2007). The proportion of British citizens who believe that EU membership has been a good thing, has dropped, and support for the single currency and EU Constitution has been lower than in many other member states. Europe has also become a more important issue for voters and one that cuts across the traditional left–right dimension. Europe is then a potential vote winner for the Conservatives. A clear majority of those who switched to the Tories in 2001 were opposed to European integration. But most voters did not change allegiance. Hague's 'save the Pound' campaign was widely criticized for appealing primarily to the Conservative core vote and for prioritizing an issue that was well behind health and education among voters' concerns. However, as Jane Green points out, the Conservatives were concentrating on one of the few issues on which they were close to voters (Green, 2005). Indeed, the party adopted a more moderate position on Europe than that of its supporters. The Tories were acting in a manner consistent with salience theory – emphasizing issues favourable to them and de-emphasizing unfavourable ones. But many voters were unsure about the Conservative position on Europe, prompting eurosceptics to argue that a harder, more consistent message was required.

Ideology, the predominance of euroscepticism in the party, and the proximity of the Conservative position to public opinion all suggest that the Tories should prioritize Europe. But Conservative leaders have not done so since 2001, recognizing that it is not an easy issue to exploit because it does not figure highly among voter concerns and can expose divisions within the party. Iain Duncan Smith defied predictions by closing down the issue. Michael Howard structured the case against the EU Constitutional Treaty around the issue of democracy, rather than the traditional Tory theme of sovereignty. Europe did not feature prominently in the Conservatives' 2005 general election campaign and when it did, it was in relation to a referendum on the Constitution.

Cameron has followed his predecessors by removing Europe from centre stage in the Conservative narrative, and concentrating on democracy and trust when the Lisbon Treaty came on the agenda. He has done so with greater conviction and purpose than Duncan Smith or Howard, his wish that the Conservatives should not 'bang on about Europe' being part of a broader modernization project that seeks to 'decontaminate the brand' and change voters' perceptions by downplaying traditional Conservative issues and focusing instead on new ones (e.g. the environment) or ones on which Labour has made the running (e.g. health). The Blair and Brown governments also contributed to the reduced salience of the European issue (Oppermann, 2008). Their proposals for referendums on the single currency and the EU Constitutional Treaty, neither of which came about, took the heat out of these issues. Brown's negative verdict on the five economic tests in 2003 removed EMU from the agenda and his refusal to hold a referendum on the Lisbon Treaty allowed for a much more manageable parliamentary ratification. In the period from Cameron's election in 2005 to the start of 2009, fewer than one in ten voters identified Europe as 'one of the most important issues facing Britain today'.[28]

Cameron's treatment of UKIP also echoes that of previous Conservative leaders. Howard called UKIP members 'cranks and gadflies', Cameron dismissed them as 'fruitcakes, loons and closet racists'. UKIP had polled 16 per cent of the vote and won 12 seats at the 2004 European elections, but averaged just 3 per cent in the constituencies it contested at the 2005 general election. Nonetheless, where UKIP performed best the Conservatives were the party to suffer most (Curtice et al., 2005). Many Conservative eurosceptics view UKIP as an irritant, fearing that it harms the prospects of a eurosceptic government by fielding candidates in Tory target seats. But some diagnose a more robust eurosceptic message as the optimal means of negating the UKIP challenge. UKIP's fortunes declined after 2004 as Robert Kilroy-Silk launched an acrimonious leadership challenge before quitting the party. Nigel Farage has sought to broaden its appeal and position UKIP on the centre-right by adopting positions (e.g. tax cuts and grammar schools) that Cameron has steered away from. But it is unlikely to make significant inroads into Conservative support at the next European and general elections.

Conclusion

The Cameron effect in Conservative European policy is less pronounced than in the other fields examined in this book. He has maintained the 'soft' eurosceptic position developed by his predecessors, his policy on the Lisbon Treaty mirroring Howard's on the EU Constitutional Treaty. The change in presentation and discourse that has been such an important feature of Cameron's modernization project is also less pronounced on European matters. The emphasis on positive themes such as democracy and the environment when discussing the EU resonate with Cameron's broader strategy, but the low salience of European issues has been a feature of Conservative politics since Iain Duncan Smith became leader in 2001. Maintaining this low profile has been helped by the near-unity of the Conservative parliamentary party on Europe, Labour's desire to neutralize the issue, and public disinterest. The one European matter on which Cameron, as a leader of the party in opposition, could make a real difference was group membership in the European Parliament. Cameron's pledge to leave the EPP-ED helped secure him eurosceptic support in the 2005 leadership contest, but he was unable to deliver it in the short term.

The failure to find suitable members for a new group in the European Parliament, and the dissent (albeit muted) that Cameron's pledge and its postponement produced in the party, suggest that the course of

Conservative European policy is unlikely to run as smoothly in the future. Cameron will be expected to deliver a new group after the 2009 European elections. Failure to do so will damage his credentials with eurosceptics in his party, but the formation of an unstable group will provoke accusations that the Conservatives are isolated and extremist. The Lisbon Treaty is a ticking time-bomb. If it has not been ratified by all member states when a Cameron administration takes power, then a referendum on the treaty will provide a defining moment early in its spell in office. Should Lisbon already be in force when the Conservatives take office, the party's position is that it 'will not let matters rest'. Cameron might expect that a government elected with a mandate to renegotiate will enjoy a degree of cooperation from other member states who will not relish the prospect of another period of British awkwardness.[29] But securing anything beyond limited concessions and opt-outs will prove difficult and time-consuming. If he cannot deliver, then Cameron will have to manage dissent within his party from eurosceptics pressing for a more profound renegotiation of British membership.

In the 1990s life became very difficult for a Conservative government that was in a minority in the EU and suffered internal divisions at home. History is unlikely to repeat itself in quite such stark terms, but a period of difficult relations in the EU and eurosceptic discontent at home looks likely. On Conservative European policy, Cameron's first three years as party leader may be remembered only as the lull before the storm.

Notes

1. http://www.iwantareferendum.com
2. Dominic Grieve, House of Commons debates, 29 January 2008.
3. David Lidington, House of Commons debates, 5 February 2008.
4. James Clappison, House of Commons debates, 6 February 2008, cols 985–6.
5. House of Commons European Scrutiny Committee, *Subsidiarity, National Parliaments and the Lisbon Treaty*, 33rd Report, 2007–08, (para. 37) doubted whether the Lisbon Treaty provisions 'would make much practical difference to the influence presently enjoyed by the UK Parliament'.
6. Hague (2006c). Many Conservative eurosceptics promote a 'hyperglobalist' version of this that views current EU policies as constraining British competitiveness in the global economy; see Baker et al. (2002).
7. Mark Francois, House of Commons debates, 22 February 2008, cols 844–5.
8. The Conservative Friends of Turkey group was launched in 2008 with 18 MPs among its founder members, http://www.cfot.org.uk/index.html
9. Presidency Conclusions of the Laeken European Council (14–15 December 2001): Annex I: Laeken Declaration on the future of the European Union.
10. 'Tories would seek to scupper EU treaty', *Financial Times*, 23 July 2008.

11. On a different, but relevant, matter Cameron plans to replace the Human Rights Act 1998 with a British Bill of Rights. The Conservatives have also looked with interest at the power of the Federal Constitutional Court of Germany to rule whether EU treaties are consistent with the Basic Law.
12. W. Hague, House of Commons debates, 11 March 2008, col.167.
13. Q. Davies, letter to David Cameron, 26 June 2007, http://www.quentindaviesmp.com/node/55
14. No Conservatives rebelled on the second reading of the bills ratifying the Amsterdam and Nice Treaties. Kenneth Clarke, David Curry and Quentin Davies defied the whip on the second reading of the European Union Bill ratifying the EU Constitutional Treaty.
15. http://www.revolts.co.uk/cat_news.html
16. Cameron appointed Clarke as chair of the party's Democracy Task Force in 2006. Two other prominent pro-Europeans, Michael Heseltine and John Gummer, also led policy review bodies.
17. 'Kenneth Clarke promises no Europe meddling as Tory reshuffle announced', *The Times*, 19 January 2009.
18. http://www.tfa.net/betteroffout/ (accessed 28 January 2009).
19. Nine Conservative MPs attended the BOO launch in May 2006. Those whose names no longer appear on the list of BOO supporters are the late Eric Forth, Christopher Chope, David Davies and Bob Spink who defected to UKIP in 2007. See 'MPs throw their weight behind Better Off Out campaign', *The June Press*, 2006.
20. Interviews with Conservative MPs and MEPs, 2006.
21. This section draws upon Lynch and Whitaker (2008).
22. Seven Conservative MEPs signed a letter welcoming the promise to leave the EPP-ED (*Daily Telegraph*, 1 October 2005); 13 signed a counter-letter supporting EPP-ED membership (*Daily Telegraph*, 5 October 2005).
23. 'Hard' eurosceptics Roger Helmer and Daniel Hannan have been suspended from the EPP-ED and sit as non-attached MEPs, but retain the Conservative Whip (although Helmer lost this too for a time).
24. The Bulgarian Union of Democratic Forces joined briefly in 2007 but left when its leader resigned after failing to win seats in the European Parliament. Details of the work of the MER (or lack of it) can be found at http://www.europeanreform.eu
25. A UEN-ED alliance is the preferred option of some Conservative MEPs. See C. Tannock, 'Conservative MEPs – what are the options for alliances', 2 December 2008, http://conservativehome.blogs.com/centreright/2008/12/conservative-me.html
26. Eurosceptics were, though, unhappy about a candidate selection process that ensured that incumbents would top the regional lists. See 'The story of how the party's EU enthusiasts fixed the MEP selection process', http://conservativehome.blogs.com/goldlist/2008/04/the-story-of-ho.html
27. 'The EPP declaration that MEP candidates must sign', http://conservativehome.blogs.com/goldlist/2007/12/the-epp-declara.html
28. http://www.ipsos-mori.com/content/the-most-important-issues-facing-britain-today.ashx
29. See 'Charlemagne: Europe's Tory nightmare', *Economist*, 10 July 2008, and Aaronovitch (2007).

13
Conclusion:
A Cameronite United Kingdom?

Matt Beech

> I am clear about the new direction we must set for Britain. To
> meet the challenges of the twenty-first century, and to satisfy
> people's aspirations today, this country needs a responsibility
> revolution.
>
> (Cameron, 2006e: 2)

If David Cameron wins the next general election he will be the first
Conservative Prime Minister of the twenty-first century. He will be the
first in at least 12 years and the first that many British citizens will have
voted for. Whether Cameron and the Conservative Party will prove to
be the victors is a matter of speculation. What is certain is that the size
of the Conservative Party's parliamentary majority will dictate the level
of power Cameron has to implement his vision of a more 'responsible'
United Kingdom. But with some scholars predicting a hung parliament
at the next general election (Kalitowski, 2008) Cameron may experience
minority government and therefore the scope of his ambitions might
be restricted. In spite of such uncertainties I want to attempt to sketch a
picture of what a Cameronite United Kingdom would look like through
the lens of existing constraints, policy commitments and political
relationships that will likely be encountered.

Without doubt, the major existing constraint that Cameron would face
is the state of the economy. This year, 2009, will be the year of recession
as 2008 was the year of the credit crunch and if the UK economy begins
to show signs of growth in 2010, it will be gradual. Firstly, for Cameron,
New Labour's borrowing will eventually need paying off and he requires

a long-term plan to achieve this. He has already declared his intention not to raise the top rate of income tax but, how his government will attempt to recoup the spent funds is a difficult issue for a self-styled 'low tax Conservative' (cited in Jones, 2008: 280). Until the economy returns to a period of greater stability and growth, the prospect for tax cuts – so important to the Conservative Party and its supporters – is very distant. Cameron, therefore, faces the prospect of a first term of damage limitation, austerity and little realistic chance of reducing the burden of income tax on British citizens and the burden of public debt on the nation's balance sheets.

Secondly, and added to the bleak economic outlook is the social cost of recession: rising unemployment and the poverty it causes. The rate of unemployment as of 21 January 2009 according to the Office for National Statistics was 6.1 per cent and the total number of people unemployed was 1.92 million (Office for National Statistics, 2009). This will be a central challenge for the new breed of Conservatives and may well be the intellectual litmus test in deciding whether their Thatcherite inheritance outweighs their centrist, post-New Labour appearance. How will they respond to the escalating social misery that deep and chronic unemployment brings? If Cameron's speech on fiscal responsibility is an indication of his intentions it could be argued that he believes that, ultimately, government and citizens must face the cost of such phenomena and ride out the storm; and, moreover, that government should not borrow further to spend further but instead it ought to cut back on 'waste' and other measures outlined by the government to create jobs in the short term (Cameron, 2008b).

Thirdly, Cameron has an economic policy commitment not to match New Labour's level of public expenditure. This was a recent change of policy in light of the pre-budget report and the ensuing recession, and it was delivered in a speech to the CBI Conference:

> So I can announce today that in order to keep spending at a responsible level and to ensure the quickest possible end to the recession and the strongest possible recovery, we will not match Labour's new spending plans for 2010 and beyond. Only by taking this step can we ensure that the Government lives within its means and only by ensuring that Government lives within its means can we build the low tax, low debt economy that will be able to compete in the world and help create jobs, wealth and opportunity for our people in the future. (Cameron, 2008b)

That extract begs the following questions: what Departments will suffer? What programmes and services will be axed? Through such a commitment Cameron's Conservatives are looking more akin to traditional neo-liberals than reformed, centrists in their economic and social thinking.

Fourthly, and a further interrelated problem that currently exists and may well persist, is the lack of lending between banks and by banks to businesses and individuals. Cameron has suggested the government create a National Loan Guarantee Scheme (Cameron, 2008k), but if the issue of a lack of liquidity continues how will Cameron persuade the lenders to lend? The Conservatives are ideologically and often socially close to the leaders and financiers of the City of London. Will this be a help or a hindrance? How effectively will Cameron be able to reprimand such people and encourage them to lend and thus to act in the interests of the nation?

The nature of the global recession and its impact on the British economy will dictate to what extent Cameron can implement his two main political reforms: taxation and public service reform; and social policy and welfare reform. The first question here is whether he will be able to return power and meaningful choice to British citizens in the form of tax cuts and greater personalization of public services in such an austere economic climate. Tax cuts will be extraordinarily hard to achieve even if his ministers ruthlessly cut programmes from their various budgets. However, Cameron could succeed in the delivery of greater personalization of public services if what he means is greater privatization of health and social services or further outsourcing of services to the third sector. Whether it will prove to be cost-effective in the long run is at present a moot point, but if he seeks a bold programme of privatization for certain existing public services such as social care then the state may well make substantial savings as the full financial burden will fall to individuals and families.

The second question is: with low tax receipts and a new commitment not to borrow further (unlike New Labour) will Cameron's government have sufficient resources to support their policies to mend Britain's 'broken society'? On a more optimistic note for Cameron's plans his second goal of mending Britain's 'broken society' is a thesis which at root argues for greater parental and personal responsibility on a range of issues and in one sense is not an expensive state-centric enterprise. For example, 'talking up' life-long marriage and removing the disincentive to marry from the benefits system does not cost much. Nevertheless, tackling welfare dependency is of a different order of magnitude in terms of public policy problems as the Secretary of State for Work and Pensions, James

Purnell, is currently discovering. Despite the fact that third sector groups such as family support charities and Christian social action organizations bring deeper compassion, commitment and fresh thinking to the issues surrounding poverty and deprivation (including drug and alcohol addiction, worklessness, illiteracy, family breakdown and dysfunction) than the state and its practitioners, the state is still required as regulator and funder of last resort. The sheer number of people that are affected by these issues is enormous and thus for reforms to be effective Cameron's 'broken society' thesis will require inter-generational investment and sustained commitment. Even with the partnership that does already exist between the state and the third sector, Cameron's goal of social reform will not be fully addressed unless he utilizes the levers of government and intervenes. Legislative reform, government guidance and modifications of existing laws will change things but ultimately the social problems that have been identified are huge, multifarious and multilayered. They will only be addressed by state and third sector partnership over several generations; and yet, some of us are not convinced of the ability of the state or the market to remedy certain issues that require personal trans-formation and an act of will.

The United Kingdom, in Cameron's eyes, will be precisely that, the Union of Great Britain and Northern Ireland. He is comfortable with the existence of a Scottish parliament, assemblies in Wales and Northern Ireland and especially with the Mayor of London, currently his friend and fellow Conservative, Boris Johnson. Cameron is an ardent unionist and like Brown and Blair is hostile towards Celtic nationalism. He does believe that something needs to be done over the West Lothian Question (Cameron, 2007g: 9). However, his Conservative Democracy Task Force chaired by Ken Clarke concluded in their report that:

> The Democracy Task Force recommends to David Cameron a modified version of 'English Votes for English Laws', incorporating English-only Committee and Report stages but a vote of all MPs at Second and Third Reading. We believe that this proposal can remove the main source of English grievance at the current devolution settlement without some of the risks to political stability that critics have seen in proposals for a completely English procedure. (Conservative Democracy Task Force, 2008: 5)

The West Lothian Question, recently dubbed 'English Votes for English Laws', is an easy political argument for Conservatives to make (though not one without merit and a sense of equality) because the Conservative

Party is in practical terms an English political organization as they hold one seat in Scotland and none in Wales. If such reforms were introduced it would likely give the Conservative Party a majority in English debates and would seriously hamper the Labour Party's ability to govern. This was noted by the Conservative Democracy Task Force, hence their less full-blooded recommendation of votes by the whole House of Commons on English-only issues at the second and third readings. However, if only English MPs were entitled to vote on issues that pertain solely to English constituents then it would be a most radical piece of constitutional reform. It would change the nature of British politics and arguably force the Labour Party to be an organization even more focused on winning a great many southern and midland English seats. Given the culture and political and economic inclination of those regions it would be highly unlikely that Labour or even New Labour would prosper. In effect, it would build a notable degree of Conservative power and influence into the majority of the debates in the House of Commons, possibly making it impractical for the Labour Party to meaningfully govern the whole country. From this view, it is understandable why the Prime Minister is against it.

In a recent speech, Cameron appeared to be courting the support of the Ulster Unionist Party as their support of a minority Conservative administration could be crucial in a hung parliament:

> I want the most talented people to form my government and that will mean people from all corners of the UK. Why are there great Ulstermen and women on our television screens, in our boardrooms and in our military but not in our Cabinet? The semi-detached status of Northern Ireland politics needs to end. It's time for Northern Ireland to be brought back into the mainstream of British politics. Northern Ireland needs MPs who have a real prospect of holding office as ministers in a Westminster government. That's what a dynamic new political force of Conservatives and Unionists offers a revival of real democracy across the United Kingdom. (Cameron, 2008m)

Cameron as a Tory is committed to established institutions and the Union is central to his understanding of Conservatism. Simultaneously his Conservatism is pragmatic and he recognizes that a possible political reality at the next election is that no party may hold an absolute majority and in this case building coalitions with like-minded parties such as the Ulster Unionists is of great importance.

With regards to the United Kingdom's relationship with the European Union under a Cameron administration it is likely that it would change in tone and in terms of positive, active engagement. Cameron will not withdraw nor will he abrogate prescribed member state responsibilities. However, he will not only seek to reduce regulations on business and perhaps gain an 'opt out' from the Social Chapter but he will also seek to align other centre-right European parties in the European Parliament who advocate free market economics, are sceptical of supranationalism and opposed to European federalism.[1] If this is achieved he can finally break with the EPP-ED. In general Cameron's tone will be less pro-European than Blair's or Brown's but, like New Labour, he will be opposed to protectionism. On reflection it seems likely that euroscepticism will be back in vogue at the elite level of British politics. But one interesting factor in the discussion of a Cameron administration and its relationship with the European Union has recently surfaced, namely the re-emergence of Ken Clarke to frontline Conservative politics. Presently, as Shadow Business Secretary, Clarke's brief is well defined: it is to shadow Peter Mandelson and add experience and gravitas to Cameron's economics team. Nevertheless, Clarke is an unapologetic pro-European and an advocate of Britain adopting the European Single Currency, yet he belongs and serves in one of the most eurosceptic parties in Europe. More than any other political issue in Conservative politics, the issue of Britain's integration into the European Union is the most provocative. Euroscepticism is totemic and ideologically central to what it means to be a Conservative in Britain. The return of the most prominent pro-European Conservative in British politics may well lead to internal problems for Cameron, especially if Clarke is perceived as shadowing Mandelson competently he will grow in his indispensability for Team Cameron.

Akin to Cameron's desire to be further from the sphere of influence of the European Union is his desire to be closer to the United States of America. To continue the 'special relationship' and to connect Britain's foreign and defence policy interests with those of the United States is a central tenet of British Conservatism and Cameron is no different. In one sense he will be in a more favourable position than Blair that it is surely beyond dispute that in President Obama, Cameron will be working with a man keen on multilateralism, nuance and not in hock to powerful ideologues behind the scene. One hopes and is optimistic that Cameron will not be 'bounced into war' in the way that Blair was. On the other hand, politically Cameron and Obama have little to mutually celebrate in their political philosophies bar the basic Western principles of democracy and market economics and this absence of political symmetry may cause some minor tensions, but often with intergovernmental relationships personality matters more.

Overall, it can be asserted that Cameron is a committed Conservative who wishes to see a very different kind of United Kingdom from the one New Labour has tried to build. He is confident in his political beliefs: neo-liberal economics; euroscepticism; a Tory regard for institutions; scepticism towards the big state; personal responsibility and environmentalism. It will be interesting to analyse the policies that he and his colleagues devise for the next general election campaign and compare them against the policy prescriptions offered by his predecessors. New Labour was genuinely new – and the reform of Clause IV; a more centrist approach to the market economy, personal taxation and the business community all attest to this fact. Of course there were ideological currents present in New Labour that existed in previous Labour governments such as high levels of public spending; active government; and redistributionism. New Labour never ceased to be centre-left and part of the social democratic family. However, there were sufficient substantive changes that made New Labour 'new' and the electorate understood this change. The same evolution has not fully occurred with Cameron's Conservatives but neither is he merely an identikit Thatcherite. The power to invoke that political change lies with Cameron. Time will tell whether he opts for the well trodden path of post-Thatcherite British Conservatism or the newer path to a more moderate centre-right politics in the twenty-first century.

Note

1. For more on Cameron's desire to realign the Conservatives in the European Parliament see Lynch and Whitaker (2008).

References

Aaronovitch, D. (2007) 'Love from Lisbon – an explosive package', *The Times*, 13 November.

Ainsworth, P. (2009) *Green Energy Bill – Power for All*, Press release, 21 January.

Alexander, M. and Garden, T. (2001) 'The Arithmetic of Defence Policy', *International Affairs*, 77(3): 509–29.

Anthony, A. (2008) 'The second coming of Iain Duncan Smith', *Observer*, 29 June.

Appleby, J. and Harrison, T. (2005) 'The War on Waiting for Hospital Treatment', The King's Fund. Available at: http://www.kingsfund.org.uk/publications/kings_fund_publications/the_war_on.html (accessed 15 July 2008).

Ashcroft, M. (2005) *Smell the Coffee: A Wake-up Call for the Conservative Party* (London: Michael Ashcroft).

Baker, D., Gamble A. and Ludlam, S. (1994) 'The Parliamentary Siege of Maastricht: Conservative Divisions and British Ratification', *Parliamentary Affairs*, 47(1): 37–60.

Baker, D., Gamble, A. and Seawright, D. (2002) 'Sovereign Nations and Global Markets: Modern British Conservatism and Hyperglobalism', *British Journal of Politics and International Relations*, 4(3): 399–428.

Baker, S. (2007) 'Sustainable Development as Symbolic Commitment: Declaratory Politics and the Seductive Appeal of Ecological Modernisation in the European Union', *Environmental Politics*, 16(2): 297–317.

Barber, B. (1963) 'Some Problems in the Sociology of the Professions', *Daedalus*, 92(4).

Baumol, W.J., Panzar, J.C. and Willis, R.D. (1982) *Contestable Markets and the Theory of Industry Structure* (New York: Harcourt Brace Jovanovich).

BBC (2002) 'Willetts outlines one nation hope', 27 February, http://news.bbc.co.uk/1/hi/uk_politics/1843763.stm (accessed 18 February 2009).

BBC (2005a) 'Howard will stand down as leader', 6 May, http://news.bbc.co.uk/1/hi/uk_politics/vote_2005/frontpage/4521941.stm (accessed 19 December 2008).

BBC (2005b) 'Cameron pressed on drugs question', 14 October, http://news.bbc.co.uk/1/hi/uk_politics/4340328.stm (accessed 15 January 2009).

BBC (2007) 'First 100 days: David Cameron', 5 October, http://news.bbc.co.uk/1/hi/uk_politics/4810212.stm (accessed 19 December 2008).

BBC (2008a) 'Tories cut Labour spending pledge', 18 November, http://news.bbc.co.uk/1/hi/uk_politics/7735113.stm (accessed 19 December 2008).

BBC (2008b) 'Russia to move missiles to Baltic', 5 November, http://news.bbc.co.uk/1/hi/world/europe/7710362.stm

BBC (2008c) 'Tories cut Labour spending pledge', 18 November, http://news.bbc.co.uk/1/hi/uk_politics/7735113.stm

BBC (2008d) 'Afghanistan "priority for Tories"', 1 October, http://news.bbc.co.uk/1/hi/uk_politics/7646323.stm

Beckett, A. (2008) 'What can they be thinking?' *Guardian*, 26 September.

Beech, M. (2008) 'New Labour and the Politics of Dominance', in M. Beech and S. Lee (eds), *Ten Years of New Labour* (Basingstoke: Palgrave Macmillan).

Bernanke, B. (2009) 'The Crisis and the Policy Response', Remarks by the Chairman, Board of Governors of the Federal Reserve System, Stamp Lecture, London School of Economics, 13 January.

Blair, T. (1999) 'Doctrine of International Community', Speech, 24 April. Available at: http://www.number10.gov.uk/Page1297 (accessed 30 September 2008).

Bobbit, P. (2006) *The Shield of Achilles* (London: Penguin).

Bosanquet, N., Haldenby, A. and Rainbow, H. (2008) *NHS Reform: National Mantra, Not Local Reality* (London: Reform).

Branigan, T. (2006) 'Blair grasped Thatcher legacy, now Tories must retake centre ground says Cameron', *Guardian*, 31 January 2006.

Brown, C. (2007) 'Osborne declares Cameron is the true "heir to Blair"', *Independent*, Thursday, 31 May. Available at: http://www.independent.co.uk/news/uk/politics/osborne-declares-cameron-is-the-true-heir-to-blair-451108.html (accessed 15 January 2009).

Brown, G. (2006) 'Meeting the terrorist challenge', Speech, 10 October. Available at: http://www.hm-treasury.gov.uk/1946.htm (accessed 7 November 2008).

Brown, G. (2007) Speech at the Lord Mayor's Banquet, 12 November. Available at: http://www.number10.gov.uk/Page13736 (accessed 22 September 2008).

Brown, G. (2008) 'Time for the third act in public sector reform', *Financial Times*, 9 March. Available at: http://www.ft.com/cms/s/0/c96a2baa-edfc-11dc-a5c1-0000779fd2ac.html (accessed 15 July 2008).

Brown, G. and Straw, J. (2007) 'Foreword' to Ministry of Justice, *The Governance of Britain*, Cm. 7170 (London: The Stationery Office).

Bulpitt, J. (1986) 'The Discipline of the New Democracy: Mrs Thatcher's Domestic Statecraft', *Political Studies*, 34(1): 19–39.

Bureau of Labor Statistics (2009) *The Employment Situation: December 2008* (Washington, DC: United States Department of Labor).

Burnham, J. and Pyper, R. (2008) *Britain's Modernised Civil Service* (Basingstoke: Palgrave Macmillan).

Bush, G. (1999) 'The duty of hope', Speech, Indianapolis, Indiana, 22 July, reproduced as 'Appendix B' in M. Olavsky (2000) *Compassionate Conservatism: What It Is, What It Does, and How It Can Transform America* (New York: The Free Press), pp. 215–26.

Bush, G. (2002) 'President promotes compassionate conservatism', Speech, San José, California, 30 April.

Butler, R. (1971) *The Art of the Possible* (London: Hamish Hamilton).

Cabinet Office (1999) *Modernising Government* (London: HMSO).

Cabinet Office (2001) *Better Policy-making* (London: HMSO).

Cabinet Office (2007) *Building on Progress: Public Services* (London: HMSO). Available at: http://archive.cabinetoffice.gov.uk/policy_review/ (accessed 15 December 2008).

Cabinet Office/CMPS (2002) *International Comparisons in Policy-making Toolkit* (London: CMPS).

Cameron, D. (2005a) 'Changing the Conservative Party', Speech at the launch of leadership bid, London, 29 September.

Cameron, D. (2005b) 'Ending the Blair era', Speech, 10 November.

Cameron, D. (2005c) 'Change to win', Speech at the Conservative Party Conference, 4 October.

Cameron, D. (2005d) 'A voice for hope, optimism and change', Speech, London, 6 December.

Cameron, D. (2005e) 'Until we're represented by men and women in the country, we won't be half the party we could be', Speech, Leeds, 12 December.

Cameron, D. (2005f) *Vision for Britain: Policy Programme*. October.

Cameron, D. (2006a) 'Modern Conservatism', Speech at Demos, London, 30 January.

Cameron, D. (2006b) 'The new global economy', Speech, 22 June.

Cameron, D. (2006c) 'The planet first, politics second', *Independent on Sunday*, 3 September.

Cameron, D. (2006d) 'A new approach to foreign affairs – liberal conservatism', Speech to the British American Project, 11 September.

Cameron, D. (2006e) 'Foreword', in Conservative Party, *Built to Last: The Aims and Values of the Conservative Party* (London: Conservative Party).

Cameron, D. (2007a) 'A liberal Conservative consensus to restore trust in politics', Speech in Bath, 22 March.

Cameron, D. (2007b) 'The Conservative approach to improving public services', Speech, 26 January. Available at: http://www.conservatives.com/tile. do?def=news.story.page&obj_id=134729&speeches=1 (accessed 15 December 2008).

Cameron, D. (2007c) 'We still don't have a proper plan for Afghanistan', 8 August, http://www.conservatives.com/News/Articles/2007/08/David_Cameron_We_ still_dont_have_a_proper_plan_for_Afghanistan.aspx

Cameron, D. (2007d) Berlin Security Conference Speech, 26 October.

Cameron, D. (2007e) David Cameron's First Speech in Washington DC, 29 November.

Cameron, D. (2007f) 'The EU: a new agenda for the 21st century', Speech to the Movement for European Reform, Brussels, 6 March.

Cameron, D. (2007g) 'Scots and English flourish in the Union', *Daily Telegraph*, 11 April.

Cameron, D. (2008a) Speech to Conservative Party Conference, in Birmingham, 1 October.

Cameron, D. (2008b) Speech to CBI Conference, in London, 9 December.

Cameron, D. (2008c) 'A borrowing binge', *Guardian*, 18 November.

Cameron, D. (2008d) 'I'm on your side, not in your wallet', *News of the World*, 9 November.

Cameron, D. (2008e) 'The choice on borrowing', Speech, 18 November.

Cameron, D. (2008f) 'Fixing our broken society', Speech in Glasgow, 7 July.

Cameron, D. (2008g) Interview on the Andrew Marr Show, 28 September, BBC 1.

Cameron, D. (2008h) 'The choice isn't between economy and environment', Speech, 16 June. Available at: http://www.conservatives.com/tile.do?def=news. story.page&obj_id=145279

Cameron, D. (2008i) 'Crossroads for NATO', Speech, 1 April. Available at: http:// www.conservatives.com/News/Speeches/2008/04/David_Cameron_Crossroads_ for_NATO.aspx

Cameron, D. (2008j) 'We must make Moscow pay for this blow against democracy', 17 August, http://www.conservatives.com/News/Articles/2008/08/David_ Cameron_We_must_make_Moscow_pay_for_this_blow_against_democracy. aspx

Cameron, D. (2008k) Speech to Policy Exchange, in London, 28 November.

Cameron, D. (2008m) Speech to Ulster Unionist Annual Conference, in Belfast, 6 December.

Cameron, D. (2009a) 'We need popular capitalism', Speech at the World Economic Forum, Davos, Switzerland, 30 January.

Cameron, D. (2009b) 'Britain's economic future', Speech, London, 5 January.

Cameron, D. and Osborne, G. (2008) 'Foreword' to Conservative Party, *Reconstruction: Plan for a Strong Economy* (London: Conservative Party).

Cash, B. (2007) 'The Dogs have Barked and the European Caravan must be Stopped', *European Journal*, November/December.

Centre for Social Justice (2008) '63% agree that British Society is broken' (London: Centre for Social Justice).

Cerny, P.G. (1990) *The Changing Architecture of Politics: Structure, Agency and the Future of the State* (London and Thousand Oaks, CA: Sage).

Cerny, P.G. and Evans, M. (2004) 'Globalisation and Public Policy under New Labour', *Policy Studies*, 25(1): 51–65.

Chauhan, R. (2005) *The Financial Times European Business Schools Ranking 2005: How the Table Was Compiled*. Available at: http://www.ft.com/cms/s/2/fd62015e-6324-11da-be11-0000779e2340,dwp_uuid=b29636b0-20ee-11d8-81c6-0820abe49a01. html (accessed 23 May 2007).

Cohen, N. (2001) 'WITHOUT PREJUDICE: Is Blair Bush's poodle? That's unfair to poodles', *Observer*, 25 February, p. 31.

Common, R. (2001) *Public Management and Policy Transfer in Southeast Asia* (Aldershot: Ashgate).

Conservative Democracy Task Force (2008) *Answering the Question: Devolution, the West Lothian Question and the Future of the Union* (London: Conservative Party).

Conservative Party (1997) *You Can Only Be Sure with The Conservatives: Conservative Manifesto 1997* (London: Conservative Party).

Conservative Party (2001) *Time for Common Sense: Conservative Election Manifesto 2001* (London: Conservative Party).

Conservative Party (2002) *Leadership with a Purpose: A Better Society* (London: Conservative Party).

Conservative Party (2005) *Are You Thinking What We're Thinking? It's Time For Action: Conservative Election Manifesto 2005* (London: Conservative Party).

Conservative Party (2006) *Built to Last: The Aims and Values of the Conservative Party* (London: Conservative Party).

Conservative Party (2007) *Power to the People: The Decentralised Energy Revolution* (London: Conservative Party).

Conservative Party (2008a) *Our Vision*. Available at: http://www.conservatives. com/tile.do?def=our.vision.page (accessed 14 March 2008).

Conservative Party (2008b) *Repair Plan for Social Reform* (London: Conservative Party).

Conservative Party (2008c) *An Unfair Britain* (London: Conservative Party).

Conservative Party (2008d) *Reconstruction: Plan for a Strong Economy* (London: Conservative Party).

Conservative Party (2008e) *Raising the Bar, Closing the Gap*, Policy green paper no. 1 (London: Conservative Party).

Conservative Party (2008f) *Building Skills, Transforming Lives: A Training and Apprenticeships Revolution*, Policy green paper no. 7 (London: Conservative Party).

Conservative Party (2008g) *Work for Welfare: Real Welfare Reform to Help Make British Poverty History*, Policy green paper no. 3 (London: Conservative Party).

Conservative Party (2008h) *Delivering Some of the Best Health in Europe: Outcomes Not Targets*, Policy green paper no. 6 (London: Conservative Party).

Conservative Party (2008i) *Where We Stand: Defence*, http://www.conservatives.com/Policy/Where_we_stand/Defence.aspx

Conservative Party (2009a) *Labour's Debt Crisis* (London: Conservative Party).

Conservative Party (2009b) 'Where we stand: Economy' (London: Conservative Party). Available at: http://conservatives.com/Policy/Where_we_stand/Economy.aspx (accessed 14 January 2009).

Conservative Party (2009c) *The Low Carbon Economy: Security, Stability and Green Growth* Protecting Security: Policy green paper no. 8.

ConservativeHome (21 September 2008) http://conservativehome.blogs.com/torydiary/2008/09/tories-set-to-s.html

Conservative Research Department (2005) *The Campaign Guide 2005* (London: Conservative Research Department).

Cowley, P. (2009, forthcoming) 'The Parliamentary Party', *Political Quarterly*, 80, and at http://www.revolts.co.uk/PhilCowleyPQ.pdf

Cowley, P. and Green, J. (2005) 'New Leaders, Same Problems: The Conservatives', in A. Geddes and J. Tonge, *Britain Decides: The UK General Election 2005* (Basingstoke: Palgrave Macmillan).

Credit Action (2009) *Debt Facts and Figures – Compiled 2nd January 2009* (London: Credit Action).

Crewe, I. (1994) 'Electoral Behaviour', in D. Kavanagh and A. Seldon (eds), *The Major Effect* (London: Macmillan).

Crick, M. (2005) *In Search of Michael Howard* (London: Simon & Schuster).

Crouch, C. (2003) *Commercialisation or Citizenship: Education Policy and the Future of Public Services* (London: Fabian Society).

Curtice, J., Fisher, S. and Steed, M. (2005) 'Appendix: The Results Analysed', in D. Kavanagh and D. Butler, *The British General Election of 2005* (Basingstoke: Palgrave Macmillan), p. 246.

Davies, A. (1995) *We, the Nation: The Conservative Party and the Pursuit of Power* (London: Little, Brown and Company).

Dearlove, J. (1989) 'Bringing the Constitution Back In: Political Science and the State', *Political Studies*, 37(3): 521–39.

Department for Work and Pensions (2008) Opportunity For All resource centre, table of indicators (London: Department for Work and Pensions).

Department of Health (2008) Summary letter by Professor the Lord Darzi of Denham KBE. *High Quality Care For All: NHS Next Stage Review Final Report – Summary* (London: HMSO).

Disraeli, B. (1998) *Sybil: or The Two Nations* (Oxford: Oxford Paperbacks).

Dodds, K. and Elden, S. (2008) 'Thinking Ahead: David Cameron, the Henry Jackson Society and British Neo-Conservatism', *British Journal of Politics and International Relations*, 10(3): 347–63.

DOE (Department of the Environment) (1990) *This Common Inheritance: Britain's Environmental Strategy*, Cm 1200 (London: HMSO).

Dolowitz, D. and Marsh, D. (2000) 'Learning from Abroad: The Role of Policy Transfer in Contemporary Policy-Making', *Governance*, 13: 5–24.

Dolowitz, D., Hulme, R., Ellis, N. and O'Neal, F. (2000) *Policy Transfer and British Social Policy* (Buckingham: Open University Press).

Donoughue, B. (2008) *Downing Street Diary*, Vol. 2 (London: Jonathan Cape).

Dorey, P. (2003) 'Conservative Policy under Hague', in M. Garnett and P. Lynch (eds), *The Conservatives in Crisis: The Tories after 1997* (Manchester: Manchester University Press), pp. 125–45.

Dorman, A. (2001) 'Crises and Reviews in British Defence Policy', in S. Croft et al. (eds), *Britain and Defence 1945–2000: A Policy Re-evaluation* (Harlow: Longman), pp. 9–28.

Driver, S. and Martell, L. (2006) *New Labour* (Cambridge: Polity).

Dudley Edwards, R. (1983) *Harold Macmillan: A Life in Pictures* (London: Macmillan).

Duncan, A. and Hobson, D. (1995) *Saturn's Children: How the State Devours Liberty, Prosperity and Virtue* (London: Sinclair -Stevenson).

Duncan, A. and Hobson, D. (1999) *Saturn's Children* (London: Politico's).

Duncan Smith, I. (2003) 'Introduction: The Renewal of Society', in G. Streeter (ed.), *There Is Such a Thing as Society: Twelve Principles of Compassionate Conservatism* (London: Politico's), pp. 30–7.

Eaglesham, J. and Parker, G. (2009) 'Conservatives go on to war footing', *Financial Times*, 13 January.

Economic Competitiveness Policy Group (2007) *Freeing Britain to Compete: Equipping the UK for Globalisation* (London: Economic Competitiveness Policy Group).

Elliott, F. and Hanning, J. (2007) *Cameron: The Rise of the New Conservative* (London: Harper Press).

Emmerson, C. and Frayne, C. (2005) *Public Spending*, Election briefing note, BN56, (London: Institute for Fiscal Studies).

Esping-Andersen, G. (1990) *The Three Worlds of Welfare Capitalism* (Cambridge: Polity Press).

European Scrutiny Committee (2007–08), *European Union Intergovernmental Conference: Follow-Up Report*, 3rd Report.

Evans, G. (2002) 'European Integration, Party Politics and Voting in the 2001 Election', *British Elections & Parties Review*, 12: 95–110.

Evans, G. and Butt, S. (2007) 'Explaining Change in British Public Opinion on the European Union: Top Down or Bottom Up?', *Acta Politica*, 42(2–3): 173–90.

Evans, M. (2004) *Constitution-Making and the Labour Party* (Basingstoke: Palgrave Macmillan).

Evans, M. (ed.) (2005) *Policy Transfer in Global Perspective* (Aldershot: Ashgate).

Evans, M. (2008) 'New Labour and the Rise of the New Constitutionalism', in M. Beech and S. Lee (eds), *Ten Years of New Labour* (Basingstoke: Palgrave Macmillan), pp. 68–88.

Evans, M. and Cerny, P. (2003) 'Globalization and Social Policy', in N. Ellison and C. Pierson (eds), *Developments in British Social Policy 2* (Basingstoke: Palgrave Macmillan), pp. 19–40.

Evans, S. (2008) 'Consigning its Past to History? David Cameron and the Conservative Party', *Parliamentary Affairs*, 61(2).

Fox, L. 'Conservative Way Forward Speech By DR. Liam Fox', http://www.theatlanticbridge.com/articles/WayForward.pdf

Fox, L. (2007a) 'State of the Royal Navy', http://www.conservatives.com/tile.do?def=news.story.page&obj_id=137725

Fox, L. (2007b) 'We need a government that honours our armed forces', http://www.conservatives.com/News/Speeches/2007/10/Liam_Fox_We_need_a_Government_that_honours_our_Armed_Forces.aspx

Freeden, M. (1995) *Green Ideology: Concepts and Structures*, OCEES Research Paper no. 4, Mansfield College, Oxford.

Freedman, L. (1999) *The Politics of British Defence, 1979–98* (Basingstoke: Palgrave Macmillan).

Friedman, M. (1962) *Capitalism and Freedom* (Chicago: University of Chicago).

Furness, D., et al. (2008) *SMF Health Project: Background Paper 1: An Overview of Health Systems Reform and the NHS* (London: Social Market Foundation).

Gamble, A. (1988/1994) *The Free Economy and the Strong State: The Politics of Thatcherism* (Basingstoke: Palgrave Macmillan).

Gamble, A. (2006) 'Shifting Sands', *Soundings*, 34 (Autumn).

Gamble, A. (2009) 'Cameron's Conservatism', in S. Griffiths and K. Hickson (eds), *British Party Politics and Ideology after New Labour* (Basingstoke: Palgrave Macmillan).

Garnett, M. and Gilmour, I. (1998) 'The Lessons of Defeat', *Political Quarterly*, 126–32.

Giddens, A. (1994) *Beyond Left and Right: The Future of Radical Politics* (Cambridge: Polity).

Giddens, A. (1998) *The Third Way: The Renewal of Social Democracy* (Cambridge: Polity Press).

Gilmour, I. (1977) *Inside Right: A Study of Conservatism* (London: Hutchinson).

Gilmour, I. (1978) *Inside Right: Conservatism, Policies and the People* (London: Quartet Books).

Gilmour, I. (1992) *Dancing with Dogma: Britain under Thatcherism* (London: Simon and Schuster).

Goldwater, B. (1960) *The Conscience of a Conservative* (Shepherdsville: Victor).

Gouldson, A. and Murphy, J. (1998) *Regulatory Realities* (London: Earthscan).

Gray, C.S. (1999) *Modern Strategy* (Oxford: Oxford University Press).

Gray, J. (1993) *Beyond the New Right: Markets, Government and the Common Environment* (London: Routledge).

Gray, J. (1997) 'Conservatism R.I.P.', *New Statesman*, 12 September.

Grayling, C. (2008) 'Welfare – the next steps', Speech to the Centre for Policy Studies, 27 May.

Green, J. (2005) 'Conservative Party Rationality: Learning the Lessons from the Last Election for the Next', *Journal of Elections, Public Opinion and Parties*, 15(1): 111–27.

Grice, A. (2008) 'How green are the Tories?' *Independent*, 31 July.

Griffiths, S. (2009) 'The Public Services under Gordon Brown – Similar Reforms, Less Money', *Policy Studies*, February.

Hague, W. (2006a) 'The special relationship', Speech at the School of Advanced International Studies, 16 February.

Hague, W. (2006b) 'Foreign affairs may be the greatest of all challenges for the next government of this country', Speech at Conservative Party conference, 3 October.

Hague, W. (2006c) 'The future of Europe: freedom and flexibility', Speech to Open Europe, 7 June.

Hague, W. (2007a) 'Constructive responsible foreign policy', Speech, 3 March.

Hague, W. (2007b) 'Thinking ahead: The foreign policy of the next Conservative Government', Speech at Chatham House, London, 31 January. Available at: http://www.chathamhouse.org.uk/events/view/-/id/489/ (accessed 10 November 2008).

Hague, W. (2007c) 'The politics of disenchantment and a question of trust', Speech to the Centre for Policy Studies, 19 September.

Hague, W. (2008) 'The European project and democratic consent: disconnection or disengagement?', Speech to Policy Exchange, London, 8 February.

Hague, W. (2009) 'Why Britain will never join the Euro', *Daily Mail*, 2 January.

Hajer, M. (1995) *The Politics of Environmental Discourse* (Oxford: Oxford University Press).

Hall, M. (2007) 'How dare millionaire Goldsmith lecture the voters on "sacrifice"', *Daily Express*, 9 December.

Ham, C. (1996) 'Contestability: A Middle Path for Health Care', *British Medical Journal*, 312: 70–1.

Hansard (2007) *House of Commons Hansard Debates for 14th March 2007*, http://www.publications.parliament.uk/pa/cm200607/cmhansrd/cm070314/debtext/70314-0020.htm

Hartley, K. (2001) 'UK defence spending', http://www.york.ac.uk/depts/econ/documents/research/rusi.pdf

Hayek, F. (1960) *The Constitution of Liberty* (Chicago: University of Chicago Press).

Hayek, F. (1976) *Law, Legislation and Liberty Volume II: The Mirage of Social Justice* (London: Kegan Paul).

Hayek, F. (1991) *The Fatal Conceit: The Errors of Socialism* (Chicago: University of Chicago).

Helm, T. and Rennie, D. (2006) 'Don't be fooled by Cameron, Tebbit to warn Right', *Daily Telegraph*, 31 January. Available at: http://www.telegraph.co.uk/news/uknews/1509210/Dont-be-fooled-by-Cameron,-Tebbit-to-warn-Right.html (accessed 15 January 2009).

Heppell, T. (2002) 'The Ideological Composition of the Parliamentary Conservative Party 1992–97', *British Journal of Politics and International Relations*, 4(2): 299–324.

Heppell, T. (2008) *Choosing the Tory Leader: Conservative Party Leadership Elections from Heath to Cameron* (London: Tauris Academic Studies).

Heppell, T. and Hill, M. (2008) 'The Conservative Party Leadership Election of 1997: An Analysis of the Voting Motivations of Conservative Parliamentarians', *British Politics*, 3(1): 63–91.

Hill, M. (2007) 'The Parliamentary Conservative Party and the Party Leadership: The Elections of William Hague and Iain Duncan Smith', Unpublished PhD thesis, University of Huddersfield.

Hirst, P. (ed.) (1989) *The Pluralist Theory of the State* (London and New York: Routledge).

Hirst, P. and Thompson, G. (1996) *Globalization in Question* (Oxford: Polity Press).

HM Treasury (2007a) *The Role of the Voluntary Sector in Service Delivery* (London: HM Treasury).

HM Treasury (2007b) *2007 Pre-Budget Report and Comprehensive Spending Review* (London: HM Treasury).

Hoggart, S. (2004) 'Old masticators dazzled by a killing machine', http://www.guardian.co.uk/politics/2004/oct/07/conservatives2004.politicalcolumnists

Honeyman, V. (2009, forthcoming) 'Gordon Brown and International Policy', *Policy Studies*.

Hood, C. (1995) 'Contemporary Management', *Public Policy and Administration*, 10(2): 104–17.

Hope, C. and Jones, G. (2008) 'Defence spending is lowest since the 1930s', http://www.telegraph.co.uk/news/uknews/1540160/Defence-spending-is-lowest-since-the-1930s.html

Horsfall, D. (2009, forthcoming) 'Comparing Competition States', *Policy Studies*, 34(4).

House of Commons Defence Committee (2008) *Defence – Ninth Report*, http://www.publications.parliament.uk/pa/cm200708/cmselect/cmdfence/111/11102.htm

Howard, M. (2005) BBC News, 6 May, cited in M. Ashcroft, *Smell the Coffee: A Wake-up Call for the Conservative Party* (London: Michael Ashcroft).

Hutton, W. (1995) *The State We're In* (London: Cape).

Hutton, W. and Cameron, D. (2009) 'Recession Britain: The Great Debate', *Guardian*, 1 February.

Independent (2008) 'Tories in brief: Ainsworth calls for a greener economy', 2 October.

Independent on Sunday (2006) 'Cameron's green edge' (editorial), 3 September.

Ipsos MORI (2008a) 'Conservatives open 28% point lead over Labour'. Available at: http://www.ipsos-mori.com/content/home-page-news/conservatives-open-28-point-lead-over-labour.ashx

Ipsos MORI (2008b) *Government Delivery Index. Satisfaction with The Chancellor Trends Agreement with Government Policies* (London: Ipsos MORI).

Ipsos MORI (2008c) *Government Delivery Index. Best Party on Key Issues: Managing the Economy* (London: Ipsos MORI).

Ipsos MORI (2008d) *Government Delivery Index. Best Party on Key Issues: Taxation* (London: Ipsos MORI).

Ipsos MORI (2008e) 'Labour may be losing support from traditional sources'. Available at: http://www.ipsos-mori.com/content/news/labour-may-be-losing-support-from-traditional-supp.ashx (accessed 15 July 2008).

Ipsos MORI (2008f) 'Voting intention in Great Britain (Certain to vote)'. Available at: http://www.ipsos-mori.com/content/voting-intention-in-great-britain-certain-to-vote.ashx (accessed 15 January 2009).

Jay, D. (1937) *The Socialist Case* (London: Faber and Faber).

Jenkin, B. (2007) *A Defence Policy for the UK: Matching Commitments and Resources* (London: Conservative Way Forward).

Jessop, B. (1988) *Thatcherism: A Tale of Two Nations* (Cambridge: Polity).

Johnson, B. (2008) 'What on earth has come over our aimless, feckless, hopeless youth?', *Daily Telegraph*, 19 August.

Johnson, L. (2008) 'Glimpses into the Gems of American Intelligence: The President's Daily Brief and the National Intelligence Estimate', *Intelligence and National Security*, 23(3): 333–70.

Jones, D. (2008) *Cameron on Cameron: Conversations with Dylan Jones* (London: Fourth Estate).

Jones, T. and Newburn, T. (2001) 'Learning from Uncle Sam? Exploring US Influences on British Crime Control Policy', *ESRC Future Governance Programme*, http://www.hull.ac.uk/futgov/

Joseph, K. (1976a) *Stranded on the Middle Ground: Reflections on Circumstances and Policies* (London: Centre for Policy Studies).

Joseph, K. (1976b) *Monetarism is Not Enough* (London: Rose).

Joseph, K. (1978) 'Proclaim the Message: Keynes is Dead!', in P. Hutber (ed.), *What's Wrong With Britain?* (London: Sphere Books), pp. 99–106.

Joseph, K. and Sumption, J. (1978) *Equality* (London: John Murray).

Kalitowski, S. (2008) 'Hung-up Over Nothing? The Impact of a Hung Parliament on British Politics', *Parliamentary Affairs*, 61(2): 396–407.

Kerr, P. (2007) 'Cameron Chameleon and the Current State of Britain's "Consensus"', *Parliamentary Affairs*, 60(10).

King, A. (2006) 'Why Labour Won – Yet Again', in J. Bartle and A. King (eds), *Britain at the Polls 2005* (CQ Press).

King, D. and Wickham-Jones, M. (1999) 'From Clinton to Blair – the Democratic Party Origins of Welfare to Work', *Political Quarterly*, 70: 62–74.

Le Grand, J. (2003) *Motivation, Agency, and Public Policy: Of Knights and Knaves, Pawns and Queens* (Oxford: Oxford University Press).

Lea, R. (2006) *The Chancellor's Record: An Audit of the Last 10 Years* (London: Centre for Policy Studies).

Lea, R. (2007) 'Tories' economic legacy has been squandered', *Daily Telegraph*, 17 September.

Lee, S. (1996) 'Manufacturing', in D. Coates (ed.), *Industrial Policy in Britain* (London: Macmillan), pp. 33–61.

Lee, S. (1997) 'Part B: Explaining Britain's Relative Economic Performance', in A. Cox, S. Lee and J. Sanderson, *The Political Economy of Modern Britain* (Cheltenham: Edward Elgar), pp. 65–253.

Lee, S. (2003) 'The Political Economy of the Third Way: The Relationship Between Globalisation and National Economic Policy', in J. Michie (ed.), *The Handbook of Globalisation* (Cheltenham: Edward Elgar), pp. 331–46.

Lee, S. (2007a) 'Building Institutions for Freedom', in M. Mullard and B. Cole (eds), *Globalization, Citizenship and the War on Terror* (Cheltenham: Edward Elgar), pp. 168–88.

Lee, S. (2007b) *Best for Britain? The Politics and Legacy of Gordon Brown* (Oxford: Oneworld).

Lee, S. (2008) 'The British Model of Political Economy', in M. Beech and S. Lee (eds), *Ten Years of New Labour* (Basingstoke: Palgrave Macmillan), pp. 17–33.

Lee, S. (2009) *Boom to Bust: The Politics and Legacy of Gordon Brown* (Oxford: Oneworld).

Letwin, O. (2003) 'For Labour There Is No Such Thing as Society, Only the State', in G. Streeter (ed.), *There Is Such a Thing as Society: Twelve Principles of Compassionate Conservatism* (London: Politico's), pp. 38–51.

Lightfoot, E. (1999) 'Connecting Policy Transfer with Ideology: A Study of Great Britain's Failed Emulation of the Americans with Disabilities Act', *American Political Science Association Annual Conference*.

Lonsdale, D. (2008) 'Blair's Record on Defence: A Strategic Analysis', in M. Beech and S. Lee (eds), *Ten Years of New Labour* (Basingstoke: Palgrave Macmillan).

Lynas, M. (2008) 'World saved ... planet doomed', *New Statesman*, 24 November, pp. 20–4.

Lynch, P. (1999) *The Politics of Nationhood: Sovereignty, Identity and British Politics* (London: Palgrave).

Lynch, P. and Garnett, M. (2003) 'Conclusions: The Conservatives in Crisis', in M. Garnett and P. Lynch, *The Conservatives in Crisis* (Manchester: Manchester University Press).

Lynch, P. and Whitaker, R. (2008) 'A Loveless Marriage: The Conservatives and the European People's Party', *Parliamentary Affairs*, 61(1): 31–51.

Macleod, I. and Maude, A. (eds) (1950) *One Nation: A Tory Approach to Social Problems* (London: Conservative Political Centre).

Macmillan, H. (1938) *The Middle Way: A Study of the Problem of Economic and Social Progress in a Free and Democratic Society* (London: Macmillan).

Macnicol, J. (1987) 'In Pursuit of the Underclass', *Journal of Social Policy*, 16(3): 293–318.

Marmor, T. (1997) 'Global Health Policy Reform: Misleading Mythology or Learning Opportunity?' in C. Altenstetter and J. Bjorkman (eds), *Health Policy Reform: National Variations and Globalization* (Basingstoke: Palgrave Macmillan).

Marshall, B., Duffy, B., Thompson, J., Castell, S. and Hall, S. (2007) *Blair's Britain: The Social and Cultural Legacy* (London: Ipsos MORI).

Martin, I. (2008) 'Britain's defence spending is a disgrace', http://www.telegraph. co.uk/comment/columnists/iainmartin/3555259/Britain's-defence-spending-is-a-disgrace.html

May, T. (2002) Speech to Conservative Party Conference, Bournemouth, 7 October.

May, T. and Timothy, N. (2007) *Restoring Parliamentary Authority: EU Laws and British Scrutiny* (London: Politeia).

McKenzie, R. and Lee, D. (1981) *Quicksilver Capital: How the Rapid Movement of Wealth has Changed the World* (New York: Free Press).

Mead, L. (1992) *The New Politics of Poverty: The Nonworking Poor in America* (New York: Basic Books).

Military Covenant Commission (2008a) *Restoring the Covenant: The Military Covenant Commission's Report to the Leader of the Conservative Party* (London: Military Covenant Commission).

Military Covenant Commission (2008b) *The Leader of the Opposition's Military Covenant Commission: Launch Document* (London: Military Covenant Commission).

National and International Security Policy Group (2007) *An Unquiet World: Submission to the Shadow Cabinet* (London: Conservative Party).

'NATO cannot afford to fail in Afghanistan', http://www.conservatives.com/tile. do?def=news.story.page&obj_id=137793

Nelson, F. (2008) 'Cameron gets ready for Number 10 – and Boris must wait his turn', *Spectator*, 10 May.

Neville-Jones, P. (2007) *Conservative Party National and International Security Policy Group Report Launch* (London: Chatham House).

Norton, P. (1990) '"The Lady's Not for Turning" But What About the Rest? Margaret Thatcher and the Conservative Party 1979–1989', *Parliamentary Affairs*, 43(1), January.

Norton, P. (ed.) (1996a) *The Conservative Party* (London: Prentice Hall/Harvester Wheatsheaf).

Norton, P. (1996b) 'Philosophy: The Principles of Conservatism', in P. Norton (ed.), *The Conservative Party* (London: Prentice Hall/Harvester Wheatsheaf), pp. 68–82.

Norton, P. (2002) 'The Conservative Party: Is There Anyone Out There?' in A. King (ed.), *Britain at the Polls 2001* (New York: Chatham House).

Norton, P. (2008) 'The Future of Conservatism', the Norton Lecture, delivered at the University of Hull, 12 February 2008. Forthcoming in *Political Quarterly*.

Norton, P. and Aughey, A. (1981) *Conservatives and Conservatism* (London: Temple Smith).

O'Hara, K. (2007) *After Blair. David Cameron and the Conservative Tradition* (Cambridge: Icon Books).

Obama, B. (2009) Speech by President-elect Barack Obama on his American Recovery and Reinvestment Plan, George Mason University, Virginia, 8 January.

OECD (2008) 'Annex Table 32: General Government Gross Financial Liabilities', in OECD, *OECD Economic Outlook 84 Database* (Paris: Organization for Economic Co-operation and Development).

Office for National Statistics (2009) http://www.statistics.gov.uk/cci/nugget. asp?id=12 (accessed 21 January).

Olavsky, M. (2000) *Compassionate Conservatism: What It Is, What It Does, and How It Can Transform America* (New York: The Free Press), pp. 215–26.

Oppermann, K. (2008) 'The Blair Government and Europe: The Policy of Containing the Salience of European Integration', *British Politics*, 3(2): 156–82.

Osborne, G. (2005) 'Principles of a Conservative economic policy', Speech to the Centre for Policy Studies, London, 12 July.

Osborne, G. (2006a) 'A tax policy that puts stability first', Speech, 1 June.

Osborne, G. (2006b) 'Stability before tax cuts', Speech, 23 January.

Osborne, G. (2007) 'The emerging battle for public service reform', Speech, 30 May. Available at: http://www.georgeosborne.co.uk/shadow_news.php?id=32 (accessed 15 January 2009).

Osborne, G. (2008) 'Recovery through fiscal responsibility', Speech, 31 October.

Page, B. and Byrom, A. (2005) 'What will people choose when choice goes live?' Research Study Conducted for Department of Health. MORI Social Research Institute. Available at: http://www.ipsos-mori.com/_assets/polls/2005/pdf/doh2. pdf (accessed 6 August 2008).

Parry, N. and Parry, J. (1976) *The Rise of the Medical Profession: A Study of Collective Social Mobility* (London: Croom Helm).

Pascoe-Watson, G. (2009) 'Cameron's well hung', *Sun*, 9 January.

Peters, B.G. and Savoie, D.J. (eds) (1998) *Taking Stock: Assessing Public Sector Reforms* (Montreal: McGill-Queen's University Press).

Policy Exchange. http://www.policyexchange.org.uk/

Politicalstuff.co.uk (2001) *Conservative Party Manifestos*, conservativemanifesto. com

PoliticsHome.com (2008) *The PoliticsHome Electoral Index: The Largest Ever UK Marginals Poll* (London: PoliticsHome.com).

Prabhakar, R. (2009) 'Reforming Public Services: The View of the Main Parties', in S. Griffiths and K. Hickson (eds), *British Party Politics and Ideology after New Labour* (Basingstoke: Palgrave Macmillan).

Public Services Improvement Group (2007) *Restoring Pride In Our Public Services* (London: Public Services Improvement Group).

Quality of Life Policy Group (2007) *Blueprint for a Green Economy* (London: Conservative Party).

Rawnsley, A. (2008) 'The latest version of the PM – Brown with added Blair', *Observer*, 10 February. Available at: http://www.guardian.co.uk/commentisfree/2008/ feb/10/publicservices.gordonbrown (accessed 15 January 2009).

Ray, L. (2007) 'Mainstream Euroskepticism: Trend or Oxymoron', *Acta Politica*, 42(2–3).

Rayment, S. (2008) 'Two thirds of Apache attack helicopters "unusable"', http:// www.uknda.org/two_thirds_of_apache_attack_helicopters_unusable_/n-180. html

Redwood, J. (2002) *Third Way – Which Way: How Should We Pay for Public Services?* (London: Middlesex University Press).

Reich, R. (1991) *The Work of Nations: Preparing Ourselves for 21st Century Capitalism* (New York: Knopf).

Rhodes, R.A.W. (1997) *Understanding Governance: Policy Networks, Governance, Reflexivity and Accountability* (Buckingham: Open University Press).

Riddell, P. (1985) *The Thatcher Government*, revised edition (Oxford: Basil Blackwell).

Riddell, P. (2009) 'Gordon Brown bounce fades as Conservatives return to huge poll lead', *The Times*, 13 January.

Rose, R. (2005) *Learning from Comparative Public Policy: A Practical Guide* (London and New York: Routledge).

Sanders, D. (1990) *Losing an Empire, Finding a Role* (Basingstoke: Palgrave Macmillan).

Santorum, R. (2003) 'The New Wave of Compassionate Conservatism', in G. Streeter (ed.), *There Is Such a Thing as Society: Twelve Principles of Compassionate Conservatism* (London: Politico's), pp. 60–7.

Schlosberg, D. and Rinfret, S. (2008) 'Ecological Modernisation, American Style', *Environmental Politics*, 17(2) (April): 254–75.

Scruton, R. (1996) *The Conservative Sense of Community* (London: Conservative 2000 Foundation).

Scruton, R. (2006) *Arguments for Conservatism* (London: Continuum).

Seawright, D. (2005) 'One Nation', in K. Hickson (ed.), *The Political Thought of the Conservative Party since 1945* (Basingstoke: Palgrave Macmillan).

Seldon, A. (2004) 'Whatever the Tories do, they're doomed', *Observer*, 3 October.

Seldon, A. and Ball, S. (eds) (1994) *Conservative Century: The Conservative Party since 1900* (Oxford: Oxford University Press; London: Macmillan).

Seldon, A. and Snowdon, P. (2001) *A New Conservative Century?* (London: Centre for Policy Studies).

Seldon, A. and Snowdon, P. (2005) 'The Barren Years: 1997–2005', in S. Ball and A. Seldon (eds), *Recovering Power: The Conservatives in Opposition Since 1867* (Basingstoke: Palgrave Macmillan).

Smith, M. and Richards, D. (2001) *Governance and Public Policy in the UK* (Oxford: Oxford University Press).

Social Justice Policy Group (2006) *Breakdown Britain* (London: Social Justice Policy Group).

Social Justice Policy Group (2007) *Breakthrough Britain: Ending the Costs of Social Breakdown*, Volumes I–VI (London: Social Justice Policy Group).

Soederberg, S., Menz, G. and Cerny, P. (eds) (2005) *Internalising Globalization: The Rise of Neo-liberalism and the Decline of National Varieties of Capitalism* (Basingstoke: Palgrave Macmillan).

Stelzer, I. (2007) 'The characters behind the promises', *Spectator*, Wednesday, 7 February.

Stone, D. (1999) 'Learning Lessons and Transferring Policy Across Time, Space and Disciplines', *Politics*, 19: 51–9.

Stratton, A. (2009) 'Heathrow expansion: Government survives Commons vote', *Guardian*, 28 January.

Streeter, G. (ed.) (2003a) *There Is Such a Thing as Society: Twelve Principles of Compassionate Conservatism* (London: Politico's).

Streeter, G. (2003b) 'Conservatives Must Change in Order to Help the Vulnerable', in G. Streeter (ed.), *There Is Such a Thing as Society: Twelve Principles of Compassionate Conservatism* (London: Politico's), pp. 1–10.

Summers, D. (2008a) 'Delegates welcome Tory plan for high-speed rail link', *Guardian*, 29 September.

Summers, D. (2008b) 'David Cameron vows to avoid US-style deadlock in dealing with economic crisis', *Guardian*, 30 September.

Taggart, P. and Szczerbiak, A. (2008) 'Theorising Party-Based Euroscepticism: Problems of Definition, Measurement and Causality', in P. Taggart and A. Szczerbiak (eds), *Opposing Europe: The Comparative Party Politics of Euroscepticism*, Vol. 2, *Comparative and Theoretical Perspectives* (Oxford: Oxford University Press), pp. 238–61.

Tax Reform Commission (2006) *Tax Matters: Reforming the Tax System* (London: The Tax Reform Commission).

Taylor, I. (2003) 'The Conservatives 1997–2001: A Party in Crisis?' in M. Garnett and P. Lynch (eds), *The Conservatives in Crisis* (Manchester: Manchester University Press).

Tempest, M. (2004) 'Tories back intervention in Africa', http://www.guardian.co.uk/politics/2004/oct/06/conservatives2004.conservatives8

Tempest, M. (2005) 'Odds lengthen on Davis for Tory leader', http://www.guardian.co.uk/politics/2005/oct/05/toryleadership2005.conservatives (accessed 15 January 2009).

Tetteh, E. (2008a) *Election Statistics: UK 1918–2007: House of Commons Library Research Paper 0//12* (London: House of Commons Library).

Tetteh, E. (2008b) *Local Elections 2008: House of Commons Research Paper 08/48* (London: House of Commons Library).

Thatcher, M. (1987) Interview with *Woman's Own*, 31 October.

Thatcher, M. (1993) *The Downing Street Years* (New York: HarperCollins).

Thatcher, M. (2003) *Statecraft: Strategies for a Changing World* (London: HarperCollins).

The Times (2008) 'Conservatives in a cold climate', 29 September.

Theodore, N. and Peck, J. (1999) 'Welfare-to-Work: National Problems, Local Solutions?', *Critical Social Policy*, 19: 485–510.

Thompson, N. (2009) 'A reply to Prabhakar', in S. Griffiths and K. Hickson (eds), *British Party Politics and Ideology after New Labour* (Basingstoke: Palgrave Macmillan).

Toye, R. (2002) '"The Gentleman in Whitehall" Reconsidered: The Evolution of Douglas Jay's Views on Economic Planning and Consumer Choice 1937–1947', *Labour History Review*, 67(2).

Toynbee, P. (2008) 'This craven airport decision hands Cameron a green halo', *Guardian*, 17 January.

Travis, A. (2001) 'Voters fail to share Hague's euro obsession', *Guardian*, 20 May.

UNICEF (2007) *Child Poverty in Perspective: An Overview of Child Well-being in Rich Countries. A comprehensive assessment of the lives and well-being of children and adolescents in the economically advanced nations*, Innocenti Report Card Seven, UNICEF, Innocenti Research Centre, Florence.

UKNDA (United Kingdom National Defence Association) (2008a) *Overcoming the Defence Crisis*, http://www.uknda.org/uknda_discussion_paper:_overcoming_ the_defence_crisis/n-154.html

UKNDA (2008b) *Defence is Now an Election Issue – Poll Reveals*, http://www.uknda. org/defence_is_now_an_election_issue_-_poll_reveals/n-158.html

UKNDA (2008c) *UKNDA Welcomes Cameron Pledge on Armed Forces – But Where is the Extra Money?*, http://www.uknda.org/uknda_welcomes_cameron_pledge_ on_armed_forces_-_but_where_is_the_extra_money/n-163.html

Usherwood, S. (2002) 'Opposition to the European Union in the UK: The Dilemma of Public Opinion and Party Management', *Government and Opposition*, 37(2): 211–30.

Uttley, M. (2001) 'The Management of UK Defence', in S. Croft et al. (eds), *Britain and Defence 1945–2000: A Policy Re-evaluation* (Harlow: Longman), pp. 88–102.

Vogel, S. (1996) *Freer Markets, More Rules: Regulatory Reform in Advanced Industrial Countries* (Ithaca, New York: Cornell University Press).

Webb, P. (2008) 'The Attitudinal Assimilation of Europe by the Conservative Parliamentary Party', *British Politics*, 3(4): 427–44.

Whiteley, P. (1983) *The Labour Party in Crisis* (London: Methuen).

Willetts, D. (1998) 'Conservative Renewal', *Political Quarterly*, pp. 110–17.

Willetts, D. (2003) 'The New Contours of British Politics', in G. Streeter (ed.), *There Is Such a Thing as Society: Twelve Principles of Compassionate Conservatism* (London: Politico's), pp. 52–9.

Willetts, D. (2005) 'Compassionate conservatism and the war on poverty', Speech to Centre for Social Justice, 6 January.

Willetts, D. (2009) 'Charlie Ellis and Neo-mutualism: A Comment', in S. Griffiths and K. Hickson (eds), *British Party Politics and Ideology after New Labour* (Basingstoke: Palgrave Macmillan).

Wolman, H. (1992) 'Understanding Cross National Policy Transfers: The Case of Britain and the US', *Governance*, 5: 27–45.

Index

Compiled by Sue Carlton